MACRO-ECONOMICS: MAKING GENDER MATTER

MACRO-ECONOMICS: MAKING GENDER MATTER

Concepts, policies and institutional change in developing countries

EDITED BY MARTHA GUTIÉRREZ

Deutsche Gesellschaft für
Technische Zusammenarbeit (GTZ) GmbH

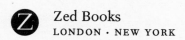

Zed Books
LONDON · NEW YORK

Macro-Economics: Making Gender Matter — Concepts, Policies and Institutional Change in Developing Countries was first published by Zed Books Ltd, 7 Cynthia Street, London N1 9JF, UK and Room 400 175 Fifth Avenue, New York, NY 10010, USA in 2003

with financial support from the Bundesministerium für Wirtschaftliche Zusammenarbeit und Entwicklung (BMZ) in co-operation with Gesellschaft für Technische Zusammenarbeit (GTZ) GmbH, Postfach 5180, 65726 Eschborn, Germany.

www.zedbooks.demon.co.uk

Translations by Anabel Torres

Cover designed by Andrew Corbett
Set in Monotype Fournier by Ewan Smith, London
Printed and bound in the United Kingdom by Biddles Ltd, www.biddles.co.uk

Distributed in the usa exclusively by Palgrave, a division of St Martin's Press, LLC, 175 Fifth Avenue, New York, NY 10010

A catalogue record for this book is available from the British Library.

US CIP data is available from the Library of Congress.

ISBN 1 84277 060 8 cased
ISBN 1 84277 061 6 limp

Contents

Abbreviations and Acronyms

BMZ	Federal Ministry for Economic Co-operation and Development
CBI	Caribbean Basin Initiative
CGE	computable general equilibrium
ECLAC	Economic Commission for Latin America and the Caribbean
GPR	global participation rate
GTZ	German Technical Cooperation Agency
HDI	Human Development Index
HIPC	Highly Indebted Poor Country
IADB	Inter-American Development Bank
IDRC	International Development Research Center
IDS	Institute of Development Studies
IICA	American Institute for Cooperation on Agriculture
INSTRAW	International Research and Training Institute for the Advancement of Women (UN)
NSA	National Satellite Accounts
NTAE	non-traditional agricultural export
OECD–DAC	Organisation of Economic Co-operation and Development–Development Assistance Committee
PAR	Participatory Action Research
PLA	Participatory Learning and Action
PRA	Participatory Rural Appraisal
RMSM	Revised Minimum Standard Model
RRA	Rapid Rural Appraisal
SAP	structural adjustment programme
SEWA	Self Employed Women's Association (India)
SHD	sustainable human development
SNA	System of National Accounts
UNDP	United Nations Development Programme
UNIFEM	United Nations Development Fund for Women
UNSNA	UN System of National Accounts

Introduction

Traditionally, economics has been viewed as the baseline of development. Yet the empirical research of the last two decades shows us that the relationship between them can be highly ambiguous, and such ambiguity is making the lives of policy-makers increasingly difficult and their decisions on occasion the subject of great controversy.

In view of these difficulties, many policy-makers and practitioners are left with the crude option of either backing or rejecting today's economic models. What is more, they can always tap into a wealth of competing theories and findings in order to substantiate their views. And when the results of particular economic interventions turn out to be dysfunctional or even counterproductive, they are often faced by volumes of 'lessons learnt' and an ongoing uncertainty as to how to improve their strategies.

Many economists who are also policy-makers are progressively more open to new arguments as growing public scrutiny demands higher returns on investment in development. They are looking for ways to increase the impacts of their policies on the ground, thus reassessing the canon of macro-economic approaches.

This book offers concepts and tools to bring macro-economics and state reform processes closer to the realities on the ground by focusing on a crucial determinant: gender relations. Its underlying premise is that gender relations are not only embedded in people's culture, but also make their mark on the economic domain. Earning a living, having access to markets and even paying taxes is influenced by whether you are male or female. Gender differences foster unbalanced rights and obligations, which translate into very contrasting economic opportunities and constraints on the overall behaviour of the macro-economy. By considering these differences when analysing macro-economic aggregates and institutional frameworks, policy-makers can ensure a higher coherence between macro targets, especially for poverty eradication, and the real impact of policies and programmes on people's lives.

The authors included in this volume, who come from the academic world, from international agencies and from both the public and private sectors, illustrate the potential of using gender as an analytical tool at multiple levels. The authors propose new approaches to macro-economic models and policies and put forward suggestions to design more just institutions. This book has been put together for macro-economists as well as for policy-makers, researchers, practitioners and activists from other disciplines concerned with development issues.[1]

Many of the contributions on Latin America were present during a seminar on macro-economics, gender and the state, organized by the Colombian National Planning Department (DNP) and the German government.[2] The event brought together civil servants from national planning ministries and women's divisions in various Latin American countries, civil authorities from national and regional entities, academics, members of NGOs and representatives from international development organizations. The seminar, as well as this book, were funded by the German Ministry for Economic Co-operation and Development. The present volume reflects the commitment of the Ministry and its agency for technical co-operation, GTZ, to enriching the debate on macro-economics and gender, as agreed by the OECD–DAC members.

The book is organized in four parts. The first deals with macro-economics and gender, the second with gender in state reform, and the third with institutionalizing gender in national and international organizations. The last part contains case studies from Latin America. Each section puts forward conceptual frameworks and applications, either as specific studies or as models for possible replication.

PART I deals with macro-economic analysis, the intersection between macro-economics and gender, the effects of the alleged neutrality of economics as a discipline and the new perspectives opened up by innovative approaches. *Barbara Evers* brings us the most recent insights on integrating a gender approach into macro-economic models. Starting from empirical evidence on the relation between gender inequalities and economic growth, she runs through the problems faced when introducing gender into macro-economic frameworks, offering alternatives and highlighting their implications for policy. *Nilufer Çagatay* indicates the relevance of gender in the different aspects of macro-economic analysis: its concepts, models and policy formulation. She then turns to the implications of gender inequalities at both micro and macro levels, and the conceptual aspects that demand new approaches to examining the relationship between macro-economics and gender.

Ingrid Palmer provides a comprehensive review of social and gender issues in macro-economic policy advice. She details the areas of macro-economic concern and their micro linkages, paying close attention to how gender issues are incorporated into development policies and economic management, public finance and poverty alleviation strategies. She analyses gender asymmetry, showing the high social costs of inequality between men and women, which supports the contention that policies would be much more effective if they were to include a gender analysis.

Joerg Freiberg-Strauss points out the changes in macro-economic theory during the past 20 years, which have led to integrating variables usually not regarded as economic. He portrays the linkages among the micro, meso and macro levels of the economy, and proposes criteria for analysing the impact of gender relations at the macro level. *Rebeca Grynspan* highlights the effects that economic policies and public spending may have on men and women. These differential effects, she argues, lie at the heart of the discussion over state reform processes, privatization and decentralization. She believes the capacity of a development strategy to create growth and sustainability depends on its commitment to social policy and its ability to bring about a more equitable society, with gender equality as a priority.

Several perspectives on the relationship between productive and reproductive work are included. *Fabiola Campillo* discusses the gender biases typical of the connection between the reproductive, non-paid sphere and the productive, paid sphere. Campillo explores the effects of unpaid household labour and its link to market subsidies, labour markets and employment patterns, as well as social services. She reviews various tools available for measuring unpaid household work on an empirical basis. *Tatjana Sikoska* tackles the methodological aspects of measuring and valuing unpaid household production in more detail. After comparing the existing methods and techniques, she presents INSTRAW's innovative methodology, which applies the United Nations 'satellite accounts' concept which has been promoted in the context of the UN valuing domestic labour.

The study carried out by *Thelma Gálvez* shows the construction of gender statistics. It offers a bird's eye view of statistics compiled via national systems and their shortcomings, which the author then uses as a starting point to examine what is needed to produce gender-sensitive statistics that help facilitate a change in gender relations as a whole.

PART II   takes a look at the often difficult process of integrating gender issues into the state's agenda. The contribution by *Maria Cristina Rojas* and *Elvia Caro* explores various conceptual interpretations of the state's role in the search for gender equality: the state as a reproducer of gender relations, as an autonomous entity, as a constituent part of gender relations, and as an institutionalized system of interpretation. Rojas and Caro also propose interesting new terms for the women's movement to view the state in their quest for gender justice. *Annette Backhaus*, focusing on gender and state modernization, examines the factors that hinder state intervention from promoting a change in gender relations, institutional bias being one such factor. She holds that the processes of state modernization in Latin America favour institutional change and contain key elements relevant to designing such a strategy.

PART III   As part of the experience of institutionalizing gender in formal national and international settings, three chapters deal with integrating a gender approach into ongoing organizational processes. *Ana Rico de Alonso* and *Barbara Hess* describe step-by-step how to deal with the institutional integration of a gender approach at the national level, with specific reference to the Colombian National Planning Department. *José Antonio Ocampo* takes a broader perspective on the subject. He describes international, regional and national tools to promote gender equality and puts forward the conceptual approach of the United Nations Economic Commission for Latin America and the Caribbean (ECLAC). ECLAC focuses on diagnosis of macro-economic conditions, plus the need for an efficient state and a healthy, open economy. In his view, knowing accurately who benefits from policies and who may be adversely affected is crucial.

Maria Nieves Rico reviews the actual process followed by ECLAC in mainstreaming a gender approach into its procedures and tools. Its achievements, difficulties and learning experiences may help other organisations embarking on similar processes as they encounter the all too familiar stumbling-block called 'institutional habits'.

PART IV   The last section of this book focuses on case studies from Latin America. These may well be relevant to other developing regions. With regard to the productive sector, *Cecilia López Montaño* explains the salient changes, but also persistent biases, in Colombia's rural and urban labour markets. She identifies women's growing insertion into the labour market as the principal nexus between the macro-economic and social universes, in which gender inequalities so strikingly continue to surface.

The contribution by *Rosemary McGee* entails a gender analysis of the methodologies and instruments used in Colombia to record poverty, and the country's poverty alleviation policies. She argues from two perspectives, one analysing how poor men and women in rural communities experience poverty and the other describing how poverty is perceived by the public authorities in charge of designing and implementing poverty alleviation policies. In the last chapter of the book, *Jasmine Gideon* offers a detailed analysis of how a series of economic reforms was implemented in Central America in the 1990s, pointing out how they often failed to meet their objectives. Drawing on empirical data, she highlights the impact of economic reforms on women and men and the impact that gender relations have had on the reform of Central American economies.

We hope this publication contributes to the debate on gender and macro-economic policy that is flourishing throughout the world. We know, however, that much still needs to be done to come up with feasible approaches. Further research is certainly needed to address pressing questions. To point out just a few examples as regards the labour market, there is the extent to which women's more active participation in the economy affects consumption and saving patterns in the home; how domestic well-being is influenced by women's increased presence in the labour market; how women's growing education and engagement in the labour market have resulted in higher productivity of the economy as a whole; and the question whether women's broader participation has discouraged or displaced men's participation. We look forward to new findings on these and other issues.

Many people and entities have made this publication possible. First and foremost, I would like to thank the authors for engaging unstintingly with this endeavour. My highest appreciation goes to Elvia Caro, who compiled and edited many of the documents originally published in Spanish. My special gratitude goes to Robert Molteno from Zed Books, who was a most patient and valuable ally. Writer and translator Anabel Torres merits special recognition for translating many of the articles from Spanish into English. Finally, I would like to express our special appreciation to the former planning minister of Colombia, Cecilia López Montaño, for so wholeheartedly hosting the International Seminar on Macro-economics, Gender and the State, which was the starting point for this book.

Martha Gutiérrez on behalf of
the Gender-Project of GTZ[3]

NOTES

1. For an introduction to the gender dimensions within key concepts of macroeconomics, refer to the BRIDGE–GTZ publication: *Glossary on Macroeconomics from a Gender Perspective* (www.ids.ac.uk/bridge/reports_gend_ec.html)

2. The seminar's findings and all the papers presented were published by the Colombian National Planning Department through Tercer Mundo Editores in the book: *Macroeconomía, Género y Estado*, 2nd edn, May 1999.

3. Martha Gutiérrez is a political scientist and currently heads GTZ's policy project on Democracy and the Rule of Law (Germany).

BIBLIOGRAPHY

Alexander, P. and S. Baden (2000) *Glossary on Macroeconomics from a Gender Perspective*, Brighton: BRIDGE.

Bakker, I. (1994) 'Engendering macroeconomics' policy reform in the era of global restructuring and adjustment', in I. Bakker (ed.), *The Strategic Silence. Gender and Economic Policy*, London: Zed Books.

Benería, L. (1995) 'Toward a greater integration of gender in economics', *World Development*, 23(11).

Blackden, M. and E. Morris-Hughes (1993) *Paradigm Postponed: Gender and Economic Adjustment in Sub-Saharan Africa*, Washington, DC: World Bank.

Cagatay, N., D. Elson and C. Grown (1995) 'Gender, adjustment and macroeconomics', *World Development*, 23(11).

Elson D. and J. Gideon (1997) 'Género en el análisis de las economías nacionales. Crecer con la mujer. Oportunidades para el desarrollo económico centroamericano', San José: Royal Embassy of The Netherlands, Manchester University.

Palmer, I. (1995) 'Public finances from a gender perspective', *World Development*, 23(11).

Van Osch, T. (1996) 'Aspectos de género en el proceso de globalización', in T. van Osch (ed.), *Nuevos enfoques económicos*, San José: UNAH-POSCAE, Honduras Women's Study Centre, Royal Embassy of The Netherlands.

Walters, B. (1995) 'Engendering macroeconomics. A reconsideration of growth Theory", *World Development*, 23(11).

PART ONE

Macro-economics and Gender

CHAPTER I

Broadening the Foundations of Macro-economic Models through a Gender Approach: New Developments

BARBARA EVERS[1]

§ Since the mid-1980s economists working within a gendered analytical perspective have produced a substantial body of work that critically evaluates macro-economic theory, macro-economic policy and its gendered impacts (see Beneria 1995 for a review of this literature; for recent work see Bakker 1994; Darity 1995; Elson 1995, 1998; Elson and McGee 1995; Palmer 1995; Grown et al. 2000; Walters 1995 and chapters by Çagatay, Gideon and Palmer, this volume). Although the focus of this chapter is on gender inequalities, much of the work on gender and macro-economics is part of a wider effort to develop a 'a more humane economics centred around the provisioning of human needs rather than around the notions of scarcity, efficiency and maximization of economic growth without a human purpose' (Beneria 1995: 1847). We would argue that a gendered macro perspective, incorporating social reproduction, is integral to the development of more equitable and sustainable approaches to growth, poverty reduction and human development (see for example, Elson and Cagatay 2000; Elson et al. 1997; Picchio 1992; UNIFEM 2000).

This chapter summarizes recent efforts to broaden and transform the analytical foundations of macro-economic models through the integration of a gender analytical approach. This is not a formal discussion, but one that summarizes many of the key issues and developments in the area of gender and macro-economics which may be of interest to macro-economists who have little understanding of gender and to those familiar with gender analysis, but with little background in macro-economics.

The chapter is organized as follows: the first section summarizes selective empirical findings on the relationship between gender inequalities and economic growth and introduces the idea of conceptualizing the economy from a gender perspective at the micro and meso levels; the second section discusses problems of introducing gender into macro-economic frameworks and notes the fundamental differences between two main streams of contemporary macro-economic thought: individualist micro-foundations and structural macro-oriented approaches; the third section presents a critical view of the current micro-foundations orthodoxy in macro-economics; the fourth section points to recent developments in engendering macro-economic models; the fifth section discusses the importance of social reproduction as an analytical concept in macro-economic theory and as a focus for empirical investigation for economic policy; and the sixth section briefly reviews some implications for policy.

GENDER INEQUALITIES AND GROWTH

There is now a substantial body of evidence and theoretical reasoning that demonstrates important links between gender inequalities and women's excessive time burdens, on the one hand, and prospects for economic growth, on the other. In particular, gender inequalities are understood to be not only bad for women, but also constraints to development and growth. 'Constraints can be seen as hampering the smooth interaction of the different dimensions of the economy, creating disabling rather than enabling environments, and preventing the outcome of the international and national policy and of individual decisions adding up to sustainable, well balanced development' (Elson et al. 1997: 13).

In the context of sub-Saharan Africa, there is convincing evidence that gender inequalities constrained the supply response in agriculture (for example, see Brown 1995; Tibaijuka 1994; Palmer 1991). The World Bank (1993) draws attention to the particularly heavy workload of women, 'the significance of which is that women's labour time is highly inelastic and that female labour availability (whether for economic activities or for community-based mobilisation for self-help schemes) requires explicit assessment of the opportunity costs involved ... This is especially the case in reference to agriculture' (pp. 33–4). Not only is women's labour time over-utilized, but strict gender divisions of work mean that there is little flexibility with regard to the substitutability of male and female labour (Evans 1992).

In addition to the constraints that arise from the micro-level division of labour, distribution of time burdens and access to resources within individual households, firms or farms, there is a social and institutional dimension to these gender-based constraints. This becomes apparent with the examination of the meso dimension of the economy, which mediates between the micro and the macro. The meso consists of social norms, as well as social and physical infrastructure and collections of micro agents in organizations such as trade unions and chambers of commerce, and in markets for labour, goods and credit (Elson et al. 1997; Elson et al. 1998). At the meso level, gender inequalities and gender biases in labour, credit and goods markets have been shown to have costs for the economy as a whole in terms of misallocation of resources, inefficiencies and depressed economic growth (Elson et al. 1997; Palmer, 1991, 1995, and this volume). For instance, research in Latin America shows that gender inequality in the labour market has a cost to women, in terms of lower wages, but also in terms of national output, which would be some 5 per cent higher if gender inequalities were reduced and women's wages were higher (Tzannatos 1991). Palmer's work analyses the links between gender discrimination in credit markets and notions of economic efficiency (see Chapter 3, this volume). Women face higher interest rates than men, partly because the risks of lending to women are over-estimated (Baden 1996). Although this perception is changing with more micro-credit targeted specifically to women, women entrepreneurs still face gender-based institutional barriers in financial and credit markets. Local perceptions of trust and the informal rules of a male-dominated households and business ethic are still likely to disadvantage women over their male counterparts (Goetz 1995, 1997). In addition, gender bias in training and education means that women often lack the necessary accounting and marketing skills needed to make the most efficient use of the credit (Snyder 2000). The consequence is a distortion in the allocation of credit, which is known to be a constraint to rural agriculture as well as urban-based micro, medium and small enterprises.

Conceptualizing the economy from a gender perspective: micro and meso levels Before looking at the macro economy, we briefly review the gendered aspects of the economy at the micro and meso levels. Clearly there are huge differences in the precise nature of gender relations, gendered structures and processes, which change over time. Here we present abstractions, or stylized facts about the gendered structures of economies (see Chapter 16, this volume) which are distilled from the contextual specifics in order to present essential characteristics for the purposes of economic analysis.

The gendered structure of the micro level refers to the systematic, gender-based division of labour within commercial and domestic units and asymmetries in the rights, roles and responsibilities of women and men and boys and girls, where the distribution of household resources is often a source of conflict and subject to processes of bargaining between men and women within the household (Dwyer and Bruce 1988; Haddad et al. 1997). In practice, this means that men tend to control the majority of productive resources and decision-making while women tend to have primary responsibility for family care and for providing unpaid family labour to households, firms and farms. It also means that men and to a lesser extent boys are more likely to enjoy the benefits of household resources than girls and women.

Gendered structures and inequalities also exist at the meso level. We know this from the examination of social norms, the provision of public services and infrastructure, the structure of property rights and the operation of goods, labour and credit markets, which show that these meso-level institutions function in ways that tend to disadvantage women in comparison to their male counterparts (Elson et al. 1997; Harris-White 1998; Evers and Walters 2000).

GENDER ANALYSIS AT THE MACRO LEVEL

Gender at the macro level is more difficult to conceptualize. The macro-economy is usually described in terms of the gross national product (GNP) and the shares of agriculture, industry and services in the GNP. It corresponds to the information assembled in the System of National Accounts, which measures the value of goods and services exchanged on markets or provided by governments and non-government organizations (see Chapter 2, this volume).

Since macro-economics is concerned with abstract aggregates, not people, and certainly not men and women, how can macro-economics be made gender-sensitive? There are two general approaches to introducing gender at the macro level, which correspond to two broadly different schools of thought. One approach takes a particular conceptualization of the macro-economy as the sum total of the individual transactions of all micro-level agents. This approach roughly corresponds to the micro-foundations approach to macro-economics. It is essentially individual-istic, based on neo-classical micro-economic notions of 'economic man' who exhibits rational, optimizing behaviour. Gender-aware computable general equilibrium (CGE) models, discussed below, are structured around this micro-foundations approach to macro-economics.

An alternative approach is one that conceptualizes the macro-economy as having a life of its own, where macro-economic phenomena (the levels of and relationships between, investment, employment, growth and so on) are best understood through an analysis of the relationships between aggregates (investment, savings, interest rates, production and as we show later, social reproduction) and not through summing up the behaviour of all individual 'agents', households and firms. This approach takes a structural, not an individualist, perspective and shows how macro-economic theory and policy can be gendered, without talking about individual men and women. It looks at economic structures and conceptualizes macro-economics as a *bearer of gender* (Walters 1995; Elson 2000).

The current orthodoxy in academic macro-economics is oriented to a micro-foundations approach. The next section presents criticisms of micro-foundations as a basis for macro-economic analysis, gendered or not.

LIMITATIONS OF A MICRO-FOUNDATIONS APPROACH TO MACRO-ECONOMICS

The micro-foundations approach to macro-economics (which is the basis of Computable General Equilibrium models discussed in the next section), though technically attractive and intuitively appealing, has significant limitations as an entry point for engendering macro-economics. Kirman (1992) and Martel (1996) present forceful and convincing theoretical and empirically based objections to micro-foundations. The general sense of their arguments is summarized below.

Micro-foundations: a critical evaluation Kirman (1992) and Martel (1996) use both formal and more conceptual or intuitive arguments against the micro-foundations approach to macro-economics. The theoretical objections centre on the relationship between individual and collective behaviour and the notion of the 'representative agent', which lies at the heart of micro-foundations. It is a device that allows the aggregation of individual behaviour to represent the aggregate behaviour of society as whole, that is, it links the micro with the macro. Kirman's (1992) arguments shatter the legitimacy of the representative agent and as a consequence undermine the core of micro-foundations theorizing. Martel (1996) builds on the critique of Kirman and others and argues for a 'more meaningful' approach to macro-economics. In view of the absence of a theoretical case for the 'straitjacket of the representative agent' (Kirman 1992: 123), both Kirman and Martel conclude that its persistence in economic analysis is normative or ideological.

'It should be clear by now that the assumption of a representative individual is far from innocent; it is the fiction by which macro-economists can justify equilibrium analysis and provide pseudo-micro-foundations' (Kirman 1992: 125). 'Pseudo', because there is no formal justification for this (ibid.) ... '(T)he representative consumer is a purely mathematical result and need not have economic content ... its use ... in most macro work is an illegitimate method of ignoring valid aggregations concerns ... however ... it simplifies a great deal of macro work and thought, so is not likely to be abandoned' (Lewbel 1989, cited in Kirman 1992: 134).

The extent to which economic theories and associated models are useful for understanding economic problems and providing useful tools for policy depends to some extent on their ability to reflect essential aspects of reality. Some would argue that this is a major weakness of micro-foundations approaches found in CGE models. For example, Morishima (1984) has argued that, 'If economists successfully devise a correct general equilibrium model, even if it can be proved to possess an equilibrium solution should it lack the institutional backing to realise an equilibrium solution, then that equilibrium solution will amount to no more than a utopian state of affairs which bears no relation whatsoever to the real economy' (Morishima 1984, quoted in Kirman 1992: 121). In other words, even if these models can be made technically correct, it is argued that they are still unable to accommodate essential aspects of macro-economic reality.

ENGENDERING MACRO-ECONOMIC MODELS: RECENT DEVELOPMENTS

Recent developments in engendering macro-economic models draw on both the structural and individualistic micro-foundations schools of thought. This section draws on Çagatay et al. 2000, the most up-to-date and comprehensive account of the current state of the art of engendering macro-economic models.[2]

Computable general equilibrium models: male and female agents Despite
the objections summarized in the previous section, CGE models are
influential in both academic and policy circles. Some would argue that
these models are essentially micro-economic devices and as such will
never capture truly macro-economic phenomena and relationships
(Walters 1995). However, if we ignore for a moment the objections to
the representative agent, and view these models as heuristic devices,
they may provide important insights for macro-economists who may
not otherwise consider the relevance of gender to macro-economic
analysis. These models demonstrate how gendered behaviour and
gendered structures might influence macro-economic outcomes. This
realization can be important for the strategy of engendering the macro
policy process.

Collier (1994) is an example of the micro-foundations framework,
which models the reallocation of labour in adjusting economies where
standard macro-economic variables are simply disaggregated by gender.
With this approach stylized behavioural differences between men and
women, in investment, consumption and savings decisions for instance,
and gendered patterns of wealth and income distribution are associated
with different macro-economic outcomes. Gendered behaviour is
interpreted to arise from the exogenously determined behaviour of
representative maximizing agents (Çagatay et al. 1995: 1830). For Collier,
the overriding influence of gendered role models is a key explanation
for the gender barriers to labour reallocation in the context of structural
adjustment. However, a particular weakness of this method is that it
does not take into account the reproductive economy (see the following
section) and ignores the gendered power relations and institutions that
influence the behaviour of men and women.

More promising CGE approaches have been developed recently
which introduce new macro-economic variables representing gendered
structures and gendered power relations in the public and private sectors
and, in some cases, in the social reproduction sector (Grown et al.
2000). The new gendered macro-economic variables include measures
of the degree of gender inequality in markets (labour, credit, goods),
gender differences in decision-making and control over resources in
households and the public and private sectors. This sort of disaggregation is not based purely on biological differences between men
and women, but corresponds to the ways in which the social relations
of gender impose constraints on the overall behaviour of the macro-
economy, comparable to disaggregations by class (Walters 1995).

Arndt and Tarp (2000) adopt a more structural approach to a multi-sector computable general equilibrium model for Mozambique, which divides agricultural labour into male and female categories. The model captures gender inequalities and their influence on men's and women's behaviour and on the structure of product and labour markets. For instance, it incorporates the empirical finding that women tend to be more risk-averse than men. However, Arndt and Tarp themselves state that the most important gap in their approach is the absence of 'production within the household and other intrahousehold resource allocation issues' (Arndt and Tarp 2000: 1312). They go on to suggest that 'Improved treatment of gender and resource allocation issues as well as production activities within the household are therefore critical topics for future research and data-generation work' (ibid.).

A model that does include social reproduction is that developed by Fontana and Wood (2000). This incorporates new gendered sectors: social reproduction and leisure along with a gendered market economy sector. It applies this model to the case of Bangladesh.[3] There are clearly advantages to this approach, and again, helpful insights can be obtained by changing assumptions about women's demands and preferences with regard to work in the productive and reproductive sectors. However, some of its weaknesses are the failure to account for gendered roles in work in the characterization of labour flows and the failure to consider gendered power relations that are taken up by others.

Together these CGE models provide a means to capture ways in which gendered structures and gendered behaviour can influence macro-economic outcomes. Although there is sufficient reason to question the extent to which their outcomes reflect the reality of the macro-economy, when used in combination with other approaches, and particularly in consultation with non-technical specialists with expertise in gender, they can stimulate new approaches to thinking about the relationship between gender and macro-economic phenomena. They can suggest how actions in one sector might influence outcomes and reactions in another. This dynamism provides stimulating food for thought.

In general, CGE models are dependent on reliable and extensive data sources and are highly sensitive to the assumptions built into the models. We would argue that, at the very least, the findings of CGE models should be interpreted with a good deal of care and a heavy helping of scrutiny.

Structural approaches A different approach to macro-economics is

suggested by Walters, who argues that the limitations of micro-foundations of macro-economics 'will not be overcome by the reduction of
the macro level of analysis into a micro analysis of gendered agents'
(Walters 1995: 1878). So although gender differences and inequalities
matter, it is asserted that any disaggregations of macro-economic models
should be structural rather than individualist, based on the 'understanding of the way in which gender as a social institution impinges on
or constrains the behavior of the macroeconomy' (Walters 1995: 1871).

The structural models discussed are based on a 'two-sector' approach
that focuses on the interactions between the monetized, market-oriented
economy and the non-monetized economy of social reproduction.
Gender disaggregations of labour and resource allocation and gendered
power relations are accommodated in this type of model. But instead of
focusing on particular gender variables, the economy itself is characterized as a gendered structure (Elson 1995; Elson and McGee 1995; Elson
et al. 1997) and economic structures are either explicitly or implicitly
gendered in the way they function and in their outcomes. In this
approach gendered roles and inequalities are endogenous, that is, they
require explanation within the model.

Darity (1995) is an example of a gendered two-sector approach
particularly appropriate for analysing agricultural-based economies that
are linked to the international economy through agricultural exports.
Darity provides insights into the causes of and solutions to supply
constraints in agriculture that are generated by an inflexible gender
division of labour. This model is able to show how gendered power
relations and the gender division of labour in the household and market-
oriented economy influence both economic (agricultural output and
exports) and social outcomes (education, nutrition, well-being of
children, for example). Darity provides a good starting point from which
to 'explode' the restrictions of a formal model into a broader discussion
of women's agency and from which both social and economic policy
implications can be derived (Evers and Walters 2000). Extensions of
Darity (1995) show that women's rights in land, control over household
income as well as social norms and access to social and physical
infrastructure all affect women's bargaining power within the household.
These, in turn, influence women's responses to macro-economic policies,
particularly devaluation and trade liberalization measures and have
implications for economic growth as well as social well-being (Evers
and Walters 2000; Warner and Campbell 2000; Arndt and Tarp 2000).

Braunstein (2000) is a macro model that combines a macro disaggregation with a two-sector approach based on a female labour-intensive export sector and a male labour-intensive domestic goods sector. This model brings out the interactions of the productive and social reproductive economies by showing how gender relations in the household influence foreign direct investment. This analysis focuses on the distribution of the costs of social reproduction between men and women within the household which, in turn, influence women's labour supply to the market economy. It is argued that women's labour supply is a determinant of the profitability of investment. Braunstein argues that 'macroeconomists and development economists have not paid enough attention to the unique factors affecting female labor supply, tending to overlook how workers' productive roles outside the factory door, and the institutional and social contexts in which they live, create fundamental differences between the labor supply behavior of women and men' (2000: 1163). This model provides a framework for analysing the relationship between direct foreign investment, international capital mobility and gender relations. The depiction of the sectors and the dynamics of the model are most relevant to an East Asian and perhaps a Latin American setting.

GENDER AS A SOCIAL INSTITUTION: INCORPORATING SOCIAL REPRODUCTION INTO MACRO-ECONOMICS

From our point of view, the structural models that emphasize gender as a social institution, rather than through the gendering of economic agents, offer the most valuable analytical contribution to engendering macro-economics. Understanding gender as a social institution hinges critically on factoring social reproduction into macro-economic analysis. The rich literature on social reproduction is too vast to mention here (see for example Folbre 1994; Gardiner 1997; Mackintosh 1981). This section clarifies what we mean by social reproduction for the purposes of macro-economic analysis, drawing in particular on Picchio (1992), who traces the historical processes through which it has been removed from the sphere of economic analysis.

'(T)he significance of social reproduction as a foundation block of the classical analytical framework is almost completely lost today' (Picchio 1992: 14). Picchio contrasts the classical political economy framework with contemporary macro-economics. In the classical models, social reproduction and the market economy were linked through the idea of the subsistence wage, so that wages were seen to be directly connected to the costs of social reproduction. In modern economic frameworks, wages are viewed as prices simply set by supply and demand with no reference to social reproduction. De-linking the wage from the costs of social reproduction has meant that the processes of social reproduction, and particularly of reproducing and main-taining the labour force, were removed from the domain of economic analysis.

The exclusion of social reproduction from economic analysis is problematic for modern macro-economics where labour is treated like a commodity but it is not treated as a produced good (Walters 1995). With the removal of the sphere of social reproduction from modern economic analysis, all the processes associated with the production of the labour force are treated as *exogenous*, as if labour came out of thin air rather than through the care and toil of (largely) women. Thus current efforts to engender macro-economic models treat labour as *endogenous*, so that the production of labour itself needs to be explained within the model and not simply assumed to exist.

Modern macro-economics (both micro-foundations and structural approaches) is less amenable to gender analysis than its classical pre-decessors because of the absence of social reproduction from their analytical frameworks. This separation of 'the economy' from social reproduction, both physically and analytically, underlies and reinforces the gender bias in macro-economics. Before discussing the insertion of social reproduction into macro-economic models we clarify what we mean by social reproduction.

Social reproduction: defined We use the term social reproduction to describe the time and effort required to reproduce human beings (and the future labour force) and to maintain the well-being of people in families and communities. Although some of these activities are pro-vided by and/or supported by the state (see Pearson 2000) our central focus in this chapter is on the unpaid labour provided in the domestic sphere. It is female-intensive; men contribute a far smaller share to social reproduction than do women and this is universally true (UNDP 1995). In practice the precise nature of the activities of social repro-duction is shaped by the socio-economic and cultural context. It may include, for instance, the time and effort spent collecting water and fuel for family use, shopping, cooking, sewing, cleaning, caring for children, the elderly and the sick; the time and effort spent transport-ing children to school, health clinics and swimming lessons as well as the time spent in biological reproductive activities (childbearing and early nurturing).

Conventional economics often confuses social reproduction with leisure since time spent in unpaid labour is assumed to be non-working time (Elson 1993). Though not categorized as 'work' by the System of National Accounts,[4] it clearly has the characteristics of work: it absorbs a large proportion of time and energy, especially that of women and girls (UNDP 1995). It is an obligation that has costs in terms of time and energy. Although it is not remunerated by a wage, it is indispensable for the continuation of the entire society (UNIFEM 2000: 23). However it should be noted that the *motivations* for social reproduction are clearly very different from those that operate in the market economy. Though the outcomes of social reproduction may have economic significance, the reasons for providing care cannot be understood simply as economic optimizing behaviour. The sum total of these activities is referred to in various ways (reproductive economy, unpaid domestic economy). Here we refer to it as social reproduction.[5]

The activities of social reproduction are not normally included in official statistics either conceptually or practically. Thus, the collection of more and better data is important, as noted by others in this volume. Building up a statistical data base of social reproduction can contribute to broadening the scope of the policy framework in terms of design, implementation and evaluation. This requires time, resources, particular skills and above all commitment from key decision-makers. It is an important but doable project for strengthening the information base for more gender-sensitive macro-economic policy.

More formidable and complex constraints to engendering macro-economic theory and policy are found in the analytical limitations of modern macro-economics. The way to incorporate the insights of gender analysis into macro-economics is to understand and incorporate into the analytical and policy framework the interactions of production (aggregated outcomes of the market, official economy: GDP and so on) and social reproduction (the aggregate output of the activities of social reproduction).

Women and social reproduction Historically, in virtually every corner of the world, gendered structures of production and social reproduction mean that social reproduction has become primarily women's responsibility. Although women have always worked in both processes of production and social reproduction, in industrialized settings (including agro-processing), unpaid and paid work are often done in physically separate places and compete with one another for women's time. Before women are able to engage in production for wages, their unpaid domestic responsibilities must be fulfilled, whereas men do not face such constraints. Thus, with industrialization and the extension of the market, the problems of organizing production *and* reproduction do not disappear. Indeed, the separation of production and reproduction continues to have profound consequences for women's lives. However, historically, what did disappear with this separation was any consideration of these problems within the framework of macro-economic analysis (Picchio 1992: 82–3).

This separation generates two types of insecurities for women: women become more dependent on the wages of a husband, brother or father; and when women do enter the labour market, their wages are lower than those of their male counterparts. Thus because women reproduce the labour force not only do they work more but they earn less (Picchio 1992: 83–4). Picchio's historical analysis highlights the ways in which the separation of production and social reproduction has shifted the responsibility for care from those who own and run businesses and pay wages to those who are responsible for feeding and caring for people in the domestic sphere, largely women. As Adam Smith observed, 'a well fed and well clothed, high waged worker costs his employer less than a badly fed, poorly clothed slave' (quoted in Picchio 1992: 97). But who clothes and feeds the worker? It is largely women's work in social reproduction that covers the costs of maintaining and reproducing the labour force (see Chapter 3, this volume).

A central concern for gender analysis at the macro level, therefore, is to understand the economic implications of this and to bring these insights into the policy sphere. In particular, it means formalizing in economic analysis and policy frameworks what we already know: that women's work in social reproduction does not just support families and communities, but supports the productive economy. As Picchio puts it, 'while wages are a cost of production, housework as unpaid labour is a deduction from costs ... the surplus is realised by capitalists not in selling labour but in buying it (Picchio 1992: 97).

Elson's examination of the interaction between the unpaid and paid economies finds that 'unpaid labour plays an important role in processes of macroeconomic adjustment of the paid economy; and ought not to be neglected in decisions about macroeconomic strategy' (Elson 1993: 1). The focus is not simply on adding up the value of unpaid labour, but on looking at the interactions between paid and unpaid economies (roughly, production and social reproduction). Elson argues that the processes of structural adjustment can be better understood by examining the interaction of unpaid and paid economies in aggregate. Unpaid labour can cushion the shocks of economic adjustment, but this may place very heavy burdens on those providing unpaid labour (normally women and girls), and this increased burden is likely to have a negative feedback in terms of the ability of the economy to adjust effectively and to shift the economy on to a long-run growth path. As argued above, the principal negative feedback effects are constraints on the supply of labour to the market economy, limiting the response to new price incentives; overloading of the family and community structures, which leads to social breakdown; and instability damaging the ability of a society to educate and feed itself, and thus acquire new skills for economic growth (Elson 1993).

IMPLICATIONS FOR POLICY

Although there has been a great deal of progress in conceptualizing gender at the macro-economic level, this work has only just begun to influence the policy process itself. The work of many gender-aware social development analysts and economists – including contributors to this volume – has helped to advance this process.[6] At the same time, there has been some re-evaluation of the market dogma of the Washington Consensus (Stiglitz 1998). And for some years, many bilateral donors and the UN institutions have emphasized the influence of a broad range of factors on growth and development. Among them is the recognition of the importance of education, health and social well-being as critical inputs to economic growth. Despite these promising developments in policy circles, it is still rarely recognized that the health, education and well-being of families and communities are not just products of education and health institutions in the public and private sectors, but are also products of women's time and effort in social reproduction. At the same time, while many governments and multilateral organizations now emphasize the importance of human capabilities as an essential component of economic and social transformation, there is still virtually no acknowledgement that 'unpaid labour in the household and in the community is a vital ingredient in the transformation ... [and] for the most part, people do not simply acquire inputs through the market and transform themselves into labour power, we all rely to some extent on the unpaid labour of others to cook, clear and care for us and create the social framework of daily life' (Elson 1993: 3).

CONCLUSIONS

Gendered structures, inequalities and gender differences in behaviour are integral to the subject matter of macro-economics. The gender dimensions of economic structures and processes can be modelled in different ways but the message for policy-makers is clear: these gendered structures, including the explicit consideration of the sphere of social reproduction, must form an integral part of the theoretical and policy frameworks of macro-economics.

This chapter, along with the other contributions to this volume, attests to the need for more and better gender-disaggregated data, for more refined analytical concepts and frameworks that take into account the economic significance of gendered structures and gender relations for macro policy and programming. However, this needs to be complemented by the meaningful participation of women and the representation of women's interests and the needs of social reproduction in the macro-economic policy process in order to build a more people-centred macro-economics.

NOTES

1. Barbara Evers is professor in the Development Studies Programme at the Department of Sociology of the University of Manchester, UK.

2. For those interested in a more detailed and formal discussion of the models, see the special issue of *World Development*, edited by Grown, Elson and Çagatay (2000).

3. This is developed further in Fontana 2001.

4. Some countries produce satellite accounts, which attempt to measure the value of this unpaid work (Canada and Australia, for example).

5. See Feminist Economics website: www.facstuff.bucknell.edu/jshacke/iaffe, for a discussion of the different names for this type of work.

6. Some multilateral organizations and many bilateral donors in the OECD/DAC have produced guidelines for operationalizing more gender-sensitive approaches to macro-economic and sectoral strategies. Approaches that incorporate notions of social reproduction in the analysis include the Gender Responsive Budget Initiatives of the Commonwealth Secretariat in collaboration with the United Nations Development Fund for Women (UNIFEM) and International Development Research Centre (IDRC) (see www.gender-budgets.org for details); and guidelines produced by the OECD/DAC Working party on Gender Equality

(OECD 2000, 2001) on integrating gender into programme aid, sector investment programmes, market reforms and other forms of economic policy assistance.

BIBLIOGRAPHY

Arndt, C. and F. Tarp (2000) 'Agricultural technology, risk and gender: a CGE analysis of Mozambique', *World Development*, 28(7): 1307–26.

Baden, S. (1996) *Gender Issues in Financial Liberalisation and Financial Sector Reform*, BRIDGE Report, Brighton: Institute of Development Studies.

Bakker, I. (ed.) (1994) *The Strategic Silence: Gender and Economic Policy*, London and Toronto: Zed Books with the North–South Institute.

Beneria, L. (1995) 'Toward a greater integration of gender in economics', *World Development*, 23(11): 1839–50.

Brown, L. (1995) *Gender and the Implementation of Structural Adjustment in Africa: Examining the Micro-Meso-Macro Linkages, a Synthesis of a Three Country Case Study: Ghana, Zambia, Mali*, Report prepared for the Africa and Middle East Division, Canadian International Development Agency, Washington, DC: International Food Policy Research Institute.

Braunstein, E. (2000) 'Engendering foreign direct investment: family structure, labor markets and international capital mobility', *World Development*, 28(7): 1157–72.

Çagatay, N., D. Elson and C. Grown (eds) (1995) *Gender, Adjustment and Macroeconomics*, Special Issue, *World Development*, 23(11).

Collier, P. (1994) 'Gender aspects of labour allocation during structural adjustment: a theoretical framework and the Africa experience', in S. Horton, R. Kanbur and D. Mazumdar (eds), *Labour Markets in an Era of Adjustment*, Vol. 1, Washington, DC: World Bank.

Darity, W. (1995) 'The Formal Structure of a Gender-Segregated Low-Income Economy', *World Development*, 23(11), November.

Dwyer, D. and J. Bruce (1988) *A Home Divided: Women and Income in the Third World*, Stanford, CA: Stanford University Press.

Elson, D. (1991) 'Male bias in macro-economics: the case of structural adjustment', in D. Elson (ed.), *Male Bias in the Development Process*, Manchester: Manchester University Press.

— (1993) *Unpaid Labour, Macroeconomic Adjustment and Macroeconomic Strategies*, Gender Analysis and Development Economics: A Programme of Research and Training Funded by the Swedish International Development Authority, Working Paper Number 3.

— (1995) 'Gender awareness in modeling structural adjustment', *World Development*, 23(11).

— (1998) 'Talking to the boys, gender and economic growth models', in C. Jackson and R. Pearson (eds), *Feminist Visions of Development, Gender Analysis and Policy*, London and New York: Routledge.

— (2000) 'Gender at the Macroeconomic Level', in J. Cook, J. Roberts and

G. Waylen (eds), *Towards a Gendered Political Economy*, Basingstoke and London: Macmillan and New York: St Martin's Press, pp. 77–97.

Elson, D., S. Baden and G. Reardon (1998) *Gender and Market Liberalisation*, Paper presented to the Workshop on Integrating Gender Issues in Programme Aid, Sector Investment Programmes, Market Reform and Other Forms of Economic Policy Assistance, DAC Working Party on Gender Equality, OECD, Paris, 6–7 May.

Elson, D., B. Evers and J. Gideon (1997) *Gender Aware Country Economic Reports*, Concepts and Sources; Uganda, Nicaragua and Pakistan, University of Manchester Graduate School of Social Sciences, Genecon Unit, Working Papers Nos 1–4.

Elson, D. and R. McGee (1995) 'Gender equality, bilateral program assistance and structural adjustment: policy and procedures', *World Development*, 23(11): 1987–94.

Evans, A. (1992) 'A review of the rural labour market in Uganda', May, mimeo.

Evers, B. and J. Harrigan (2001) 'Seaga Macro Manual', produced for the Seaga Programme, FAO, Rome, final draft, mimeo.

Evers, B. and B. Walters (2000) 'Extra-household factors and women farmers' supply response in Sub-Saharan Africa', *World Development*, 28(7): 1341–45.

FAO (1999) *Filling the Data Gap: Gender-sensitive Statistics for Agricultural Development*, Rome: FAO.

— (2000) *Gender and Food Security, the Role of Information: Strategy for Action*, Rome: FAO.

Folbre, N. (1994) *Who Pays for the Kids? Gender and the Structures of Constraint*, New York: Routledge.

Fontana, M. (2001) *Modelling the Effects of Trade on Women: A Closer Look at Bangladesh*, Working Paper 139, Brighton: Institute of Development Studies, September.

Fontana, M. and A. Wood (2000) 'Modeling the effects of trade on women, at work and at home', *World Development*, 28(7): 1173–90.

Gardiner, J. (1997) *Gender, Care and Economics*, London: Macmillan.

Goetz, A. M. (1995) 'Macro-meso-micro linkages: understanding gendered institutional structures and practices', Paper prepared for the SAGA Workshop on Gender and Economic Reform in Africa, Ottawa, 1–3 October.

— (ed.) (1997) *Getting Institutions Right for Women in Development*, London and New York: Zed Books.

Grown, C., D. Elson and N. Cagatay (eds) (2000) *Special Issue: Growth, Trade, Finance and Gender Inequality, World Development*, 28(7), July.

Haddad, L., J. Hoddinott and H. Alderman (eds) (1997) *Intrahousehold Resource Allocation in Developing Countries, Models, Methods and Policies*, Baltimore, MD and London: Johns Hopkins University Press.

Harriss-White, B. (1998) 'Female and male grain marketing systems: analytical and policy issues for West Africa and India', in C. Jackson and R. Pearson (eds), *Feminist Visions of Development: Gender Analysis and Policy*, London and New York: Routledge, pp. 189–213.

Joekes, S. (1999) 'A gender-analytical perspective on trade and sustainable development', in UNCTAD, *Trade, Sustainable Development and Gender*.

Kirman, Alan (1992) 'Whom or what does the representative individual represent?', *Journal of Economic Perspectives*, 6(2): 117–36.

Lewbel, A. (1989) 'Exact aggregation and a representative consumer', *Quarterly Journal of Economics*, 104, August: 622–33.

Mackintosh, M. (1981) 'Gender and economics: the sexual division of labour and the subordination of women', in K. Young, C. Wolkowitz and R. McCullagh (eds), *Of Marriage and the Market: Women's Subordination in International Perspective*, New Delhi: CSE Books, pp. 1–15.

Martel, R. (1996) 'Heterogeneity, aggregation, and a meaningful macroeconomics', in D. Colander (ed.), *Beyond Microfoundations, Post-Walrasian Macroeconomics*, Cambridge: Cambridge University Press, pp. 127–44.

Morishima, M. (1984) 'The good and bad uses of mathematics', in P. Wiles and G. North (eds), *Economics in Disarray*, Oxford: Basil Blackwell, pp. 51–73.

OECD (2000) *Gender and Economic Reform, Note by the Task Force on Gender and Economic Reform*, DCD/DAC/GEN 2000(2), Paris: Development Co-operation Directorate Development Assistance Committee of the Organisation for Economic Co-operation and Development.

— (2001) *Proceedings and Main Findings of the Consultative Workshop on Gender Equality in Sector-wide Approaches*, CDC/DAC/GEN 2001(3), Paris: Development Co-operation Directorate Development Assistance Committee of the Organisation for Economic Co-operation and Development.

Palmer, I. (1991) *Gender and Population in the Adjustment of African Economies*, Geneva: ILO.

— 1992, 'Gender equity and economic efficiency in adjustment programmes', in H. Afshar and C. Dennis (eds), *Women and Adjustment Policies in the Third World*, London: Macmillan.

— 1995, 'Public finance from a gender perspective', *World Development*, 23(11): 1981–6.

Pearson, R. (2000) 'The political economy of social reproduction: the case of Cuba in the 1990s', in J. Cook, J. Roberts and G. Waylen (eds), *Towards a Gendered Political Economy*, London: Macmillan and New York: St Martin's Press, pp. 77–97.

Picchio, A. (1992) *Social Reproduction: The Political Economy of the Labour Market*, Cambridge: Cambridge University Press.

Snyder, M. (2000) *Women in African Economies, from Burning Sun to Boardrooms*, Kampala: Fountain Publishers.

Stiglitz, J. (1998) *More Instruments and Broader Goals: Moving Toward the Post-Washington Consensus*, paper presented to the World Institute for Development Economics Research Annual Lecture, Helsinki, 7 January.

Tibaijuka, A. (1994) 'The cost of differential gender roles in African agriculture: a case study of smallholder banana–coffee farms in the Kagera region, Tanzania', *Journal of Agricultural Economies*, 45(1): 69–81.

Tzannatos, Z. (1991) 'Potential gains from the elimination of gender differentials in the labour market', in G. Psacharopoulos and Z. Tzannatos (eds), *Women's Employment and Pay in Latin America*, Washington, DC: World Bank.

UNCTAD (1999) *Trade, Sustainable Development and Gender*, Geneva and New York: United Nations Publications, UNCTAD/EDM/Misc.78.

UNDP (1995) *Human Development Report, 1995*, Oxford and New York: Oxford University Press.

UNIFEM (2000) *Progress of the World's Women 2000, UNIFEM Biennial Report*, New York: United Nations Development Fund for Women.

Walters, B. (1995) 'Engendering macro-economics: a reconsideration of growth theory', *World Development*, 23(11).

Warner, J. M. and D. A. Campbell (2000) 'Supply response in an agrarian economy with non-symmetric gender relations', *World Development*, 28(7): 1327–40.

World Bank (1993) *Uganda: Growing Out of Poverty*, Washington, DC: World Bank.

CHAPTER 2

Engendering Macro-economics

NILUFER ÇAGATAY[1]

§ The economic analysis of gender relations is quite recent. Even though economists have in isolated instances debated 'women's issues' since the 1930s and 1950s, the concept of gender relations as a socially constructed category that could have systemic links to the economy began to emerge only after the early 1970s.[2] Looking at gender and gender relations from a macro-economic point of view is even more recent. In the 1970s, it began to be recognized that economic development had generally affected women differently from men in the developing world. Likewise, in the 1980s, feminists in general and feminist economists in particular argued that macro-economic policies that were being implemented throughout the decade in the developing world in the context of structural adjustment policies were not gender-neutral in their effects. It was also recognized that the direction of causation between the macro-economy and gender relations could go both ways. Thus, a line of analysis that began with the recognition of the gender non-neutral effects of macro-economic policies evolved in a direction where it focused on the feedback effects of gender relations on the macro-economy.

Macro-economic analysis can be described as the analysis of the economy-wide interaction of a few highly aggregated markets. Usually, at a minimum, macro-economists define three such aggregated markets: the labour market, the asset market and the goods market. Building on a conceptual understanding of how these markets are constituted, macro-economists functionally specify the connections and the nature of the interaction between them. This makes it possible to build models that can capture these relations in varying degrees of detail and complexity depending on the question at hand.

After developing a working model, it also becomes possible to add on what had been left out initially, such as the government and the income and in decision-making can act as barriers in the effective and productive use of human resources in meeting human needs. Just to cite a few examples, research by Tzannatos (1992) has shown that total output could be increased considerably by eliminating gender discrimination in occupational patterns and pay. King and Hill (1995) show that gender gaps in education have an adverse effect on growth. Likewise, especially in sub-Saharan Africa, evidence suggests that gender inequalities in the control of resources in agriculture constrains output responses that structural adjustment policies are designed to induce (Palmer 1991; Gladwin 1991).

Along similar lines, in his analysis of why structural adjustment policies have failed to be effective in Africa, Collier (1994) emphasizes the importance of constraints women face in their labour supply decision, which in his view can be summarized in terms of the following four processes: a) discrimination against women outside the household; b) copying of gender-specific role models; c) asymmetric rights and obligations within households leading to weak incentives for women to undertake tasks in male-controlled cash crop production; d) the burden of reproduction, leading to confinement to a restricted range of economic activities that are more easily compatible with motherhood.

Collier's analysis concentrates on the obstacles these processes create for labour mobility and how that negatively affects output adjustment at the macro level. However, other macro-level feedback loops caused by asymmetric rights, or, more specifically, inequalities in decision-making within the household, can also be equally important. A striking example is the so-called 'good-mother' thesis. Evidence from a diverse group of countries, for instance, shows gender differences in the pattern of consumption expenditures. Whereas women tend to spend more on children and household needs, the pattern of expenditures by men tend to be skewed towards leisure commodities (alcohol, tobacco, gambling, etc.) and goods that are status symbols. In a social environment characterized by economic insecurity and uncertainty it might not be surprising that women save and invest in their children, while men focus their energies, and channel their expenditures, in order to gain privileged access to networks of other men outside the household. Thus the expenditures of women enhance capabilities that are directly productive while those of men tend to be channelled to 'unproductive' uses. These examples make it clear that gender inequalities in the distribution of income and wealth along with male biases in the legal and institutional structure of the economy are likely to have significant short-term, as well as long-term effects on the way the macro-economy functions.

ENGENDERED MACRO-ECONOMIC MODELLING

Formal modelling can be expected to fulfil three useful functions. First, it can help us organize our body of knowledge and state our arguments with theoretical precision. We can thereby identify and isolate key variables, specifying in an unambiguous way the nature of interaction between these variables. Second, it can ease the difficulty of communication with those economists who have little knowledge of the stylized facts on how gender matters in the way the macro-economy functions. Finally, and perhaps most importantly, formal modelling is a crucial step in policy-making. Simple models can be quite effective in demonstrating the potential effectiveness of gender-aware policies to policy-makers.

Four different approaches can be distinguished in gender-aware macro-modelling (Çagatay et al. 1995a). The first method entails disaggregation by gender. In this class of models, the objective is to highlight the implications of the difference in behaviour between the two genders. An example is Collier's (1994) model of labour reallocation during structural adjustment. Here, the objective of the exercise is to show how the introduction of a key stylized fact alone – in this instance, restrictions on the mobility of female labour – can significantly alter the way the model behaves. By implication, it can then be argued that because policies that ignore gender differences in behaviour will fail to produce desired outcomes, a new gender-aware set of policies needs to be designed. Another example of this method of modelling involves taking into account differences in the patterns of consumption by gender. As discussed above, women tend to have a higher marginal propensity than men to spend on goods that enhance the capabilities of children. By introducing differences in gender patterns of consumption into the New Growth Theory models, where investment in human capital and educational attainment are important explanatory variables of long-term growth, it might be possible to trace out the long-term implications of distributing income towards women.

In this group of models, gender differences in behaviour are exogenously given, as it is assumed that they arise from a pattern of life characterized by pervasive gender inequalities. The disaggregation method is clearly more applicable in some countries than in others. In those economies where petty commodity production predominates, it is more likely that men and women control different streams of income or differ explicitly with respect to their productive activity in a clearly identifiable way. By contrast, in economies characterized by large public or private enterprises, gender differences in behaviour will be more subtle and less uniform.

The second approach to macro-economic modelling with gender involves the introduction of the gender dimension of certain macro-economic variables into the model. This approach is based on the insight that the way in which labour, credit and goods markets function is predicated upon the degree of gender inequality. Likewise, decision-making within the household, or in the private and public sectors, is made to depend on particular aspects of gender relations. As an example, we can envision what potential changes can be introduced to standard macro-economic models such as the Revised Minimum Standard Model (RMSM) used by the World Bank. For one, the incremental capital-output ratio, which plays a very important role in this model as the gauge of overall efficiency, ignores unpaid labour in the reproductive sector. If unpaid labour were taken into account, the value of this ratio, and the policy prescriptions of the model, would change. Another important variable in this and in all other macro-economic models with a clear gender dimension is the savings rate. Again, the relative importance of non-monetized goods in the wage basket, and the gender distribution of income as the 'good-mother' thesis discussed above suggests, are likely to have an impact not only on the composition of consumption expenditures but also on the overall savings rate.

The third approach divides the economy into two sectors as productive and reproductive. The former sector comprises the traditional macro-economic variables while the latter includes unpaid labour, non-monetized goods and services and human resource networks within the reproductive sector. Here, the objective is to focus on how the two sectors interact in terms of both flow and stock variables. As the model by Taylor (1995) exemplifies, these models can be developed on the basis of a social accounting matrix and different hypotheses about the linkages between the two sectors can be examined.

A fourth approach consists of using a combination of the approaches outlined above. For example, Darity (1995) combines the third approach with the first. He divides the economy into two sectors. The first sector is the household/subsistence sector in which it is assumed that production is carried out exclusively by women. The second sector is the cash crop sector where both men and women work together, but their activities are gender-typed. Men control both the production process and the income from cash crops. When needed, they try to pull women from the household/subsistence sector and enlist their labour in the cash crop production by a combination of coercion, cooperation and inducement through compensation. Exploring how the loss of female labour to the cash crop sector affects the output of the household sector, the model shows that in a gender-segregated, low-income economy where women shoulder the time/work burden, an export boom can possibly cause nutritional deprivation for women.

Another model that combines different modelling approaches is the one by Erturk and Cagatay (1995). In the context of a growth cycle model, they examine how secular and cyclical changes in the degree of feminization of the labour force and the intensity of female household labour influence the behaviour of the macroeconomy. They argue that an increase in the feminization of the labour force is likely to have a positive effect on investment, and that the savings rate would be positively related to the intensity of female household labour. They use this model to investigate under what conditions an adjusting economy would be able to experience an economic recovery in the monetary economy by shifting costs to the reproductive sector. On the basis of their analysis, they conclude that a recovery is likely to succeed when the impact of feminization of the labour force on investment is stronger than the impact of the intensity of female household labour on savings. This, they argue, is more likely to be the case in high- and high-middle-income countries.

These models illustrate the ways in which gender differences play a role in macro-economic outcomes. More complicated models can be built to shed light on economic policy.

GENDER AND MACRO-ECONOMIC POLICY

A cardinal rule of economic policy-making involves the principle that policies should target problems at their source, rather than dealing with their manifestations. Various macro-economic problems discussed in the earlier sections of this chapter emanate from gender inequalities at the micro and meso levels. Thus long-term solutions can be achieved only if and when these inequalities are eradicated at their source. Creating conditions of equality in sharing reproductive responsibilities and decision-making within the household; providing women with equal access to economic resources, education and job training; eradicating legal, institutional and cultural barriers that prevent or disadvantage women's participation in economic activity and decision-making at the political level are just a few examples of the objectives long-term policies need to target at the meso and micro levels.[7] However, this does not imply that macro-economic policies cannot or need not be made gender-aware. It must be recognized that the traditional macro-economic policies that are presumed to be gender-neutral are in fact gender-blind, since they have clearly identifiable gender-asymmetric effects at the micro and meso levels.

Fiscal policy is a good example of how macro-economic policies need, and can, be scrutinized with respect to their gender effects. In countries as diverse as Canada, the UK, Australia and South Africa, women's budget statements and initiatives have been developed as a device of intervention at the macro-economic level of policy-making. They are used to review and analyse national budgets and expenditures to determine which groups benefit from fiscal policies and whether biases against women, poor people or other disadvantaged groups are built into them. In these efforts, the ultimate objective has been to make macro-economic policy responsive to the needs of the disfranchised groups.[8]

For instance, the South African Women's Budget Initiative recognizes that women are not a homogeneous group and that African women are particularly poor as a result of the legacy of apartheid. Thus, targeting women is viewed as an effective strategy of poverty reduction. In the analysis of budgetary allocations, a checklist of questions is drawn up, to be asked of any type of public expenditure:

- How much is to be spent and on what?
- How will services be delivered?
- How does expenditure relate to provision by business organizations, voluntary organizations and community groups?
- How does expenditure relate the informal and unpaid provision of services through households and family networks?
- Who will benefit in terms of access to services?
- Who will benefit in terms of public sector employment?
- How can poor women access more time, better nutrition, health and better skills?

A similar checklist is prepared with regard to revenue-raising measures, such as taxes and user fees. This list included questions about the effects of such measures on various groups in terms of a reduction in income, consumption, access to services (e.g. through user fees) as well as a question on which groups would bear an increased workload in terms of *unpaid labour time* as a result of the revenue-raising measures. Another question that is asked addresses the role of fiscal policy in promoting norms, morals or ways of life.

The South African Women's Budget has also helped identify built-in biases in the budgetary process. For instance, it has revealed that the national budget was designed on the assumption of a stereotypical male (white) citizen with a nine-to-five job in the urban formal sector with a wife and children dependent on him. Yet in relation to the total economically active population formal sector employment is small; women, who are just over half the population, predominate in the informal sector, among the unemployed and in rural areas, which are the most disadvantaged. Another example in the area of transportation policies reveals a similar bias built into the underlying assumptions made in the design of policy. In South Africa, the majority of users of public transport are women and Africans. For poor families, transportation is the second major expense after food. Yet transport subsidies apply only to those who hold weekly or monthly tickets, discriminating against those who do not hold regular jobs. Unemployed people in search of jobs as well as those in the informal sector – most of whom are women – who travelled at irregular intervals and on a variety of routes do not qualify for the subsidy. Moreover, it was also found that subsidies to private transport, in the form of income tax relief, free parking provisions and the like, are often larger than subsidies to the public transport system. Yet those who use private transport come from the relatively affluent households who need government subsidy the least.

These examples show that it is important to consider not just the size of the national deficit/surplus, which macro-economists are traditionally concerned with, but also the combination of expenditure and revenue that produces it. It is usually argued that in the budgetary process there ought to be two overriding concerns: efficiency in the use of resources and mobilization of new resources (Pyatt 1993). As Elson (1996) points out, in relation to both of these concerns, gender analysis can play an important role, by ensuring the following:

1. Efficiency in the use of resources must be properly defined. Macro-economic policies that seem to increase efficiency in the formal economy might simply be an artefact caused by the transfer of costs to the reproductive sector of the economy.

2. Efforts to mobilize new resources should take into account the fact that women's labour is an over-utilized resource. This means that, because households do not necessarily pool all their resources, the impact of different taxes will vary by gender.

3. Policy design of the pattern of expenditures should take into account the gender-specific externalities. An important example of this is women's caring work, which has wide spillover effects on the economy at large beyond the family.

4. Sustainability must be understood in a broader sense to include the intangible social/human resources, underpinning goodwill, trust, social stability and networks of solidarity. It is being recognized that the social framework is not invariant to macro-economic policies and that excessive reliance on contractionary policies in macro-economic stabilization can severely tax the social framework by creating widespread unemployment and idle capacity.

ENGENDERING MACRO-ECONOMICS AND THE UNDP

For the UNDP, as for other development institutions, incorporating a gender perspective into all policies and programmes is a mandate of the Beijing Platform for Action. However, for the UNDP, this mandate goes beyond a formal compliance in that *the development paradigm*, sustainable human development, advocated by the UNDP has gender equality as one of its cornerstones, others being poverty reduction, environmental regeneration, and employment growth and sustainable livelihoods. Among these, the UNDP's main focus is on poverty reduction and freedom from poverty is viewed as a human right. However, the other cornerstones of SHD are equally important, since, for example, without women's empowerment and advancement, that is, promotion of gender equality, poverty cannot be reduced (UNDP 1998). Within the framework of SHD, the UNDP also promotes good and democratic governance, respect for human rights in general and participatory people-centred approaches to policy-making. Women's empowerment and poor people's empowerment are seen as critical for participatory and democratic policy-making processes.

However, this does not mean that gender equality is approached in an instrumentalist way.[9] Just as freedom from poverty is viewed as a human right by the UNDP, women's rights are also viewed as human rights. The question, then, is not whether gender equality or poverty reduction are goals in and of themselves, but how and through which policies and programmes these rights, gender equality and freedom from poverty can be realized. From a macro-economic point of view, this involves identifying macro-economic policies that promote gender equality and types of growth that help reduce poverty and social inequalities in a sustainable and environment-friendly way.

Thus engendering macro-economic policies is consistent with the overall development policy framework of the UNDP. Along these lines, several initiatives at the UNDP have been undertaken towards engendering macro-economics policies.

1. With other partners such as the Ford Foundation and the University of Utah, UNDP has been supporting research in the area of engendering macro-economics and international economics. An international working group of economists has been conducting research to further the conceptual, modelling, empirical and policy levels of analysis.[10] The next step in this process will be to produce manuals or training materials that can be used both by UNDP country offices and by a range of policy-makers, civil society groups and other development partners.

2. The ultimate purpose of engendering macro-economics is to produce gender-aware policy tools. For this purpose, another initiative is being undertaken to support the production of more detailed simulation models and to engender such models in order, for example, to predict the impact of a variety of policies on women and men as well as the impacts on the poor.

3. Along with a number of other agencies and foundations, the UNDP has supported the South Africa Women's Budget Initiative and is interested in supporting other similar initiatives, which bring together governments and civil society groups for examining gender and anti-poor biases in fiscal policy.

4. Engendering macro-economics or any other type of policy presupposes the availability of gender-disaggregated data. The UNDP, along with the ILO, the UN Statistical Division and the IDRC (International Development Research Center, Canada) and statistical offices of a number of countries, has initiated a pilot project on 'Engendering Labor Statistics'. The project involves the improvement of engendered data collection on both paid and unpaid labour in about a dozen countries. In the paid labour data collection, one particular area of concern is the better documentation of informal employment, which is disproportionately made up of women. This

project will also involve time-use surveys, which are necessary for gender-aware macro-economic analysis and policy-making.[11]

It is hoped that such initiatives will contribute to the design and advocacy of policies that promote gender and other types of social equality and the elimination of poverty and destitution, not only by policy-makers but also by civil society groups, whose efforts were crucial in making the connection between gender and macro-economics.

NOTES

1. Nilufer Çagatay is professor at the University of Utah and previously economic adviser for the Social Development and Poverty Elimination Division of the UNDP. Copyright © UNDP.

2. See Beneria (1995) for a detailed exposition.

3. One implicit assumption is that increasing levels of per capita income increase the well-being of societies or are synonymous with 'development.' Higher per capita incomes are indeed correlated with a number of indicators of well-being, such as educational attainment and longer life expectancy. Achieving high growth rates is also important for reducing poverty, although obviously, high growth rates do not guarantee an automatic trickling down of economic benefits to everyone. The sustainable human development approach advocated by the UNDP is one of the paradigms that has challenged the equation of growth with development, without denying the significance of growth for achieving human development. See *Human Development Reports*, various years.

4. See Çagatay et al. (1995b) for examples of such work.

5. For examples of work in this literature, see Standing (1989), Commonwealth Secretariat (1989), Elson (1991a, 1991b), Moser (1992, 1996, 1998), Beneria and Roldan (1987), Sen (1991), Beneria and Feldman (1992), Afshar and Dennis (1992), Bakker (1994), Sparr (1994), Çagatay and Ozler (1995), Gonzales de la Rocha (1994), Floro (1995).

6. In its assessment of the effectiveness of adjustment programmes in increasing the overall efficiency of the economy, the World Bank relies on the statistics of incremental capital output ratio. A fall in this ratio is interpreted to reflect an improvement in the overall efficiency of the economy. However, incremental capital-output ratio statistics are typically calculated from statistics that ignore unpaid work. Thus, given the invisibility of the reproductive sector, a fall in this ratio might just as well hide increasing inefficiency (Elson 1995).

7. However, some micro- and meso-level policies may have to be undertaken globally. For example, it may be politically difficult to increase women workers' rights (or labour standards in general) in open economies where women are mostly located in export-oriented sectors because of fears of loss of competitiveness. So in an increasingly integrated world economy, some micro- and meso-level interventions need to be undertaken by all countries (or regions), hence they would require transnational collective action and global governance structures.

8. See Budlender (1996, 1997) for detailed analysis of the South African Women's Budget Initiatives. The following discussion of the South African case draws from these volumes. See Elson (1996) for a general discussion of women's budget initiatives.

9. Some feminists have argued that gender equality should be pursued within a framework of 'human rights', rather than as an instrument of achieving other goals such as 'efficiency'. However, there is no contradiction between pursuing gender equality as a human right and also at the same time trying to design policies that enhance goals such as growth (without necessarily subscribing to a neo-classical concept of efficiency). Gender equality and macro-economic goals such as growth do not necessarily involve a trade-off, although sometimes gender inequality may be associated with higher profitability and perhaps a higher growth rate for a period of time. For example, keeping women's wages in export sectors such as apparel or textiles low may be a part of a country's international competition strategy. However, a low-wage strategy of competition may not be sustainable in the long run. Continuous upgrading of technology and increased productivity are essential for the creation of competitive advantage (Çagatay 1996). A similar argument holds for other social inequalities, which may be associated with high profitability or growth under certain circumstances; however, growth strategies that rely on social inequalities, besides being ethically objectionable, become socially and therefore politically unsustainable by giving rise to ethnicity-, race- and class-based conflicts.

10. The group has been in existence since 1994 and the first results of research were published in Çagatay et al. 1995a.

11. There has been a debate about evaluation of unpaid labour and the its incorporation into National Income Accounts. Some in the feminist movement fear that making (mostly) women's unpaid labour visible will lead to demands of 'wages for housework', which they believe will lock women into 'housework' and perpetuate gender inequalities. Others find the efforts to assign a value to unpaid labour as problematic on grounds that any evaluation based on market prices will be gender-biased since market prices are gender-biased. What is being argued here is that in order to trace the feedback effects between the paid and the unpaid economy, we need to have time-use surveys and ideally they need to be conducted yearly over the course of the business cycle to investigate, for example, who bears the cost of adjustment during macro-economic crises. However, such exercises do not necessarily require evaluation of unpaid labour at gender-biased market prices. The problematic of gender-biased market prices raises more difficult questions about the accuracy of income accounts in general and about the wisdom of policy positions that advocate 'getting prices right'. Unfortunately, these questions are beyond the scope of this chapter.

BIBLIOGRAPHY

Afshar, H. and C. Dennis (eds) (1992) *Woman and Adjustment Policies in the Third World*, London: Macmillan.

Agarwal, B. (1994) *A Field of Her Own*, London: Macmillan.

Bakker, I. (1994) *The Strategic Silence: Gender and Economic Policy*, London: Zed Books.

Beneria, L. (1979) 'Reproduction, production and the sexual division of labour', *Cambridge Journal of Economics*, 3(3).

— (1992) 'Accounting for women's work: the progress of two decades', *World Development*, 20(11).

— (1995) 'Toward a greater integration of gender in economics', *World Development*, 23(11), November.

Beneria, L. and S. Feldman (eds) (1992) *Unequal Burden: Economic Crises, Persistent Poverty and Women's Work*, Boulder, CO: Westview Press.

Beneria, L. and M. Roldan (1987) *The Crossroads of Class and Gender: Homework, Subcontracting and Household Dynamics in Mexico City*, Chicago: University of Chicago Press.

Beneria, L. and G. Sen (1981) 'Accumulation, reproduction and women's role in economic development: Boserup revisited', *Signs*, 7(2).

Bergman, B. (1974) 'Occupational segregation, wages and profits when employers discriminate by race and sex', *Eastern Economic Journal*, 1(1–2).

Budlender, D. (ed.) (1996) *The Women's Budget*, Cape Town: IDASA.

— (ed.) (1997) *The Second Women's Budget*, Cape Town: IDASA.

Çagatay, N. (1996) 'Trade and Gender', in ESCAP (ed.), *Asian and Pacific Developing Economies and the First WTO Ministerial Conference: Issues of Concern*, Proceedings and papers presented at the ESCAP/UNCTAD/UNDP meeting of Senior Officials to Assist in Preparation for the First WTO Ministerial Conference, New York: United Nations.

Çagatay, N., D. Elson and C. Grown (eds) (1995a) *World Development*, special issue on Gender, Adjustment and Macroeconomics, 23(11), November.

— (1995b) 'Introduction', *World Development*, special issue on Gender, Adjustment and Macroeconomics, 23(11), November.

Çagatay, N. and S. Ozler (1995) 'Feminization of the labour force: the effects of long-term development and structural adjustment', *World Development*, 23(11), November.

Collier, P. (1994) 'Gender aspects of labour allocation during structural adjustment theoretical framework and the Africa experience', in S. Horton, R. Hanbur and D. Mazumdar (eds), *Labour Markets in an Era of Adjustment*, Vol. 1, Washington, DC: World Bank.

Commonwealth Secretariat (1989) *Engendering Adjustment for the 1990s*, London: Commonwealth Secretariat.

Darity, W. (1995) 'The formal structure of a gender-segregated low-income economy', *World Development*, 23(11), November.

Edholm, F., O. Harris and K. Young (1977) 'Conceptualizing Women', *Critique of Anthropology*, 3(9/10).

Elson, D. (1991a) 'Male bias in the development process: an overview', in D. Elson (ed.), *Male Bias in the Development Process*, Manchester: Manchester University Press.

— (1991b) 'Male bias in the development process: the case of structural adjustment', in Diane Elson (ed.), *Male Bias in the Development Process*, Manchester: Manchester University Press.

— (1995) 'Gender awareness in modeling structural adjustment', *World Development*, 23(11), November.

— (1996) 'Gender-neutral, gender-blind, gender-sensitive budgets? Changing the conceptual framework to include women's empowerment and the economy of care', Paper prepared for the Fifth Meeting of Commonwealth Ministers Responsible for Women's Affairs, Port of Spain, Trinidad, 25–28 November 1996.

Elson, D. and R. Pearson (1981) 'The subordination of women and the internationalization of factory production', in K. Young, C. Wolkowitz and R. McCullogh (eds.), *Of Marriage and the Market*, London: Routledge.

Erturk, K. and N. Çagatay (1995) 'Macroeconomic consequences of cyclical and secular changes in feminization: an experiment at gendered modeling', *World Development*, 23(11), November.

Ferber, M. and B. Birnbaum (1977) 'The "new home economics": retrospects and prospects', *Journal of Consumer Research*, 4: 19–28.

Ferber, M. and J. Nelson (1993) *Beyond Economic Man: Feminist Theory and Economics*, Chicago: University of Chicago Press.

Floro, M. (1995) 'Economic restructuring, gender and the allocation of time', *World Development*, 23(11), November.

Folbre, Nancy (1982) 'Exploitation comes home: a critique of the Marxian theory of family labour', *Cambridge Journal of Economics*, 6(4): 317–29.

— 1986) 'Hearts and spades: paradigms of household economics', *World Development*, 14(2): 245–55.

— (1994) *Who Pays for the Kids?*, New York: Routledge.

Gladwin, C. H. (1991) (ed.) *Structural Adjustment and African Women Farmers*, Gainesville, FL: University of Florida Press.

Gonzales de la Rocha, M. (1994), 'The urban family and poverty in Latin America', *Latin American Perspectives*, 22(2).

Hartmann, H. (1979) 'Capitalism, patriarchy, and job segregation by sex', in Z. Eisenstein (ed.), *Capitalist Patriarchy and the Case for Socialist Feminism*, New York: Monthly Review Press.

King, E. and A. Hill (1995) 'Women's education and economic well-being', *Feminist Economics*, Summer.

Moser, C. (1992) 'Adjustment from below: low income women, time and the triple role in Guayaquil, Ecuador', in H. Afshar and C. Dennis (eds), *Woman and Adjustment Policies in the Third World*, London: Macmillan.

— (1996) *Confronting Crisis: A Comparative Study of Household Responses to Poverty and Vulnerability in Four Poor Urban Communities*, Washington, DC: World Bank (Environmentally Sustainable Development Series and Monograph Series No. 8).

— (1998) 'The asset vulnerability framework reassessing urban poverty reduction strategies', *World Development*, 26(1).

Palmer, I. (1991) *Gender and Population in the Adjustment of African Economies: Planning for Change*, Geneva: ILO.

Picchio, A. 1992. *Social Reproduction: The Political Economy of the Labour Market*, Cambridge: Cambridge University Press.

Pyatt, G. (1993) 'Fiscal politics, adjustment and balanced development', Inter-departmental Project on Structural Adjustment, Occasional Paper 8, Geneva: ILO.

Rubery, J. (ed.) (1988) *Women and Recession*, London: Routledge & Kegan Paul.

Sawhill, I. (1977) 'Economic perspectives on the family', *Daedalus*, 106(2): 115–25.

Sen, A. (1990) 'Gender and cooperative conflict', in I. Tinker (ed.), *Persistent Inequalities: Women and World Development*, New York: Oxford University Press.

Sen, G. (1991) 'Macroeconomic policies and the informal sector: a gender sensitive approach', Working Paper No. 13, Poughkeepsie, NY: Vassar College, Department of Economics.

Sen, G. and C. Grown (1987) *Development, Crises and Alternative Visions: Third World Women's Perspectives*, New York: Monthly Review Press.

Sparr, P. (1994) *Mortgaging Women's Lives: Feminist Critiques of Structural Adjustment*, London: Zed Books.

Standing, G. (1989) 'Global feminization through flexible labour', *World Development*, 17(7): 1077–95.

Taylor, L. (1995) 'Environmental and gender feedbacks in macroeconomics', *World Development*, 23(11), November.

Tzannatos, Z. (1992) 'Potential gains from the elimination of labour market differentials', in 'Women's Employment and Pay in Latin America, Part 1: Overview and Methodology', *Regional Studies Program Report* No. 10, Washington, DC: World Bank.

UNDP (1995) *Human Development Report*, New York: Oxford University Press.

— (1998) *UNDP's 1998 Poverty Report*, New York: United Nations.

Young, K., C. Wolkowitz and R. McCullogh (eds) (1984) *Of Marriage and the Market*, London: Routledge (first published 1981).

CHAPTER 3

Social and Gender Issues in Macro-economic Policy Advice

INGRID PALMER[1]

§ This chapter is addressed to macro-economists and to their agenda of concerns. It explores ways to incorporate gender in three major areas of macro-policy concern: development policies and economic management, public finance and poverty alleviation.

It starts from the position that there is nothing wrong with the standard *tools* of economic analysis. The problem has been that economists have failed to appreciate the actual *context* to which they apply those tools. The explicit or implicit assumptions of macro-economic analytic frameworks may only fortuitously coincide with the reality of the market (the meso-level) or of individual (micro-level) choices. Much of new development literature is premised on this need to place contextual caveats on economic theories. The new 'socio-economics' that is emerging covers a very broad spectrum of opinion. Some of those who emphasize social structures virtually write off economics. But the viewpoint that is held in this paper is that economics matters very much and that it is important to improve the grounding of macro-economic policies. This corresponds to Solow's point (Swedberg 1990: 275, 273):

> I think that many economists would like to think that economics is a universal science, just like physics, and that all the sociological stuff is pointless. People maximise this or that, and that is really all you need to know. That is why I disagree with the notion of economics as physics. But what I personally have in mind is that I would like to do as rigorous theoretical and empirical economics as possible. I want to preserve the analytical structure of economics, and I would also like to improve it by including or somehow incorporating into it the understanding that the objectives of individual economic behaviour are modified by social institutions.

If gender means the social construction of relations between men and women, then gender is one social institution to take account of in that economic analysis. Although this chapter focuses on gender *per se*, it is understood that both the absolute and relative statuses of men and women, and the prevailing gender relations, are strongly influenced by class, age, family formation, culture and ethnicity. Any particular gender situation arises from the associated social matrix of these features of the population.

Gender issues in macro-economic policy can be approached in two ways. One is to focus on the different outcomes of macro-economics for men and women and on changes that are required to bring about gender equality. The other is to examine the implications that gender relations and disparities hold for macro-economic analyses and policy options. It is the latter that provides the primary orientation of this chapter, which attempts to show that embedding gender in analysis is good economics. It is not intended to show how macro-economics can serve women as a special interest group. Nevertheless, it is obvious from experience, and can be cogently argued theoretically, that gender-differentiated outcomes of macro-policies rebound on the success of those same policies. If gender equality figures strongly in this chapter it is because of its crucial importance to the macro-economists' goal of efficient and sustainable growth.

In no way should this approach be seen as a substitute for activists' promotion of gender equality. The advances in special support to women in their reproduction work and in relevant reforms of institutional and legal structures do much to create gender equality. But to leave it at that would give credence to the frequent claim of macro-economists that they plan at too high a level to be relevant to women's needs, or for gender to be relevant to policy analysis.

The next section gives a summary of the scope of macro-economics and its shortcomings, as well as pointers to some newly emerging ideas that are taken further under the relevant area of policy concern. This is followed by logically arguing the significance of gender to macro-economic analysis supported by illustrations from the women-in-development literature. The argument is presented in the language of economists. Then comes the section that deals with the implications of this argument for the three areas of macro policy concern. Finally, conclusions are drawn in terms of suggesting useful ways to take the discussion further: areas of research or analysis that might be developed and likely entry points in government.

Although the chapter is addressed to economists and the argument is presented in the language of economics, it is hoped that it will be used by non-economists interested in gender. To that end a glossary of economic terms is supplied in the appendix as a guide through the economic arguments. The summary of what macro-economics is about has also been written in part consideration of this readership.

THE SUBJECT MATTER OF MACRO-ECONOMICS

Ultimately macro-economists are the guardians of external and internal economic balances. Prosperity may be possible in the short term while ignoring imbalances, but the shocks to the economy from later debt payments and import restrictions, as well as the corrosive uncertainty and distributional effects of inflation, are in very few people's interests in the long term. Nothing is to be gained by vilifying macro-economists for doing their job. At the same time it should be recognized that there is no single, unique packaging and sequencing of policies to secure future sustainable national balances.

Monetary and fiscal policies have their effects via sectoral and sub-sectoral variables. Assumptions have to be made about the likely behaviour of these variables when establishing macro objectives, approaches, means. On the basis of those assumptions, judgements then have to be made about targets, foci, emphases, linkages, leakages, preconditions and phasing. If the assumptions made upstream are based on misconceptions, a lot of policy detail unravels downstream at the local level.

This is what is meant by linking the macro and the micro. In plain language if macro-economic policy is to be effective it must be informed by what the micro level can and wishes to deliver in response to macro-level signals, directly and via the meso level of the market. The principle of individuals trying to maximize their positions is unimpeachable. But these positions are arrived at not only after weights are attached to risk and leisure, but after consideration of losses and gains (including violence, personal security, social membership, reputation and so on) inherent in seeking those positions. Uncertainty surrounding some of these gains and losses will mean individuals seek margins for 'error', often interpreted by economists as conservative tradition or irrational behaviour. The social constructs of gender and class, in particular, are powerfully expressed in the economic domain through these, seemingly obscure, influences.

The main macro policy instruments for managing the external balance are the exchange rate and foreign trade tariffs. In the last decade and a half the manipulation of these instruments has been in the direction of freeing the one and eliminating the other with the objective of making production of exports more profitable and purchases of imports more costly. The policy instruments also place domestic producers in open competition with international producers. Therefore, in addition to promoting external balance they start the process of adjustment: eliminating distortions in factor and product markets.

Guardians of the internal balance (between demand and supply of domestic resources) operate on the amount of effective demand through determining public expenditure (controlling budget deficits) and influencing the price of borrowing (interest rates). The need for such monetary stabilization is indicated by the rate of inflation. But inflation also distorts markets by discouraging savings and encouraging borrowing to spend today in order to beat the price rise tomorrow. In addition, the uncertainty that always accompanies inflation makes production planning difficult and turns investors away from production to rent-seeking, leading to further distortions in factor and product markets. Probably the most damning indictment of inflation is that 'the production costs of high unstable inflation are associated with the increasingly widespread use of the short term as a decision-making horizon' (ECLAC 1992: 64). And '... any evaluation of a stabilisation programme should compare its costs with the costs of high and unstable inflation rather than with those of a normal economic situation'. An internal imbalance left unaddressed also has a knock-on effect on the external imbalance by gradually overpricing the currency and necessitating eventual devaluation.

These are the strict concerns about inflation widely held by economists. But what of the supply side to the internal balance? Recent economic orthodoxy promoted the idea that a 'hands-off' market liberalization strategy would remove obstructions to greater efficiency, which would increase production. Freeing markets allows switching of resource use and calls forth greater quantities of resources. There may be hiatuses in supplies during this switch and, of course, there is always a risk of a surge of inflation when demand is not met. But this is a transitional problem.

The problem with the diagnosis of external and internal imbalances is that it is framed in macro aggregates. There is a 'demand overhang', there are market distortions that theory states has certain effects, inflation has to be wiped out. Likewise, prescriptions are seen in abstract terms at a high level. Markets, once freed from interference, and enjoying more monetary stability, will see producers and consumers responding to new price relatives in the manner of seeking to maximize gains.

Macro-economic analysis does not normally extend to a close scrutiny of likely price and income elasticities of supply and demand of different categories of people acting as producers, consumers and intermediaries. Until this is done there is no real way of assessing slack capacity, ability to create new capacity, flexibility of factor substitution within production functions, lead times and the competence of the market. Market competence includes issues of access, entry and participation. For some a market may effectively not exist while for others it appears well developed.

The elasticity of supply also involves incentives and freedom to respond. Incentives to make the effort of all this switching are not simply a case of new price relatives getting through imperfect intermediary institutions. There are questions of directing incentives to those who actually make the effort of response, social freedom to redeploy or expand resources, competing demands on resources between economic and non-economic purposes, trade-offs with social objectives. The freedom, as distinct from the physical capacity, of individuals to respond is socio-culturally determined. There may be a total prohibition or a degree of freedom with a cost (effectively a transaction cost) attached.

On the other side of the market the elasticity of demand depends on real purchasing power, the necessity of the good and the availability of near substitutes. To construct an aggregate demand for a good there first has to be some deconstruction by way of asking 'whose purchasing power, whose necessity, and whose income or price substitution effects?'

The above refers to a diagnosis of the pre-existing ability or willingness of individuals and markets to respond to macro prescriptions. There is the additional problem that the prescription to control inflation, an engineered squeeze on domestic spending, has the effect of reducing people's capacity to respond to any new incentives. This usually comes through reduced social sector and infrastructural supports, and by raising the price of credit, makes it more difficult to expand the supply of resources or redeploy them. In effect, these budget reductions can increase some kinds of transaction costs normally incurred during any change in production patterns. It is notable that this increase tends to be greatest for the poorest. The concept of transaction costs need not be confined to market situations. Redeployment of resources or intensifying the uptake of resources in self-provisioning production can also involve transaction costs.

Macro-economists need to have some sense of whose elasticity of response they implicitly have in mind when these difficulties, which are not experienced in a uniform manner, are raised.

Repackaging and resequencing the various policy instruments can ease conflicts. For instance, strategically targeting public expenditure and credit, or prolonging the implementation of price changes, can help. But essentially this is merely reshuffling the old prescription. That it has been applied is due to recognition at the macro level that previous schedules for markets to deliver the desired changes were too tight.

But macro-economic thinking is evolving beyond this. A major new concern is bringing the issue of social structures to the macro-economic agenda. This has been forced by noting that where prescriptions succeed in creating new patterns of production that were more competitive and better reflected the efficient allocation of (utilized) resources, this process seemed to halt at a smaller volume of production leaving a great deal of unused resources, notably labour. The new competitive economic efficiency was returning costly externalities in the form of worsening unemployment and poverty. A sizeable bill was landing on the doorstep of government. Efficiency gains were accruing to some private in-dividuals whereas losses were accruing to society. For a proper economic accounting of overall macro-economic efficiency this bill ought to be subtracted from the gains of greater partial efficiency.

This has changed concepts of efficiency – in effect moving from private efficiency to social efficiency. At the very least if an economic system is not sustainable it can hardly be regarded as efficient. Con-ceivably an economy that is efficient in the neo-classical sense of each resource equating its marginal revenue product over all uses and equating its price could be sliding to a state of implosion through chronically deficient demand. However, it is the poverty arising from exclusion that is giving rise to new ideas of allocative efficiency based on inclusiveness. But to reach allocative efficiency with inclusion depends on the state 'investing long' (and in what amounts to greater equity): in human resources and productivity (equal personal endowments), in infrastruc-ture (equal access), and in institutional reforms (equal transaction costs). This implies a much more active role for the state than prescribed in recent years. The highlights of this role must be designing overarching policies to accommodate meso and micro realities, more strategic public finance, and poverty-reduction programmes that are allied to equity and inclusiveness.

While these are still new ideas there is no sound reason to believe macro-economists will have serious theoretical problems with them. Economists have always understood that the notion of economic efficiency (or of Pareto optimality) was compromised by subjective distributions of income and wealth, as well as by the presence of externalities. Change either of these distributions, or internally cost an externality, and patterns of demand and supply will change and, with that, prices. What might formerly have been an efficient allocation of resources is no longer. Investing in greater equity means investing in new distributions of income and wealth, and, as we shall see, giving proper account to positive externalities provided by people. In this way moves towards equity force new scenarios of economic efficiency and ones that will be more inclusive of the whole of society.

The increasingly broad horizons of macro-economic thinking offer scope for introducing gender constructs in economic analysis and, thence, for arguing a case for specific long-term investments in changing those constructs.

INFORMING MACRO-ECONOMICS OF GENDER REALITIES

Macro-economic strategies and policies will be more effective if they are grounded in the correct identification of the circumstances and motivations of subject economic agents. These are shaped by, among other things, gender relations and disparities and familial obligations. Macro-economists have generally not allowed that their assumptions could be anything but gender-neutral. Men and women are the same and, if there is a difference, macro-policy is too distant to discriminate. Particular problems women have, as women, can be dealt with through welfare programmes. These problems do not intersect with economic roles. In the family, men and women together form the economic unit and, if there is some separation of powers, that has nothing to do with economists. Economists do not interfere in family relations. Well, willy-nilly, they have. Extensively. And in ways that do little good for the macro-economic policies they espouse. It is believed that the relevance of gender relations to economic analysis can best be explained through three subjects:

- biased and absent markets;

- identification of the primary unit of response; and
- socio-cultural relations between men and women.

Biased and absent markets There are two aspects to market bias: inequalities of access to and of participation in markets. Access to a market is obviously weaker for those at a distance and who are denied the use of competitively priced transport. Access is also limited by inconvenience of hours of market functioning and imperfect availability of information. There may even be severe social obstacles or outright prohibition of market entry facing categories of individuals. Privilege and power can effect degrees of exclusiveness.

Class and gender interact with these determinants. Poor men suffer from biases in access too, but poor women are likely to suffer much more, not just because of their greater poverty but because of women's great immobility, social obstacles and family gender relations. Often women's own produce has to be marketed by men, effectively interposing another (middleman) market.

Once in a product market a supplier's standing is determined by contacts, reputation, credibility and acceptance. Where a supplier is unable to go to market on a regular basis and deals only with small quantities, reputation and credibility can affect the price. Formal buying institutions may accept only consignments of a certain minimum size or accept smaller quantities but at lower unit prices. Again the poor experience these biases, and women most of all. Women with young children are the most disadvantaged.

Much more 'perfect' are the localized markets offering daily consumer needs, especially perishables, to which suppliers come on a regular basis. It is no surprise that these markets are often dominated by women.

The conundrum, and dilemma, for macro-economists is that many of the goods they wish to see produced in larger quantities to earn foreign exchange or to hold domestic prices down may be produced by women, but gender factors add significantly to the already high class-induced transaction costs of a positive response. Raising further the price incentives, were that possible, would only give greater abnormal profits to others. Economic efficiency dictates that structural interventions should be made to eliminate or counterbalance gender-based transaction costs.

The markets for factors of production – raw materials and (particularly) credit – should be of greater planning concern, for this is the stage at which entrepreneurship can be blocked completely regardless of efficiency of production and any smoothness of product markets. In factor markets we focus on the demand side. Purchasers of raw materials may face similar cost-incurring biases in availability of transport and information, of minimum size quantities and regularity of exchange, as suppliers in product markets.

Underlying access to all other factors is the need for working capital or postponement of payment until the output is sold: credit of one kind or another. Macro-economists are well aware of the biases and distortions in the credit/capital market emanating from unequally distributed economic and political clout. Interest rates and terms of repayment vary greatly by customer even in formal banking institutions. In addition to these class-based determinants there is gender discrimination, which either raises transaction costs to women enormously or (*de jure* or *de facto*) simply blocks women's access to formal sector credit and obliges them to face interest rates several times higher in the informal credit market. The official image of women as poor credit risks, though changing in the face of overwhelming evidence to the contrary, is still an obstacle to women's equal access to cheap credit. Women's particular problem with collateral is also still a sticking point, despite it being increasingly dismissed as a red herring.

The high per unit administrative costs of small loans is really the main issue. It ought to apply equally to small male borrowers, of course.

BOX 3.1 *The social opportunity cost of gender-biased credit*

A World Bank study of small-scale urban enterprises illustrates the potential social gains from greater gender equality in the allocation of credit. A factorial analysis of informal sector enterprises in Peru found that '"on average" the productivity of female firms is neither better nor worse than that of male or mixed firms with the same factor endowments (capital, expenses and labour). But firms with smaller endowment tend to have much higher factor productivity' (that is, higher marginal returns). A much higher proportion of female firms than male/mixed firms have low endowments (Smith and Stelcner 1990). The implication is clear: assuming diminishing marginal returns with increasing output, in order to equate marginal returns to capital endowments across all informal sector firms, credit must be extended – or switched – to female firms.

But it tends to be conflated with the collateral issue when raised in relation to women borrowers. The result is that the overall attitude to women as borrowers is worse than would be suggested by the sum of the separate obstacles of having no collateral and being small borrowers. An important macro-policy issue here is what weight to give the profit-maximizing position of a commercial bank (private efficiency) and what weight to give allocative efficiency of credit use throughout the economy (social efficiency). (See Box 3.1 for an example of allocative inefficiency in the credit market.) The latter is more likely to create a long-term economic dynamic and return a much greater total social dividend than the market short termism of the former. Are commercial banks' maximizing positions to be allowed to hold hostage a significant long-term social opportunity cost? Is there a case here for an infant industry (financial services) argument permitting the use of subsidies to attain that social opportunity? For instance, it is not yet clear that the original Grameen Bank in Bangladesh can operate free of subsidy dependency after its many years of business, although that dependency

---

BOX 3.2 *High per unit credit administrative costs revisited*

One of the most telling points of a World Bank evaluation of the Grameen Bank was that when localities in which the Bank had been operating acquired electricity and roads, and therefore became 'developed', formal commercial banks moved in and the Grameen Bank lost customers to it. 'The more developed is the local economy and the more alternative income-earning opportunities, the higher is the dropout rate of Grameen Bank members' (Khandker et al. 1994: 11, 13). It appears that the 'additional per unit administrative costs of small loans' may not arise from the filling in and stamping of forms as much as from the cost of outreach and spreading information and working up investment ideas in 'undeveloped' localities. If this is true, then it is not smallness of loan that is the major obstacle to granting credit but the cost of extension work in, as yet, undeveloped localities. Roads and electricity in effect reduce transaction costs for both women clients and banks. For the poor, the attraction of the commercial banks was their better banking skills. Good advice is tantamount to good information: another transaction cost is reduced.

has fallen sharply since 1991. But such interim subsidies may not be for long, as Box 3.2 makes clear.

Gender bias in the labour market is extensive. Much of it emanates from segmentation and gender-typing of jobs. Women tend to be crowded into low-status, low-skilled, temporary or part-time jobs. There has been a sharp growth in numbers of women undertaking casual or part-time, home-based work under contract (ILO 1994). These women are generally young and poorly educated. But evidence found in the women-in-development/gender literature indicates that wage disparities cannot always be excused by the existence of different productivities or tasks. That women systematically receive lower wages than men because of socio-cultural values placed on women's work means that women's labour is effectively subsidizing the returns to other factors of production or product prices. Nor is this referring to a small subsidy. Women's wages tend to average 66 per cent of men's but can be much lower.

Gender relations in the labour market are also manifest in the informal sector. Sethuraman (1985: 721) implies that one reason why earnings in the informal sector are so low is due to the malfunctioning of the labour market and lack of mobility between the formal and informal sectors, as well as within the informal sector. Women are less likely to move to higher-yielding activities within the informal sector or to use the informal sector as a stepping-stone to the formal sector. This is often attributed to child care difficulties, but women do not have small children for ever. Such gender-based disparities suggest malfunctioning of labour and credit markets.

When labour and skills are not moving freely to their best use, social (as well as private) opportunity costs are involved. Subsidies create distortions, with one distorted market sending derived ripples of distortions in other factor and, thence, product markets. One study (Tzannatos 1992: 4.1–4.8) demonstrated theoretically that when gender differentials in occupation and pay were eliminated, total output as well as women's pay could increase considerably. While men would take a smaller share of the total wages bill, they need not suffer in real terms in the long term.

But another important aspect of labour markets is their increasing internationalization. The emergent international division of labour has tended to favour the employment of women in developing countries. Footloose off-shore capital, which formerly sought out cheap young female labour that was easily trained for simple repetitive jobs, is now using older better-educated women in developing countries to move computer services around the globe through telecommunications. For instance, at least two international airlines employ women in India to enter transactions into their computer networks. Software companies are running three shifts of female programmers a day; one in Asia, followed by one in Europe, with the last in America when the Europeans close down for the day.

But it is in the unmodernized sector where markets are absent that the massive misallocation of women's resources occurs. Because of biology women spend part of their most active years concerned with maternity. But it is because of gender that the 'social reproduction' work of nursing, child care, cleaning and instilling social behaviour in children is done by women. For the majority of women the market for these tasks is absent. Inasmuch as this extra work of women reproduces the labour force at no obvious direct cost to the internal costed economy, it becomes a positive social externality. Labour's remuneration is for current maintenance only. Together with its multiplicity of units spread throughout the economy, labour is therefore a part-free public good. Like defence it enjoys a government input; in the case of labour health and education services. But unlike defence the major input comes as a socially engineered labour tax on private resources – and paid by a disadvantaged section of the population at that. It is a public good funded in a sharply regressive way.

If the conditions of this labour reproduction become too arduous, something has to 'give', usually its quality. Without being open to market forces, it is difficult to see where productivity increases in the tasks of reproduction will come from unless the state intervenes with targeted public investment. There are issues here of allocative efficiency, of moving from a highly suspect Pareto optimality to a much improved one, of more comprehensive inclusion, and of elimination of a serious externality. A leaf can be taken from environmental accounting. Missing markets are known to environmental economists working on externalities. The underlying rationale of environmental economics is to confront this total market failure by trying to price these goods to the internal costed economy. As Winpenny (1991: 2) puts it: 'The workings of markets do not always achieve the most efficient allocation of resources ... In environmental economics, externalities and public goods are two of the main reasons for market failure.'

However, in the case of the externality of labour reproduction, attributing true cost would mean not only impinging on intra-household distribution of resources and income but applying levies throughout the economy.

Aside from these reproductive services, markets are also absent from the production and consumption of a range of goods and services. Among the poor, particularly in rural areas, there is much self-provisioning of the essentials of life: water, fuel, food, health care, cleaning and sanitation. When these goods and services are produced for own consumption almost all the work is done by women. The proportion of total hours worked by women in this sub-sector varies with environmental and economic endowments, proximity to markets and socio-cultural background. Although it is rare now to find women working exclusively in self-provisioning production, for many a great deal of their labour and other resources are deployed here. It is reasonable to assume that within the combined reproduction and self-provisioning sector allocative principles of a kind are followed, dominated by prioritization of essential use-values. To the extent that these use-values provide the essentials of life which are not available to women in accessible markets, the work involved is a fixed overhead from which time cannot be subtracted however 'profitable' the production of market-oriented non-essentials may be. When women are responsible for finding the essentials of life the portfolio of goods and services they settle for will be low-yielding, but gilt-edged. The returns to any new market-oriented activity that is adopted have to be high enough to include a premium on top of the combined economic opportunity costs of the resources it absorbs.

The temptation for economists is to ignore this and to suggest that the non-marketed and marketed sub-sectors compete for resources such that marginal (monetized and imputed) net returns are equated. But self-provisioning situations are usually strongly structured by gender and other social relations. In some circumstances, such as when women are heavily cloistered, the competitive pull of the market would be so weak as to be entirely missing. Where women have at least some freedom to be 'factor mobile' it is more likely to be a case of transaction costs impairing the influence of market forces by degrees. A close scrutiny of these transaction costs might reveal that markets are not so much absent as 'out-priced' by the burden of such gender-based costs.

There is clearly a huge social opportunity cost to continuing with so much of women's labour time locked up in low-productivity reproduction and self-provisioning work. Some obstacles to unlocking it are described in the rest of this section. But the concepts of neo-classical efficiency and optimality, never realized in real life, should be the spur to doing something about absent markets for up to eight hours a day of women's work. As Stevens (1993: 28) puts it:

> In contrast to determining output levels for market goods, there is no built-in incentive to consider opportunity costs in determining the level of output for public goods. However, the concept of Pareto efficiency is still relevant; the resources that are used to produce either non-market or market goods almost always have opportunity costs or values in alternative uses. These costs are what labour and capital could earn by doing other things ... The challenge in evaluating the efficiency of a non-market good is to determine the nature and size of the opportunity costs, but the concept of Pareto efficiency remains the same.

The influence of market density, with road networks substituting where population is not dense, is worth noting. For instance, World Bank research in Nigeria and Kenya found that men are shifting to more remunerative activities in rural areas in such a way that the traditional pattern of intra-household rights and obligations has definitely changed (World Bank 1992). Women are growing more export crops and performing tasks, such as ploughing, that they did not do before.

New roads can demonstrate the effect of markets more vividly. In northeastern Thailand women transformed their farm economy by growing vegetables when roads provided access to the Bangkok market. The impact of a road was included in a case study in Cameroon, where wives stopped working on their husbands' coffee to grow cassava and other foods for the Yaoundé market (Guyer 1977). In these two cases new infrastructure provided sufficient incentive to overcome any culturally determined transaction costs in redeploying labour. In the latter case the proper costing of farm labour (thanks to its new mobility) meant a private gain to women, as well as a social gain through an expansion of the food sector and improved food supplies to the urban economy. But an opening up of the household economy to market forces revealed a source of former subsidy to coffee production by ending a gender bias.

Neo-classical marginal analysis offers a 'default position', a position that reflects nobody's reality but from which all analyses of reality could start out. Reality is then approached by exploring transaction costs and externalities.

Identification of the primary unit of response   Discussion of absent markets, a missing meso level in effect, has already led the argument to micro-level influences. But it is useful to start afresh with micro issues.

The success of macro-economic policy depends on a good assessment of the capacity and willingness of micro-level units to adapt and respond to that policy. A precondition of that is the correct identification of the micro decision-making unit, and recognition that transaction costs apply within personal relations and are felt in non-economic ways.

Economic textbooks deal separately with the producer/worker and the consumer. These individuals are deemed to be autonomous and self-standing. Unconditional command over resources and rights of appropriation of earned returns have been implicit assumptions of micro-economic theory. The producer/worker sets out to maximize net income (unless leisure is valued), and is assumed to be free to do this. Consumption preferences with given incomes and prices constitute a separate analysis. This separation of producer and consumer, and the assumption of freedom to pursue maximizing positions, with no extraneous claims on income, go to the heart of miscalculations of macro strategies that ignore gender relations of production and exchange and the socio-economic arrangements for reproducing the human population. Galbraith (1974) wrote that neo-classical theory has buried the subordination of the individual (woman) within the household.

In reality the primary units of earning, producing, managing, consuming and saving/investing may constitute individuals or groups of individuals. The composition of each of these primary units within one household need not be the same. Let us take the points separately.

One, the household will be a collection of individuals formed by family or other social bonds. There may be one, two or three generations, each with rights concerning the utilization of household resources. These (*de facto* or *de jure*) contractual rights will be permeated by both gender and age relations. These sets of relations vary with the asset status of the whole household. Within the household-level economy all, or some, members may work in a joint economic enterprise or individuals may work separately. The latter is taken to mean a separate economic accounting unit, managed by an individual responsible for mobilizing factors of production and with rights of appropriation to all returns. The analytic meaning of this is that economic returns (monetized or use-value) are internalized in that primary economic accounting unit. Household-level economies can be any mixture of joint and individual accounting units.

Two, managing a separate accounting unit does not necessarily mean labouring exclusively in that unit or without the labour of other household members. There is usually significant labour (and other) exchange between accounting units within households: effectively *quid pro quo*s. With so much gender-typing of different tasks this is inevitable. What is of concern for economic analysis is the terms of input (and sometimes product) trade between these accounting units. Terms of trade will influence the relative rates of return of the different accounting units. Marriage and inheritance patterns and gender relations at the personal level and in the wider society will influence relative bargaining powers, and therefore the terms of exchange. Household members frequently work on their own account and jointly with other members. This complicates terms of exchange and individuals' rights to have adequate time for their own-account activities. Uncertainty surrounding the authority and motivation of the head of household, and the scope for consultation, make the outcome unpredictable. This and the personal relations involved make for a range of transaction costs, some of which are obscure to the outsider.

Three, it is common to have mixed economic portfolios. Hence a single accounting unit may cover two or more lines of primary production, value-adding work, repair and wage labouring, over all of which there would, logically, be one internal rate of return.

Four, all incomes and produce from these various accounting units are not necessarily pooled in one common household budget to meet some rationalized order of consumption needs. Degrees of pooling from separate purses usually vary by purpose – food, clothes, school fees, medical expenses and so on. In some situations different combinations of household members may eat together in the morning, at midday and in the evening. Likewise contributions to these cooking pots will come from different individuals, via cash purchases or own-grown food. Seniority plays a role in these distributions of responsibility for provisioning the family, but gender is the overwhelming influence. Again there are obscure transaction costs in negotiating this pattern of appropriation even in the most 'close-knit' households.

Five, produce may be directed to a combination of market exchange and household provisioning. Self-provisioning of the household is, in nearly all cases, women's responsibility.

Factor mobility in pursuit of adaptation and change is often limited by gender divisions of responsibility to provide family essentials. Gender divisions of family budgetary responsibilities are often accompanied by corresponding access to household-level resources to produce that essential. Switching the use of those resources is an option that would require more than straightforward economic calculation, and it may well provoke a change in management and appropriation.

Identification of the micro unit should also extend to the terms on which the micro manager has access to and control over resources, including own labour. Unequal access to productive resources and unequal terms of exchange can combine with unequal responsibilities to give a gender-based asymmetry of rights and obligations. This means that women have less room than men for manoeuvre and, therefore, less capacity to respond to macro-economic policies.

The most important service the women-in-development literature has given economics is to show how crushing transaction costs can be for women when they would like to respond to events above the household level. What is certain from the substantive library of reports on how structural adjustment programmes (SAPs) affected women is that without some sensitive structural changes and public investments directed towards gender equity in production and exchange at the micro level, macro-economic policy is likely to set up a chain reaction of external diseconomies whose costs will have to be met by future generations.

The socio-cultural base to gender in economic relations   Cultural factors are not immutable. All cultures adapt and change in order to survive population increase and the introduction of technology and market encroachments. The issue is not whether socio-cultural influences on gendered relations of production and exchange alter, but 'how'. Who decides? Women's interests so far appear to have been weakly represented in choices. Long-standing traditional checks and balances which supported women have been disrupted, often in a manner which retained women's duties but eroded their rights to resources to fulfil those duties. In the modern economy culture does not always act to protect women.

Recognition of how women's weak bargaining power can lead to increasingly inefficient resource allocations, diseconomies and threats to sustainability should provide indications of the kind of interventions that good economics would identify. A simple and widely known example makes the point. One apparent consequence of the narrow economic adjustment orthodoxies was to make social reproduction more arduous while obliging women to spend extra hours either in seeking low prices for consumption items (if they were wage-earners) or responding to their menfolk's new price incentives (if they were in export-oriented production). Why did this happen? Why is intra-household work not more fairly distributed? We have to turn to the basis of gender asymmetries in rights and obligations.

Virtually all cultures prescribe the male head of household as a custodian of household resources and welfare as well as interlocutor with the wider world. The 'new household economics' accepted that there were gender divisions of labour and decision-making but not that there might be anything irrational or exploitative in the deployment of resources and income.

This is essentially also the planners' model of the micro-level producer: male, and the reasonable custodian of family resources and needs. He works as hard as his wife. His whole earnings become the family budget. What is good or bad for him is good or bad for his wife. Nothing of this is made explicit, but it is, unmistakably, the implicit assumption of how the grand strategy works. This view is now widely discredited. It has also led to some opposing theoretical modelling of gender relations in the household. The assumption that effort and return are democratically distributed and that some harmonious unit exists under an altruistic 'head' is rejected. In reality the terms of gender exchange are heavily weighted against women. (See Guyer and Peters 1987; Sen 1990; Elson 1992; Dreze and Sen 1989). What has emerged is a view that bargaining goes on between men and women in the form of 'cooperative conflict', meaning coexistence of conflict and congruence of interests. Women have bargaining power but it is inferior.

Women's limited powers of direct appropriation are a good example of this. The common expression 'women's unpaid labour' is analytically useless. The quick rejoinder must be: 'So why do they labour?' Of course there is a return. It comes in that proportion of the proper returns to women's work that passes into the household budget and obviates the need of a woman to find that value of consumption from elsewhere. But if the full return to her work is not surrendered for family consumption, why does she not take her labour elsewhere? Is the opportunity cost of working in the family so low? The answer must be that if socio-gender relations do not forbid her outright, they sufficiently intimidate her. Violence is a common means of intimidation. There is also the issue of immobility of young mothers, although why so many other women are so immobile gives the main point. High transaction costs of an occupational change lower the *de facto* opportunity cost of working in the family.

The foundation of what appears from a distance as irrational economic behaviour and abandonment of any maximizing position stems from men's superior position lying in their superior entitlements: legal rights to resources and services. Women do not have their own entitlements in equal measure, and entitlements vested in men are not automatically vested in their wives.

The case study material referenced above comes from Africa. It is often said that the Asian family production unit works and consumes more corporately. How much more is debatable. Sen (1985) has commented negatively on the application of the new household economics model to the Asian family too. There is some evidence from Asia to suggest that the status of women is higher in the poorest and best-off families, and lowest in middle-income families (Acharya and Bennett 1981; Sajogyo et al. 1980). The poorest families have to hire out labour. In the process women experience cash-in-hand and this gives them bargaining power. The middle families depend almost exclusively on family labour. The better-off hire in labour. This socio-economic stratification is also spreading in Africa, starting with fertile, more heavily populated areas with roads. Already reference has been made to instances of market density in Nigeria, Kenya and Cameroon.

For an economist what is at stake in general is that true economic opportunity costs in the wider economy are not being allowed to exert their influence because social factors and gender relations inhibit women from seeking them out. The result is gross misallocation of resources that puts past urban and import-replacing biases into the shade. Yet culture is not written in stone. Poverty has forced women to break seclusion and sell their labour visibly. Young unmarried women, the family silver in terms of national virtue, are being released by parents to become the first to be hired by new secondary industries, often far from home. We see that underlying economic forces have changed cultural mores. There is obvious scope to do more, this time consciously making offers of economic gains for women and their children which neither women nor their menfolk can refuse.

KEY AREAS OF GENDER RELEVANCE AT THE MACRO LEVEL

Development policies and economic management   In the first section of this chapter the perennial mandate of macro-economists and their policy instruments were explained. Here it is useful to begin with a summary view of how recent evolution in macro-economic management failed to modernize gender economic relations and in some ways made them more regressive. The potential of new ideas for incorporating gender equity is then discussed.

Much of post-independence macro strategies in developing countries emphasized import-substitution and heavy industry. The consensus seems to be that this discriminated against women in two main ways:

- protected import-substitution (as against an open economy) results in slow overall economic growth and by implication leads to a slow emergence of women's participation in the modern economy; and
- heavy industry favours male employment because of its traditional association with male labour.

Moreover, in so far as import-substitution was accompanied by the subsidization of credit for capital investment and a preferential exchange rate for imports of capital, the resulting manufacturing processes tended to be large-scale and capital-intensive. This also has been inimical to women's employment in the modern sector.

However, in a minority of countries where import-substitution was of light, labour-intensive manufacturing, women benefited. This was particularly true of Korea, Hong Kong, Taiwan, Thailand after 1960, and Malaysia after 1968. This was premised on a pricing of capital and foreign exchange which discouraged capital intensity. Therefore although 'flexibility of the labour market' was pursued, the government was shaping demand for labour. Its investments in education and health and infrastructure were also shaping the supply of labour.

The experience of protection and the profligate use of capital led to the adoption of open, export-oriented strategies fostered by what are called structural adjustment programmes (SAPs). These relied heavily on developed markets and institutions. At the outset of SAPs the importance of these preconditions was not appreciated. Trying to copy the East Asian experiences in much truncated form had a particularly uneven impact on gender relations and associated welfare. Where it was negative it could reach life-threatening proportions (Moser 1989).

Instead of the relatively benign neglect of women in the earlier strategy, an open competitive economy and fiscal restraint had the effect of shifting costs from the state to women. Health and local infrastructural cutbacks made social reproduction more difficult, with women substituting more of their labour to cover the deficit of state provision. Urban unemployment rose as the mobility of factors from old industries to new industries failed to materialize strongly. The new family poverty forced women into greater participation in the labour force for extremely low remuneration. Gender heterogeneity in the labour market offered women these little niches in the economy if they were ready to accept the terms. Flexibility of the labour market sometimes meant women would find work where men could not, or where men would not accept the wages that women accepted. Very poor women, sometimes abandoned by male partners who could not face the stress of unemployment and poverty, extended the use of their labour time virtually to a state of attrition. Competing demands meant reducing standards of child care and health and family welfare.

Rural areas generally enjoyed a surge of demand for primary products. The extra effort required interacted with gender-typing of tasks such that it can be argued that greater increases in effort were demanded of women than men. And this could be on top of their now more onerous social reproduction work. Gender flexibility of the labour 'market' within households was also highly imperfect. Worse, in the case of production within the household, new production incentives gave male heads of household reason to appropriate and redirect household resources. Whether they used their uncertain authority to do this depended on women's bargaining power in influencing the asymmetries of rights and obligations. Where women had inadequate bargaining counters or real socially acceptable alternatives, the forced redeployment of resources would not only have added stress to women but could have led to long-term social costs in the form of disinvestment in children and moves away from a demographic transition. Any exacerbation of gender asymmetries would worsen allocative efficiency and raise long-term social costs.

Judging from the literature it led to, the outcome of SAPs for the great majority of poor women seems to have been their seriously reduced capabilities (Elson 1989; Moser 1989; Lockwood 1992; Afshar and Dennis 1992).

There is little doubt that over the long term price stability and market liberalization benefit women more than men in terms of wage employment creation. This is so obvious in East Asia. An analysis of the impact of outward-oriented trade regimes and domestic economic liberalization concluded that the subsequent success was related to fast growth in output of labour-intensive light manufacturing which is a major employer of women. Monetary stabilization and low inflation gave confidence to small-scale businesses. Female participation and the openness of the trade regime were particularly correlated (ESCAP 1992: 109–16).

The example of East Asian 'miracle economies' devising their own economic strategies has encouraged a still ill-defined 'new growth theory'. This theory combines emphasis on structural investments (education, health, infrastructure, market access), acceptance that higher incomes mean higher growth, and a favourable policy climate. It incorporates the complementarity of efficiency and equity, and the state investing 'long' in order to achieve this, as mentioned at the beginning of this chapter. As such it gives a space for issues of gender equity.

An ECLAC publication advocates a very similar approach, although understandably, given the recent history of hyperinflation in Latin America, it is particularly exercised by the dangers of inflation (ECLAC 1992: 19, 20). The approach emphasizes the interdependence of growth and equity. An 'integrated approach' of combining social and economic policies will strengthen the areas of complementarity and reduce areas of trade-offs between equity and growth. The publication showed awareness of the threat of inflation posed by the lead time of investment in human capital. Therefore the promotion of productive employment (and hence supply of goods) is the priority. This is to be done by 'technological spread' and priority given to small and medium-sized enterprises. The prescription rests on strategic interventions in technology, the modernization of basic infrastructural support, and development of markets, especially those of capital and labour. The formula also includes open competitiveness with the international economy. All this is almost a carbon copy of the principles behind the East Asian experience.

There are two points in this strategy that are worth pausing over because, without specifying gender, they offer macro-economists guidance on overcoming gender-related economic inefficiencies. The first point (reflecting the emphasis on capital and labour markets) notes that the apparent conflict between productivity and employment stems from incorrect concepts of efficiency and productivity. In fact, technology can lead to a saving of capital by increasing *its* productivity, while increasing or decreasing labour inputs. Technology becomes a powerful shaper of labour markets. This introduces two ideas: (i) existing capital input can be so technically inefficient that switching to new equipment actually increases the output-to-capital ratio, and (ii) co-factor productivities of capital and labour can be designed to suit social purposes by saving on capital while either creating employment or saving on labour input. These could be the basis of a strategy to bring technology to women's non-marketed work and release women's labour for incorporation in the marketed economy without incurring the large amounts of capital outlay usually anticipated. It may well be that the assets currently used in non-marketed work are inefficient in the use of capital.

The second point spotlights the folly of ignoring non-market production. It is that the effective functioning of markets not only involves market-based prices and deregulation but also often calls for *active* intervention in order to create or stimulate markets that do not yet exist or are insufficient or segmented.

Socially directed technology can therefore combine economic efficiency and gender equity. If strategizing public investments to crowd in private enterprise and entrepreneurship (see below) is also put through a gender lens then the relation between economic efficiency and gender equity can be further strengthened.

The critical equation for macro-economists is between public investment and low inflation. Van der Hoeven quotes some empirical analyses that defy traditional macro-economics (1993: 22–3):

- inflation is negatively correlated with investment; and
- budget surpluses are negatively correlated with investment.

He points out that this is possible if public investment is targeted such that it 'crowds in' private investment instead of crowding it out. New growth theory assumes that public investment in human resources and infrastructure does just that. Current economic literature is 'deconstructing' public investment to show how it can improve and release labour, improve the functioning of markets and attract private investment. Earlier we saw how roads can crowd in women's entrepreneurship. Infrastructure was shown to crowd in gainful opportunities in rural Bangladesh such that commercial banks were poaching Grameen Bank members. A clear example of what happens to female labour effort when the social wage (tertiary income) is crowded *out* through withdrawal of the social services comes from Tanzania. In a critique of the mainstream view of the agricultural crisis Mbilinyi (1988) claims that villagers, especially women, withdrew their labour from export crops when social services funding declined. They argued like this: they were constantly told by state functionaries that they must produce more export/food crops to earn/save foreign exchange. In return peasants expected to share in benefits like social services. Women in particular valued the schools, water supplies and medical clinics because they knew they would not get a just economic wage via their husbands or through access to village equipment.

The mainly public investments envisioned by the new growth theory coincide with much of the particular needs of women if gender relations are not to obstruct economic development.

There is a case, then, for putting public investment through a gender lens to make it more effective. Van der Hoeven (1993: 27) summarizes

---

BOX 3.3 *Putting economic principles to the gender test*

An example of how deconstructing public investment and giving it a gender dimension can add to growth and long-term social gains was given in a meeting with a senior government economist in Jamaica. Jamaica is to embark on a large programme to promote micro-enterprises. One objective is to ensure that women, a large proportion of whom raise families on their own, are at last properly represented. Many women live alone up in the hills ekeing out meagre livelihoods, growing their own food and selling small surpluses via a tortuous path down the mountains: in effect marginalized, excluded and so on. Many are on welfare.

When asked what she was planning for the women – credit and training schemes perhaps? – the government economist replied: 'Oh no! Before all that I want to go through the entire tariff regime for possible changes in price relatives of inputs and exportable micro-enterprise products. Then I want to screen the large road building plan to see whether provision is made for small roads into the hills, instead of just widening trunk roads.' Her argument, in detail, covered incremental capital-output ratios, capital gestation periods, income and employment multipliers, social returns to capital investment as well as to health and education budgets, the efficient allocation of credit resources, reductions in welfare payments and long-term social gains. The external economies of road provision came through bringing a neglected but hardworking section of the community, responsible for raising the next generation, into the market economy with high productivity. Her case was devastating. Her argument never veered from the economic. The alternative was widening trunk roads, with the dubious benefit–cost ratio of more of the same.

the new theory thus: 'The new growth theory thus offers, especially through the link between tertiary income, income distribution and the generation of future primary incomes, a more dynamic element than traditionally was the case of the relationship between income inequality and economic growth. In this, macroeconomic policy variables can play a positive role.'

Economists will see in tertiary income elements of external economies to the internal costed economy. It could, in fact, supply a counterbalancing bias, a second best option, to overcome the massive misallocation of resources represented by women's reproduction labour overhead. It shifts the costs of providing the externality of a renewal of the labour force from women to the public purse. It should also reduce some of the transaction costs that obstruct women from pursuing their economic opportunity costs. More of this later.

The World Bank is signalling its support for this approach. The Bank still believes in a free-flowing labour market unobstructed by union bargaining, minimum wages and costly regulations on work conditions. But it values labour productivity as a means to income generation. An indication of this is proposed research in the Dacca labour market. Wages in the Dacca garments industry, dominated by a female labour force, must be just about the lowest in any secondary industry anywhere. Yet among the hypotheses the World Bank hopes to test in a study is that female labour in the garments industry is not cheap because of its very low productivity due to little human resource development. This returns us to the ECLAC publication's point of the efficiency of capital lowering the capital-to-output ratio and influencing co-factor productivities. In this case capital investment in female human resources can actually lower the capital-to-output ratio and improve labour productivity.

Of course, macro-economic policy is itself not concerned with targeting and fine-tuning. But it is concerned with major allocations of public resources and clear pronouncements on the philosophy and assumptions behind the overall development strategy. All this sets the framework for the design of public finance guidelines and activities. There is ample hard-nosed economic argument for introducing gender in these macro directions.

Public finance   The new growth theory with its stress on investment in human resources and infrastructural externalities requires a great deal of public investment. Some expenditures will have short lead times, others long ones. In general the arguments for increasing tax are long-term whereas the arguments against it are short-term. In the long term growth and higher productivity will raise incomes. On the other hand, there are present limits to taxation set by disincentives to invest and work, and the ever present danger of a flight of capital. However, balancing public finances is only the outer aggregate framework.

In short, sources of revenue can be patterned to emphasize the strategy of growth as well as to contribute to equity, while expenditures cannot only target certain capacities but the effectiveness of those targeted allocations can be improved. At the same time an important consideration of public finance must be administrative convenience and ease. Opportunities to avoid a tax devalue it immediately. It can be argued that when revenue-raising and expenditure are disaggregated and restructured to meet the goal of growth with equity there is no reason to assume that fiscal stringencies must worsen gender relativities.

The goal of equity requires direct income taxation to be progressive. Starting taxation after a certain minimum of income is a great advantage to the poorest. Administrative convenience and cost-effectiveness of tax collection are also likely to dictate that those earning small sums in the informal sector or from diverse portfolios (predominantly women) are given a miss. This is a straightforward *quid pro quo* for the inevitable rise in prices of essential consumer items.

The great advantage of indirect taxes, such as VAT, is the ease and low cost of collection. Its regressive nature can be ameliorated by its being selectively applied. The exemption of a range of essentials can turn it into a modestly progressive tax. Even where this is not possible, the fact that its size could finance major restructuring to bring about equity and inclusion of the poor in the long term has to be given serious consideration. The likely substantial long-term social opportunity cost of not taking up this option has to be weighed against its price effect on the poor today. VAT can also be used for applying price signals to producers since it changes relative prices. Since men and women partly purchase and produce different things, VAT is also a policy instrument to advance gender equity.

What has earlier been discussed under macro-economic policies has implications for the direction of public expenditures, both between and within sectoral ministries, and between (re)current and capital expenditures. Sectoral ministries should now have a more proactive role in contributing to macro designs and therefore influencing their own expenditure patterns. Those designs include scope for ministries to influence gender disparities and gender relations in present access to resources and in capabilities. But in addition to this gain ministries should be aware of the relevance of gender to expected marginal returns to their expenditure allocations.

User charges for publicly provided goods and services have been widely introduced since the early 1980s, primarily to bring revenue to sectoral ministries. Like VAT it can be highly regressive as it constitutes a tax on what were often formerly free public goods. User charges predominantly concern human resource development, which is a long-term private, as well as a social, investment. As an expenditure with postponed benefit it is likely to fall victim to both income and price substitution effects of a VAT imposed on it. User charges can also activate gender discrimination, especially among children's needs, in a way that accessing a free public good would not.

But the potential range of user charges is very large and there is scope for their flexible, or discriminatory, application. A way to mitigate the price and income effects is to apply user charges at levels and on particular services where gender disparities already exist and would not be significantly worsened by attaching a price-tag. Thus user charges on university education or on services of large urban hospitals and specific curative services might not add to discrimination against female human resources in the way user charges on primary and secondary education and on dispersed primary and maternal health care would. Such graded user charges would be as administratively convenient to collect as VAT.

But it cannot be stressed enough that without strategic targeting the price and income substitution effects of user charges are bound to do particular damage to women and girls, and therefore put in jeopardy the success of the kind of growth strategy seen in East Asia and now seemingly advocated by ECLAC. Girls could be withdrawn from school to be included in family labour, so reinforcing the value of female child labour. Any user charges for primary health care would reinforce this regressive trend because women would need more help in child care and nursing household members.

Subsidies are negative taxes. If they can be eliminated public revenue is saved for other purposes. It is now widely recognized that many of the subsidies directed to social and equity purposes were captured by the middle classes. If the poorest have not had an equitable, let alone favoured, access to subsidies, it is certain that women too did not have equal political clout with men to obtain equal access to subsidies. The elimination of many subsidies, then, would save revenue and reduce a regressive distorting effect.

Extending disaggregation and strategizing to the expenditure side of public finance also strengthens the complementarity of gender equity and economic growth. To this end, human resources and infrastructural development need to be scrutinized for 'infant industry' arguments for subsidies whose pay-offs come in the form of external economies and long-term social gains.

In most countries that have suffered years of economic decline and the effects of SAPs the health status of poor women is at a very low level. These women are also in need of child care facilities if they are to participate less arduously, and more equitably and effectively, in the labour force. There are strong social and economic arguments for putting special rings round these two items on social sector budgets. It puts public expenditure where equity and long-term growth start – with the children. It is interesting to note that East Asian countries emphasized universal access to primary education many years before they gave the kind of attention to higher education seen now.

SAPs made sectoral ministries acutely aware of the need to get the balance between capital and current expenditures right in order to maximize the effectiveness of the total reduced total budget. There is always scope to further refine this balance in the cause of advancing a strategy of growth with equity. For instance, agricultural ministries have their own experiences of higher returns to extension services when women farmers are reached. Likewise the nature of agricultural research, a capital investment expenditure, could be altered to serve an agricultural technology that helps to rationalize the gender divisions of labour and management. It is also important to understand how gender influences the cross-productivities of current and capital expenditures. Allowing these issues to play a role in economic analysis could do much to make public expenditures cost-effective and responsive.

The relevance of gender to efficiency and growth should also compel sectoral ministries to recognize mutuality of interests. Because women's lives are multi-faceted the efficiency of one sectoral ministry's expenditure may be dependent on certain actions taken by another sectoral ministry. For instance, in agricultural areas the rains coincide with peak labour demand periods, making rises in the incidence of water-borne diseases coincide with reductions in cooking and infant care. Indicators of seasonal disorder among the local population, and the importance of gender to it, are weight losses of pregnant women, low birthweights and high infant mortality. Ministries of agriculture have an interest in advocating additional pertinent health services at seasonally critical times, while ministries of health should see an opportunity to improve overall health by this kind of targeting. Other examples are the common investment interests in urban management, development of the urban labour market and credit to the informal sector of industry and local government. Put through a gender lens these interests become better focused, with consequent benefit in the form of allocative efficiency.

Poverty alleviation Earlier it was shown how important it was for macro objectives to look more closely at people's capacities to respond to macro-economic policy instruments, and to the preconditions and revised package of instruments to draw a more positive response. Without this, adjustment programmes would lead to some successes in greater efficiency and competitiveness but also to external diseconomies in the form of unemployment and poverty. Efficient and securely sustainable growth throughout the economy implied inclusiveness; and that meant investing in preparing people for efficient and competitive contributions. At the same time the evolution of ideas on poverty alleviation were arriving at similar solutions.

Around 1987, with the impact of SAPs on poverty levels becoming apparent, there was debate over the response: fire-brigade action in the form of succour or strengthening the capabilities of the poor to participate effectively in the new economy. The latter is now seen as the only means to sustainable poverty reduction, especially since it has been persistently difficult to reach the poorest with effective succour. Poverty alleviation therefore comes mainly through markets, and the labour market is the single most important market for this. Both the World Bank and the UNDP emphasize the role of human resource development in poverty alleviation. Whereas the Bank uses the term 'human capital formation', the UNDP softens this to human development as a process of 'enlarging people's choices by expanding their capabilities and opportunities' (Elson 1992: 5). But when it comes down to means, the UNDP shares with the Bank things such as sensible pricing to reflect opportunity costs, opening of market systems, supportive investment policies and expanding employment opportunities.

There has been a growing recognition of gender disparities in the intensity and nature of poverty, per class, age and ethnic group. Women heads of household are generally believed to be poorer than women with resident husbands. There is frequent mention of the 'feminization of poverty'. Women's poverty is compounded over a lifetime, due to their unpaid domestic work and discriminatory wage employment. 'The feminisation of poverty plays a necessary part in the perpetuation and deepening of poverty at the same time as it plays a key role in the perpetuation and reinforcement of discrimination against women' (Townsend 1993: 108).

Ultimately only equal participation in markets, especially the labour market, can overcome women's structured greater poverty and their dependence on men for passing welfare benefits on to them. But such are the structures of discrimination against women that only a strategic package of counterbalancing affirmative actions can bring them to equal participation. The social returns to this are now widely accepted. 'There is compelling evidence that improving women's productivity can have important effects in terms of growth and distribution ... market forces have great potential to influence gender relations and increase the perceived value of women' (Bennett 1992: 58).

There are two major causes of women being over-represented in the less profitable, more crowded parts of the unprotected labour market and under-represented in the protected labour market and in expanding self-employment. These are their lower education and training attainments and their responsibility for social reproduction.

The importance of education and training for gaining productive, higher-income employment and for enjoying occupational mobility is fairly well established. Such personal endowments also help to reduce gender segmentation of the labour market by increasing mobility from the unprotected labour market to self-employment and the protected market. Poor women of low educational and other human resource endowment are trapped in the unprotected market (Khandker 1992: 23–5). In effect, women must have such an access to education and training as to bring them out from behind men. The macro-economic returns of this are patently evident in East Asian economies.

The second cause of women's lower economic status in the labour market is their burden of social reproduction. To impose the cost of maternity leave on individual employers is a recipe for discrimination against female employees. It also creates distortions of markets by imposing an effective production tax on some enterprises but not others. ECLAC has put it squarely. Serious consideration should be given to 'socializing' the cost of maternity leave to neutralize its effect. The way to do this is to levy a tax on all enterprises, regardless of the gender ratio of their employees, to pay for maternity leaves as they occur. ECLAC suggests instead of a payroll tax (which would be anti-employment) a percentage of value added (which would be anti-capital). In the same way vouchers for child care could be funded.

There may be debate about the merits of different kinds of tax, but the principle that the whole should contribute to funding reproduction is unimpeachable. The argument is that it is the collective that should fund the 'free public good'. The collective will benefit, *en passant*, by enabling women to pursue economic opportunity costs that were previously impossible because of prohibitive transaction costs attached to social reproduction. Other transaction costs, of course, remain.

But this facility to improve gender equity applies only to the protected part of employment. It could be extended to self-employment (as sickness benefit sometimes is). However, for women in non-market work it becomes irrelevant. Here it is difficult to see how the effect of social reproduction can be directly neutralized. Indirectly, the social wage of supports in the form of water, sanitation, electrification, commuter transportation and health services should reduce the distortion and release women's time for income earning.

Credit on easy terms based on the infant industry argument would help to reach these women with higher productivity means and even training (cheap credit, for instance, being a concession in return for finding hours to train).

Socializing the costs of social reproduction can go a long way to developing the labour market in a gender-neutral way. But there are other forms of social security – unemployment and sickness benefits, old age pensions – that are still exclusive to formal-sector-protected employees, who are predominantly men. Without social security of their own women can hope for some derived benefit only by being married. Their dependence on children for security in old age will continue.

SEWA (the Self Employed Women's Association) in India has developed group social security schemes among women in the unprotected labour market and in self-employment. These include coverage for maternity and child care.

A developed labour market means that labour moves to where it can be most efficiently employed. This does not happen when a mass of workers move through a market without directives or guidance. The labour market is no exception to the need for regulation and structures to deal with transaction costs to the individual and external diseconomies to the whole market. Social security insurance helps to do just that. Earlier in this chapter the nature of transaction costs was described.

The poorest participants face the greatest transaction costs – including risks and having to make judgements on imperfect information. Social security minimizes transaction costs for the individual and internalizes the cost of negative externalities. Entrants or mobile workers must have knowledge of the market to make the best choice. They need to be able to afford a waiting time to gain that knowledge and to find the appropriate employment.

Schemes of social insurance allow that waiting time. They can also support a worker through sickness or unemployment to avoid urgency of re-entry in the market at a point that is efficient neither for the worker nor for the overall allocation of labour. In short, social security brings order to the labour market and helps to price human resources efficiently.

Access to social insurance does not come easily for women. There are, effectively, transaction costs in accessing social insurance. This stems from women's weaker starting point and tenuous hold in the labour market. Yet they badly need social insurance. Women, more than men, tend to take any job to underwrite the survival of the family. They cannot indulge in unsupported waiting time. Because of reproduction responsibilities they have less time to seek out market information and assess it. Their poorer education and training and work experience make it difficult for them to negotiate strongly.

A developed labour market, as distinct from the merely flexible promoted by early orthodox adjustment programmes, offers dividends to the whole economy. It therefore pays society to invest collectively in that development. The infant industry argument is strong in the case of subsidizing the spread of social insurance. Government could begin with group social security schemes among unprotected women to counter the risks of sickness and unemployment, the need for maternity leave, and the need for waiting time to return. SEWA's initiative in India has already been mentioned. With some subsidy this innovation could spread more quickly. Schemes for collectivized child care could accompany them. These beginnings cover immediate risks. A later stage would be to add pensions. Such extras of social insurance schemes could be designed to meet the particular risks of the informal sector, which may require a different package of supports – and different for men and women.

While strong links can be forged between poverty alleviation programmes and growth strategies, there is also need for immediate support to the poor. Social funds of one kind or another have been set up to compensate the newly unemployed as well as to reach the long-term poor. In this and in other welfare payments gender poses difficult trade-offs. Women experience poverty more acutely than men. But resources targeted on the family have to pass through the spectrum of gender relations of distribution before they settle on individual family members. The cost-effectiveness of assistance programmes is determined by their intra-family distribution and by the administrative ease of releasing the resources. The latter has to be traded off against fine-tuning of targeting to arrive at gender equity.

Public assistance seeks to improve the outcome for the poorest. The guiding principle must be that 'equal outcomes might have to entail unequal inputs'. Appleton and Collier (1992) begin from this position when they advocate gender-targeting of in-kind transfers. They reject the claim that gender is overwhelmed by other criteria of poverty, that the model of the household economy with an altruistic head should be held as the base unit for distribution, and that money transfers are superior to in-kind transfers. They argue that food, health care and education are not, in fact, 'household public goods' but have to be treated as private to the individual. Money transfers are a blunt instrument in targeting both the neediest and securing the most appropriate needed items. If the intra-family distribution of other resources is anything to go by, this argument has to be taken very seriously. Targeted transfers are also said to increase the intended recipients' bargaining power. On the other hand, if the fine-tuning of targeting in-kind transfers becomes too complex and expensive to administer this could reduce the effective coverage of the neediest women. It is difficult to 'attach' some services to the most marginalized. A percentage of a money transfer might have a more positive outcome. Leakages have to be tolerated.

Macro-economists need help to deconstruct aggregates and to forge links between poverty alleviation and macro-policy instruments. Participant identification of issues and appropriate strategies could improve the efficacy of their work. This is particularly true for gender-related aspects of forging links.

A preliminary step, the mapping of gender disparities in poverty and their resolution, is well suited to participatory methods. But the quality and sensitivity of the process are crucial. Welbourn (1991) mentions a case where village men and women were asked to mark desired changes on a village map. In one village women replied that the kind of changes they wanted could not be drawn. How could you draw things which would help to deal with overwork, breakdown in co-wife support, beatings from their husbands? Advocates of participatory methods would argue that they can lead to the empowerment of women which was so obviously lacking in that case.

However, Chambers (1992: 56) cautions that 'Whether empowerment is good depends on who are empowered, and how their new power is used ... The natural tendency is for this to be men rather than women, the better-off than the worse-off.' The dangers of misrepresentation of the needs of the poorest women in participatory research have been vividly illustrated by Hosain (1991). Identification of symptoms or end-products of poverty, and mapping gender disparities in these, is one thing. Identification of gender-related causes is more difficult, if only because it is more contentious. But identification of gender-related remedies, and prioritized remedies, is very difficult.

There are other limits to participation in designing macro-policy. De Kadt (1993: 18), writing on Chile, raises the issue of participatory groups applying for social funds: 'there must be doubts not only in relation to the efficiency of having large numbers of separate small scale projects ... but also about the extent to which participation in those can really help the poor "participate" in resolving the broader problems of poverty'.

Other commentators take the concept of participation further into forms of activist advocacy. Doubt over the ability or willingness of local community institutions to represent women's interests in inter-action with state agencies and markets has led to support for the idea of women's adversarial groups calling for change. The problem with these groups is that many are not ready to argue for new economic structures or resources. They are strong on legal advice and reforms, and they devise credit schemes and income-generating projects for women. But they are not yet equipped to present the case to macro-economists for putting new gender-related entitlements into macro strategies. Worse, from Chile comes an example of how activist women's groups are reluctant to use social fund resources to even enter economic activities (personal communication). The Fund for Social Solidarity is dispersed through local groups, including women's groups, which may formulate requests for assistance via participatory processes. Men's or mixed groups are strongly interested in economic schemes, whereas women's groups want to strengthen their group relations (personal communications). The urban women of NGOs advising local groups seem to have had an influence. Their argument was that economic schemes tend to break up the solidarity groups.

This points to a fundamental problem for macro-economists and a dilemma for gender advocates. While it can be logically argued that including the gender dimension makes for good economic analysis and better planning, the impact of past macro-economic policy on women has been, on the whole, so bad that economists start with a credibility problem. Many knowledgeable gender activists who have much to contribute to a dialogue 'don't want to know'.

SUGGESTIONS FOR AN AGENDA OF CONSOLIDATING ACTIVITIES

Gender in macro-economic policy is a new subject, still on probation. It is therefore helpful to think in terms of activities that would establish its credibility and credentials, and which would consolidate gains as they come.

One way of thinking systematically about developing an agenda of activities is to start with critical questions and to see where the answers overlap. The first question might be 'What are the *substantive policy areas* that demonstrate in high profile the relevance of gender to economic criteria such as strengthening complementarities of equity and efficient growth, infant industry arguments, social opportunity costs, transactions costs and externalities?' In effect, what is on a government's agenda which could most clearly be put to the 'gender test'? This combines opportunity and need in terms of subject material.

The next question might be 'Where are the institutional opportunities for entry points?' The answers would come in terms of sympathetic senior civil servants, personal contacts, as well as annual plans, mid-term reviews, preparation for five-year plans, and agency missions.

A third question might be 'What are the priority areas of focused policy-oriented research that have great gender relevance?'

Any overlapping of the answers to these three questions would indicate most propitious activities. But it is more likely that choices will be made on the basis of answers to any two questions overlapping. Some entry points in government might prefer argument to research, or willingness to consider research after probing of arguments.

Areas of policy interest Interest in gender issues is now emerging parallel with interest in new development strategies. The two are not unrelated because concern about alternative development routes has partly arisen from past erroneous assumptions, some concerning gender.

There are signs of willingness to disaggregate the socio-economic context and be more selective with policy instruments. But most countries are still concerned with *structural adjustment programmes* as well as development strategies. Although these are merging into long-term development strategies there remain areas of economic policy where adjustment is a precondition for new growth, and where gender is relevant. Here four main policy issues of adjustment are mentioned:

• An accurate assessment of market distortions cannot be made without referring to women's supply of goods and services in absent or very weak markets.

• The success of proposed trade regime reforms and market liberalizations will be influenced by gender divisions of labour, access to resources, production management and powers of appropriation.

• If monetary and fiscal options are, *inter alia*, to support capacity to produce essentials, to limit inflationary pressures, and to attract private investment, the design of those options can be more effective if gender determinants of response are taken into account.

• Designing the most effective means to improve the functioning of markets (especially the credit and labour markets) will also need to take into account gender biases and disparities.

We have seen that *new growth theory* is tantamount to adopting social market economics with its emphasis on public investment in infrastructure and human resources. That this approach is in its very early days means that there are opportunities to place gender in its early formulations instead of trying to add gender later. In fact there is so much complementarity of gender equity and the new growth economics that this approach to macro-economic planning offers a very large arena for developing gender inclusions.

Five subjects of policy advice are of particular pertinence to strengthening this complementarity:

• a gender dimension to long-term investments designed to promote efficient inclusiveness;

• means to socialize the work of social reproduction within the internal costed economy;

• development of efficient and inclusive labour markets by taking gender into account;

• consideration of infant industry arguments applied to the credit market to overcome distortions based on gender and class, and thence to serve long-term productivity improvements and allocative efficiency; and

- encouragement of technologies that raise the productivity of capital, but in the case of women's non-market work raise their labour productivity too.

Under *public finance* the obvious subjects for incorporating a gender dimension on the revenue-raising side are the implications of different patterns of user charges and VAT for the relation between gender equity and allocative efficiency. Arguing their mutual strengthening can give policy analysts a framework for designing individual taxes.

The other side of the ledger of public finance deals with the strategic targeting of capital and recurrent expenditures. Much depends on the allocation of public capital investments for laying the foundations of the macro strategy. There are numerous gender issues in meso- and micro-level responses to different options for that allocation. The patterning of expenditures on infrastructure and social sector asset-building can exert a strong influence on transaction costs, externalities and inclusiveness, and therefore on gender equity and its contribution to economic growth. So much follows from the distribution of capital expenditures in terms of the shaping of the economy and society for years to come that this must be a priority policy area for inserting gender issues into economic principles. For instance, the way in which this expenditure can attract private small-scale investment with a short lead time has a number of gender dimensions via positive externalities and reduced transaction costs from new infrastructure.

Current expenditures largely cover the running costs of human resource development and producer services (as well as transfer payments for poverty alleviation). Again, cost-effective designs of those services can be raised by taking account of gender-differentiated access and use.

Labour market development and social insurance schemes link macro policy and *poverty alleviation* directly. Much of what would be targeted in reference to public expenditure mentioned above is, in fact, tying poverty alleviation into the development strategy. One area that obviously needs more focused investigation is the usefulness of the gender criterion for targeting transfers.

But advice on poverty alleviation is also related to advice on public finance on the revenue-raising side.

Entry points and mechanisms   The entry points for initiating and assisting this policy analysis will largely be determined by the stage in the planning cycle. Annual reviews or annual planning offer opportunities for immediate interventions. The disadvantage is that they allow little time for preparatory thinking and analysis to establish the credentials of something new. If the opportunity is rushed, then dialogue is confined to putting down a few points without embedding them in a more comprehensive framework. Mid-term reviews on macro policy or public expenditure have the advantage that they are assessments of effectiveness of recent interventions, and could lead to the adoption of something within a few years. Alternatively a general or sectoral adjustment loan offers great promise if the World Bank is ready to cooperate.

Institutional entry points are clearly the appropriate ministries, individually or together. But seeing ministries as entry points only at times of planning or review is not an adequate approach to establish the incorporation of a new dimension to macro-economic policy. Activities over many years may be needed to engage the professional attention of more than a small minority of macro-economic planners. A sympathetic in-house climate for including gender in policy analyses has to be created starting from (almost) scratch. A series of seminars, *ad hoc* or related to on-going planning, could be built on a network of concerned civil servants, academics, local NGO staff and multi-bi-agency staff. Seminars might be held in ministries or local universities. Visiting researchers might give lectures. There will be many other ways of creating space for informal exchanges.

Key areas for research   The means to providing a basis for gendered policy analysis, relating macro, meso and micro levels, will have to be found in a judicious mix of gleaning secondary material and mounting new focused policy-driven research. Much of existing secondary material is descriptive, and where it is analytical it is rarely presented in the language of economists. There is a case for assessing country-based materials on women, or gender, for drawing out case material on social reality and translating it into economics. New, more focused, research on the other hand should be framed by government needs.

Consideration might also be given to developing a portfolio of generic gendered economic arguments and case studies from other countries for planners' reference. This referential portfolio of materials could be progressively expanded over the years as more arguments and case materials are available. Two kinds of case material are envisioned. One would come from past women-in-development/gender research that is relevant to the issues raised in this paper and which would strike a chord with macro-economists. The second part would comprise attempts by various governments to include gender in their planning practice with analysis of successes and failures that followed. This would give other governments ideas not only on what to adopt and what to avoid, but on what kind of preparatory, focused research is advisable.

Bringing in national partners as soon as possible to any research programme is important. Women's groups and NGOs have much to offer, as have local academics. Some of the best local NGOs are offering themselves as research partners.

The 1990s are a propitious time for placing gender integrally in policy analysis. The rapid succession of development theories in the twentieth century has ignored gender, or the theories have been phrased in such aggregate terms that any heterogeneity of economic agents was passed over. Now economics and sociology are coming together after decades of effective divorce. The rendezvous of macro-economists with social reality is beginning to take place. Gender is an important part of that social reality.

ANNEX: GLOSSARY OF ECONOMIC TERMS

Elasticities of supply and demand

A The price elasticity is defined as:
% change in quantity
% change in price

i) the price elasticity of supply is defined as:
% change in quantity supplied
% change in price
(assumed to be positive)

ii) the price elasticity of demand is defined as:
% change in quantity demanded
% change in price
(assumed to be negative)

B The income elasticity of demand is defined as:
% change in quantity demanded
% change in income
(assumed to be positive)

Externalities A positive externality is an external economy; a negative externality is an external diseconomy. These are benefits or disutilities that accrue to the whole or part economy as a result of the action of some particular source. For instance, public infrastructure and public investment in human resources produce huge externalities to the economy. They can make previously unprofitable enterprises profitable. Likewise a rundown of the infrastructure can make previously profitable enterprises unprofitable. Or, the expansion of industry A would cause positive externalities to industry B if this led to it providing inputs at a lower price to industry B (or negative externalities if the expansion raised the local wage rate).

Externalities were important to the theory of balanced growth – when joint introduction of a variety of industries would be more profitable than when they were developed in isolation. Externalities accrued from the joint development of both input and output markets via complementarity of demand.

The popularity of externalities received a boost with environmental economics. The environment gives the 'internal costed (marketed) economy' many positive externalities, but its excessive exploitation is turning these into negative externalities. There is an obvious link between positive externalities from the environment and the concept of public goods. If these 'free' resources are pushed too far, life support systems start becoming dysfunctional. The analogy in this chapter is of women's contribution of a regeneration of the labour force.

External economies are not usually brought into short-term economic analysis. They are more important to theories of development and sustainability. But structural adjustment programmes have been known to make regeneration of the labour force (or social reproduction) disordered in the short term via their impact on women.

Marginal product This is the output that results from applying the last (marginal) unit of an input. For instance, the marginal product of labour might be two pairs of shoes.

Marginal revenue product = marginal product × price of product.

Under conditions of competition the price of the input (e.g. wage) = marginal revenue product.

Diminishing marginal returns occur when marginal products become progressively smaller. This occurs for all kinds of reasons. For instance, labour cannot be expected to maintain its marginal productivity for ever with the same amount of other inputs being applied. Or, diminishing returns to women's labour may set in after eight hours of work in a day; and by the 15th hour of the day the marginal product might be close to zero.

Multipliers There are the Employment Multiplier and the Income Multiplier. The multiplier states that the total increase in employment (or income) resulting from an initial expenditure is greater than the original number of persons employed (or wages spent) because the original workers spend their earnings and this gives rise to successive rounds of employment and income generation. The multiplier originally referred to investments in some public work. Today multipliers are popularly applied to any injection of expenditure.

The multiplier is defined in terms of the marginal propensity to save (or, inversely, to consume). But a deconstruction of an aggregate propensity is much more interesting – and better economics. The final multiplier (and its tendency to cause inflation) depends heavily on who is employed, what they spend their wages on, what technologies are used in production, the infrastructural supports to production, and so on. Class and gender distribution of assets, income and employment are crucial determinants of multipliers and their inflationary tendencies. Multipliers are integral to Keynesian economics. Many of the interventions discussed in this chapter would tend to make them non-inflationary. Certainly the experience of East Asian economies was one of low-inflation multipliers.

Opportunity cost This is the economic return to the best alternative use of a resource. It is the return 'forgone' by choosing the present use. In (hypothetical) instances of perfect competition in all markets, there is practically no difference between the returns to one use of a resource (or activity) and the next most gainful use (or activity). Thus:

The 'opportunity cost principle' is this: competition for factors of production in different uses will distribute them in a way that means that the return to each factor is equal to its return in every alternative use.

In the absence of perfect competition the term is most usefully thought about in the loosest of its definitions: the opportunity cost of doing something is what has to be sacrificed by not doing the next most profitable (or beneficial) thing. All factors of production (land, labour and capital) have opportunity costs. An activity absorbing a combination of factors has the opportunity cost of what those resources might alternatively be applied to.

Opportunity cost can also imply the cost (forgone gains) of not doing something, of not investing in an alternative long-term strategy.

One can conceptualize opportunity costs other than the economic one. For instance, focusing credit and extension services on male farmers instead of female farmers could have a substantial nutritional opportunity cost (via gender relations of production and appropriation). Likewise a strategy that lengthens women's working day has an obvious child care opportunity cost. Or there may be a demographic opportunity cost (a missed opportunity to move towards the demographic transition).

Economists use the term *social* (collective) opportunity cost to distinguish it from the private (individual) opportunity cost. A forgone economic gain to the whole economy becomes a social opportunity cost. Finally, there are short-term and long-term opportunity costs of all kinds.

Pareto optimality   This is based on assumed perfect competition in all factor and product markets, meaning that marginal cost = minimum average cost = price of good. No rearrangement of resources can be an improvement because any rearrangement would cause some cost to be greater than price received and some cost to be less than price received. Pareto optimality represents total economic efficiency based on maximizing positions. This is assumed to represent maximum welfare. Thus private profit does not diverge from social benefit.

There have been two criticisms of Pareto optimality:

• Interpersonal utility comparisons cannot be made: a good may represent a greater utility for some people.
• It is dependent on the existing distribution of income. If that distribution changes, then prices – first of products, then of factors of production – change and this destroys the former equation, marginal cost = price.

There is a third problem. Private profit and social benefit can also diverge if there is an externality rendering a free service (or disservice) to production. That is to say, where the product (or service) of some goods is creating an externality for the production (or demand) of others calculations of optimality based on prices are compromised. Pareto optimality can begin to be assessed only if all costs and productivities go through the pricing mechanism of the market. True optimality depends on all costs and gains being attributed through prices. Clearly the whole area of women's uncosted social reproduction and self-provisioning would corrupt any attempt to calculate Pareto optimality. But the *concept* of Pareto optimality is useful to make the point of the importance of looking at social reality.

Public goods These are goods which when available to one group of individuals are available to all because it is not possible to exclude others from benefiting. Cases in point are parks and defence. These are usually denoted as goods provided by some collective action. But the environment supplies them in the form of clean air and water, and so on. There is much debate as to how 'pure' a public good really is: some may have privileged access to it, or some may be excluded from it. Debate also surrounds how to make people pay for it when each person's private benefit from it is not clear.

Reproduction of the labour force offers a public good in that labour is (theoretically) available to all employers. One would have to assume that the action of a group of employers does not affect the supply of labour to others, which is not always true. Therefore labour is not a pure public good. Labour supply can be seen as a part free good because its full cost is not covered by wages which cover only labour's running costs. Only when wages fully remunerate the reproducers of labour can it be considered to be fully costed.

Substitution effects These occur when a change in price or income leads to a new pattern of demand. For example, an increase in the price of Good A means a decrease in the relative price of Good B. If Good B is any kind of substitute for Good A it becomes relatively more attractive. So if Good A suffers a price increase there is a switch of preference from Good A to Good B. This is known as the *price-substitution effect*.

If the price of Good A increases this also means a fall in real income. A lower amount of purchasing power forces the consumer to reshuffle her buying priorities. If Good A is an essential the consumer, now poorer, will buy more of it and less of other non-essential goods. If Good A is a non-essential, its price increase will result in the consumer demanding less of it. This is the *income-substitution effect*. These effects apply also to producers buying inputs.

Transaction costs These have been defined as costs incurred in establishing or carrying out a market contract. Transaction costs are unequally distributed by class, gender, age and ethnic group. They include costs entailed through:

- obtaining and assessing information;
- deciding, planning and arranging a contract;
- successfully negotiating the contract; and
- monitoring and enforcing the contract so that the actual flow of benefits are the same as those intended and that they are not diverted.

An example of a gender-based transaction cost is when a woman farming on her own is unable to hire ploughing services as timely and as efficiently as her male counterparts. Her planting is delayed, her yields are lower. To transact the ploughing contract without these consequences (that is to obtain a contract of equal quality with male farmers' ploughing contracts), if possible at all, would require a special effort.

Transaction costs cannot always be revealed in prices. Only those transaction costs that are actually overcome to conclude a contract come to light. Transaction costs interfere with notions of perfect competition in markets and therefore of equating all costs and returns at the margin. Optimality in resource allocation is heavily compromised by transaction costs.

The notion of transaction costs can be applied to non-market activities producing goods and services; that is, costs in moving to a new pattern of non-market production or in moving to market production.

It cannot be assumed that transaction costs are smaller or do not exist in personalized exchange. They can be very high in personalized exchanges when one party to the contract is not free to approach other potential partners. Personalized transaction costs often arise in establishing access and appropriation rights. The 'New Household Economics' implicitly assume that no gender-based transaction costs arise within the household. Sen's ideas on 'cooperative conflict' and others' ideas on asymmetries of rights and responsibilities within the household point to transaction costs.

In many traditional societies third party enforcers of contracts used to be heads of large kinship groups or village elders. Privatization and modernization have lost this source of enforcement and monitoring to women. Women now have to negotiate exchange with husbands and others in a quite new situation.

NOTE

1. Ingrid Palmer is a senior consultant on macro-economics and gender issues. She has worked for GTZ, the UNDP, the FAO, the ILO, ODA, the Commonwealth

Secretariat, the OECD, USAID, the UNHCR and the World Bank. This chapter was originally published in 1994 by GTZ.

BIBLIOGRAPHY

Acharya, M. and L. Bennett (1981) 'Rural women of Nepal: an aggregate analysis and summary of eight village studies', *The Status of Women in Nepal, Vol. II: Field Studies*, Kathmandu: Centre for Economic Development and Administration, Tribhuvan University.

Afshar, H. and C. Dennis (eds) (1992) *Women and Adjustment Policies in the Third World*, London: Macmillan.

Appleton, S. and P. Collier (1992) 'On gender targeting of public transfers', mimeo, Oxford: Centre for the Study of African Economics.

Bennett, L. (1992) *Women, Poverty and Productivity in India*, Washington, DC: EDI Seminar Paper No. 43.

Chambers, R. (1992) *Rural Appraisal: Rapid, Relaxed and Participatory*, Discussion Paper No. 311, Sussex: IDS.

De Kadt, E. (1993) *Poverty Focused Policies: The Experience of Chile*, Discussion Paper No. 319, Sussex: IDS.

Dreze, J. and A. Sen (1989) *Hunger and Public Action*, Oxford: Clarendon Press.

ECLAC (1992) *Social Equity and Changing Production Patterns: An Integrated Approach*, 24th Session.

Elson, D. (1989) 'The impact of structural adjustment on women: concepts and issues', Department of Economics, Manchester University, Paper presented to DSA Annual Conference, Manchester.

— (1992) *Public Action, Poverty and Development: A Gender Aware Analysis*, Seminar on Women in Extreme Poverty: Integration of Women's Concerns in National Development Planning, Vienna: UN.

ESCAP (1992) *Integration of Women's Concerns into Development Planning in Asia and the Pacific*, Bangkok.

Galbraith, J. K. (1974) *Economics and the Public Purpose*, London: Andre Deutsch.

Guyer, J. (1997) *The Women's Farming System. The Lekie of Southern Cameroon*, Yaoundé: ENSA.

Guyer, J. and P. Peters (1987) 'Conceptualising the household: issues of theory and policy in Africa', *Development and Change*, 18(2).

Hosain, M. (1991) *Rapid Appraisal for Women in the North West Frontier of Pakistan*, RRA Notes No. 12, London: IIED.

ILO (1994) *Summary of the Discussion*, International forum on 'Equality for Women in the World of Work: Challenges for the Future', 1–3 June, Geneva.

Khandker, S. R. (1992) *Earnings, Occupational Choice and Mobility in Segmented Labor Markets in India*, World Bank Discussion Paper 154, Washington, DC.

Khandker, S. and M. Pitt (1994) *Household and Intrahousehold Impacts of the Grameen Bank and Similar Targeted Credit Programs in Bangladesh*, Washington, DC: World Bank, mimeo.

Lockwood, M. (1992) *Engendering Adjustment or Adjusting Gender? Some New Approaches*, Discussion Paper No. 315, Sussex: IDS.

Mbilinyi, M. (1988) 'Women peasants and farm workers and agribusiness', Seminar paper presented at Wye College, UK.

Moser, C. (1989) 'The impact of recession and structural adjustment programmes at the micro level: low income women and the household in Guayaquil, Ecuador', *Invisible Adjustment*, 2, New York: UNICEF.

Sajogyo, P. et al. (1980) *The Role of Women in Different Perspectives, West Java*, Project on Rural Household Economics and the Role of Women, in Cooperation with FAO and SIDA, Bogor, Indonesia.

Sen, A. (1985) 'Women, technology and sexual divisions', UNCTAQS and INSTRAW, mimeo.

— (1990) 'Gender and co-operative conflicts', in I. Tinker (ed.), *Persistent Inequalities*, Oxford: Oxford University Press.

Sethuraman, V. (1985) 'The informal sector in Indonesia: policies and prospects', *International Labour Review*, 124(6), November–December.

Smith, J. B. and M. Stelcner (1990) *Modelling Economic Behaviour in Peru's Informal Urban Retail Sector*, PHRD Working Paper 469, Washington, DC: World Bank.

Stevens, J. (1993) *The Economics of Collective Choice*, Oxford: Westview Press.

Swedberg, R. (1990) *Economics and Sociology*, Princeton, NJ: Princeton University Press.

Townsend, P. (1993) *The International Analysis of Poverty*, Hemel Hempstead: Harvester Wheatsheaf.

Tzannatos, Z. (1992) 'Potential gains from the elimination of labor market differentials', *Women's Employment and Pay in Latin America. Part 1: Overview and Methodology*, Regional Studies Program, Report No. 10, Washington, DC: World Bank.

Van der Hoeven, R. (1993) 'The design of macroeconomic policy to reduce the adverse effects on poverty of structural adjustment', Paper presented to a symposium on 'Poverty: New Approaches to Analysis and Policy', Geneva: International Institute of Labour Studies.

Welbourn, A. (1991) 'RRA and the analysis of difference', mimeo by freelance social development consultant.

Winpenny, J. T. (1991) *Values for the Environment. A Guide to Economic Appraisal*, London: HMSO.

World Bank (1992) *Raising the Productivity of Women Farmers in Sub-Saharan Africa. Volume I, Overview Report*, Washington, DC.

CHAPTER 4

Macro-economics and Gender: Options for Their Integration into a State Agenda

JOERG FREIBERG-STRAUSS[1]

ARE THEY TWO DIFFERENT PERSPECTIVES?

Until very recently, gender-sensitive policies and strategies tended to be perceived as mainly relevant to the social sector and civil society. This made it difficult for the issue of gender to penetrate the political and administrative spheres where macro-economic policies are defined and coordinated, an essential prerequisite in order to achieve more sustainable and equitable development for the sexes. At present, the link between gender and macro-economics is becoming more obvious. At the level of macro-economics, ways of drafting and implementing strategies and policies that eliminate discrimination against women are being sought. Nevertheless, a gap in communication continues to exist between gender experts and professionals in macro-economics. Among other things, this gap is due to the fact that gender still is seen as a subject related to the 'micro' level, having little connection with the essence of economic growth. This leads us to asking whether a common platform between the two groups may be found, and also whether the prevailing gap is due to institutional biases or to the fact that there are two very different professional cultures involved.

Linking gender with macro-economics demands a profound grasp of how macro-economic models are theoretically constructed, and an understanding of the political process involved in drafting and implementing macro policies, as Evers, Çagatay and Palmer imply in this book. This implies tackling several types of gaps. Economists in state-planning bodies usually adhere to a notion of 'economics' that recognizes markets alone as the main site of exchange and considers resource allocation solely upon the basis of market prices. The variables they emphasize are public spending, investment and savings. Their vision of economics is based on the supply and demand articulated in the different markets and reflected in public spending. This abstract notion of economics does not accept gender differentiation, or specifically considering political, social or institutional variables either.

In the past 20 years, a significant change has taken place in macro-economic theory, leading to the integration of new variables into its models. Structural models incorporating the impact of institutional factors into their very premises stand out among these. Institutional factors are reflected in the very definition of the sectors or parameters that such models imply. The key issue then becomes the necessary process of abstraction: that is, how to select the multiple factors having an impact on growth so as to explain economic growth in quantitative terms, and how to choose which social, institutional and political factors restrict and/or qualify growth viewed as a process of structural change. In this respect, the importance of 'gender' in the short and medium range must be understood, assuming that social structures, institutions and guidelines are stable. In the long term, the 'gender' factor is associated with a change in social structures, due, for example, to the entrance of women into the labour market under conditions of extreme exploitation of their paid and unpaid labour alike.

Viewing the economic process from a long-term perspective, the link between gender and economics becomes more evident. Applying a gender approach situates men's and women's social relations in a political, social and economic context. The disparity in their social relations results from structures that are complex but not unassailable, as the changes implied by the rise in women's labour market participation have made clear. Unequal integration is reflected, for example, in wages, legal discrimination or limited access to productive resources. Overcoming these inequalities demands deep changes in the cultural perception of male and female roles, in the economic process itself, and in the distribution of political and economic power between the sexes.

Integrating a gender perspective to macro-economic policy cannot be carried out merely by 'liberalizing' the market and therefore removing the explicit or implicit barriers blocking women's equal integration. The point is to change the system of incentives and drawbacks typical of markets through deliberate state actions. Seen from an economistic perspective, the state has two main functions: (i) to intervene in order to avoid or correct 'market failures' in the short and medium terms; (ii) to intervene in order to correct the unequal effects of the economic process found socially intolerable and restrictive of long-term economic growth.

THE LINK BETWEEN THE MICRO AND THE MACRO

The argument of 'market flaws' caused by externalities or missing markets is chiefly advanced in micro-economics. It contemplates social and economic norms and guidelines, incentive systems and the different coordination or interrelation structures that ultimately determine men and women's individual attitudes and define the social relations between them. Economic theory supports the fallacy of linking individual attitudes to aggregate results without taking into account social institutions, guidelines or norms. The concept of the 'meso level' has been developed in order to avoid advocating this unrealistic assumption. The term describes all the entities linking the 'micro level' with the 'macro level' and vice versa. Thus seen, the meso level encompasses grassroots organizations, associations, federations and state bodies at various levels. It serves as a filter to facilitate, select or prevent the transfer of macro-economic signals.

The main causes preventing the adaptation of macro-economic incentives to be expected are (i) externalities and (ii) institutional barriers. Externalities exist when prices do not reflect all relevant information. Individual actions then have a positive or negative external effect on other agents, and a difference between private and social efficiency is established. Among other examples, we can mention that: (i) investment in human capital within the family is not and cannot be reflected in the cost of labour; and (ii) domestic labour is underestimated in the informal and agricultural sectors alike, thus extending family production beyond economic profitability. The consequence of underestimating domestic work (and thus mainly women's work), or investment in human capital, is an adverse system of incentives that leads to intensifying the use of family labour, among other things.

Institutional barriers are the result of multiple formal discriminations (based on legislation) and informal biases (based on the discretionary power held by males). This leads to women not having the same property rights enjoyed by men. Women do not have equal access to social infrastructure either, nor do they participate on an equal footing in the decision-taking process at the different levels. Often discrimination involves high transaction costs: that is, costs incurred exclusively in order to gain access to labour, land or credit markets, for instance.

Externalities, therefore, exist not only at the individual (woman's) level but also at the institutional level. There are still laws in place denying women full economic and social rights. Institutional attitudes continue to hinder female access to social security systems. Due to the vulnerability and the lack of social security systems that the poor must contend with, social capital – family, kin and neighbourhood ties – allow them to offset the ill effects that such social risks entail.

An efficient alternative to broaden the scope of social security might be to support informal social security systems, by creating innovative links with the formal social security systems, making use of the potential represented by civil society organizations. What may appear to be the result of an incomplete formal social security market may be perceived as a substitute, or an organizational alternative, from the perspective of the families affected.

Thus it is essential to understand and analyse the link between the 'macro' and the 'micro' levels, through the different organizations and institutions that act as a filter and whose functions may change during the course of development. It is important to analyse price distortions and institutional barriers in order to estimate whether resources are being over or underused.

GENDER AND MACRO-ECONOMIC MODELS

Macro-economic approaches have their own identity. National accounts help to empirically deduce macro-economic ties. These ties are the result of very complex processes at the micro level. No direct link exists between micro-economic phenomena and their effects at the macro-economic level. The lack of a direct link between the deeply contrasting universes of individual decisions and aggregate results, at the macro level, makes it difficult to directly incorporate a gender perspective to macro-economic approaches. This argument must be qualified even further. The new macro-economic models try to integrate micro-economic decisions at a theoretical level. They attempt to draft macro-economic models introducing variables such as fertility, demographic growth, investment in human capital or the transfer of resources from one generation to the other (the micro-economic foundation of macro-economic models).

Dealing with the gap between market prices and social costs proves even more difficult than establishing a link between social variables and growth models. While at the micro level it may be important to consider the interplay between resource allocation via markets and via social institutions (the family, for example), at the macro level only market ties are relevant, since these define equilibrium at that level. Examining the opportunity cost of women's work may help compare different levels of development in the long term, but it does not offer any additional information about the actual supply and demand at the aggregate level. From the perspective of long-term economic growth, and in order to achieve an equitable development process, the productivity of labour and investment, the integration of social capital as a factor of economic growth, and the sub-utilization and sub-qualification of resources like the female labour force, are all key factors to consider.

Thus it is important to differentiate between short-term and long-term growth models (and processes). Short-term models are static models based on a neo-classical mode of production, accompanied by constant yields of scale and decreasing yields of inputs, that is, of work and capital. The World Bank's Revised Minimum Standard Model (RMSM) defines economic strategies that can be used to achieve stable growth. As with other macro models, the RMSM does not directly specify the economic and social contexts of the growth process, since such contexts are viewed as factors external to the model itself. Hence such a model serves to analyse restrictions but not to formulate new alternatives.

The model is gender-blind, since it does not take into account the importance of gender relations and their impact on economic growth levels and rates. It is useful, therefore, to examine the implications of gender and the assumptions around gender more thoroughly, in order to observe how the impact of gender relations remains concealed at the micro level. This does not mean that gender-differentiated variables should not be specifically introduced. We are suggesting, instead, that the impact of gender relations be considered when estimating parameters such as investment productivity (value of incremental capital/output ratio). Two examples may be mentioned here: (i) capital costs may be lowered by transferring the responsibility for social services to the 'reproductive' sector, where female labour is not valued in market terms and (ii) output may be increased by women gaining more access to productive resources, such as small and medium-scale enterprises. At the micro level, evidence of this type exists. Such evidence does not suggest direct links to macro models but it does yield significant information when it comes to estimating parameters.

A model that explicitly regards the impact of gender relations is the Collier[2] model. Collier introduces the shift in labour allocation within the context of structural adjustment, taking as a basis the tradable and non-tradable model. Such a model is not operational since its aggregate variables do not correspond to the categories used in national accounts, as the RSMS does, but it does serve as a tool to explain the impact of economic policy. Collier combines gender-differentiated disaggregation with sectorial disaggregation, specifically with respect to the export and subsistence production sectors. He identifies the various restrictions found in the rural labour market that restrain women's mobility and the option to use female labour, such as the discrimination against women in the labour market; the social and cultural factors defining women's roles; the asymmetry in rights (entitlements), obligations and access to information between men and women; and women's reproductive role in the family. Although designed to explain how the agricultural sector has developed in sub-Saharan African countries, this model may be adapted and used to understand the role of women in Latin American countries.

The models based on the 'new theory of growth' attempt to *endogenize* variables such as technological progress, labour supply and demographic growth. In this debate, Walters proposes integrating structural changes with respect to the supply of female labour into the macro-economic model, taking as a starting point the change in social norms with respect to gender relations.[3] The difficulty inherent in such models is the lack of available data, which limits their applicability to real-life situations.

GROWTH AND EQUITY IN LATIN AMERICA

Latin America has recovered its macro-economic stability in terms of growth, inflation and the public sector deficit. Nevertheless, economic growth has not sufficed to reduce unemployment and poverty. Income disparity is the most significant explanation for this unsatisfactory result, since Latin America is the continent where the largest income gaps continue to prevail.

Women's participation in the labour market has grown in Latin America, especially in the informal sector. This participation has two main characteristics. On the one hand, the expansion of female employment mostly in the low-productivity sectors has increased unequal income distribution and decreased labour productivity. On the other hand, the rise of female employment and the absence of social services have added to women's workload, exerting effects on homes and families that have not yet been fully documented. Domestic violence is bound to be an indicator of the stress and high social costs being exacted in terms of injuries and deaths.

There is not enough investment in human capital, particularly in the poorer strata. The quality and scope of services remain frail, in spite of growing expenditures in the areas of education and health. Ample sectors of the Latin American population, among these a high proportion of women, still lack adequate access to primary education and basic health services. One of the main problems of the social sector is its low efficiency and effectiveness in the production of services. A regressive investment in the social sector principally favours the middle strata. Due to the incapacity to impose guidelines for the health market, no clear and transparent norms exist, or strategies designed to channel sectorial investment either. This means high transaction costs, especially for the poor.

Programmes specifically geared to poverty alleviation such as social investment funds have very little interest – or expertise for that matter – in how to incorporate a gender approach to their processes and tools. Hypothetically, these social funds reflect the 'articulated' social demand, that is, that of men, who tend to regard women as passive recipients. Women's demands to satisfy their own specific needs or improve social conditions in the home are not reflected in what these funds provide. Ordinarily such funds have no specific guidelines for projects facilitating women's work within or outside the home. Experiences such as those had by the Community Mothers of the Colombian Family Welfare Institute seem to be concrete options for articulating women's demands in the area of social investment.

PROPOSALS FOR THE DRAFTING OF POLICIES

- Achieving gender equality and reducing poverty at the same time is not only necessary but also possible. It requires subsidizing women directly, in order to compensate for the social restrictions prevalent in the labour market through measures such as 'social' salaries for women and/or family subsidies. It also requires creating more social child care services so that women participate in the labour market without endangering their social and educational roles in the family.
- Social policies that help women take advantage of the actions promoted during the course of development exert an influence on women's fertility rates. This link merits a more exhaustive analysis and must be regarded as a central variable in macro-economic models.
- Understanding women's participation in the labour market is crucial. It requires a different methodology from the one used for collecting

data on the time and space constraints characteristic of housework. The fact that life cycles influence people's decisions must also be taken into account.

- Although an effort to document the consequences of state, economic and social reforms according to gender has been initiated, it must be more finely tuned. It is necessary to delve into the impact of gender on many economic fields, such as the internationalization of capital, labour, goods and service markets. It is vital to consider many aspects of how national policies are formulated, and strategies such as the funnelling of public investment and how such investment reaches women.

FROM THEORY TO PRACTICE

The challenge we face is how to 'ground' theoretical discussion in such a way as to influence specific policies. Several processes are taking place in Latin America that facilitate learning new trends of analysis regarding the links between macro-economics, gender and public policies, and advancing experiences that allow applying such analyses to the drafting of gender-sensitive policies.

One such experience was carried out by the National Planning Department of Colombia (DNP) through the PROEQUIDAD/GTZ Project, under the sponsorship of the German Technical Cooperation Agency (GTZ). This project began to fill the gap in communication between macro-economics and gender cited at the beginning of this document. The vital support of DNP's executive board and the expertise that the task group contributed to the project have shown how important it is to explore the subject matter the institution deals with, promoting a joint vision and a common strategy between macro-economists and gender experts (see Chapter 11).

A similar process is taking place at the Economic Commission for Latin America and the Caribbean (ECLAC), resulting in the creation of an internal working group devoted to integrating the gender approach into the organization's sectorial areas (see Chapters 12 and 13). This internal initiative, enthusiastically supported by its directors, has opened a new phase of regional cooperation among international technical assistance bodies. It presents a very favourable opportunity to promote the development and application of gender-related themes through the assistance that ECLAC provides to Latin American countries.

NOTES

1. Joerg Freiberg-Strauss has a PhD in Economics from the University of Berlin. He is currently GTZ Senior Advisor at the UN Economic Commission for Latin America.

2. Collier, P. (1994) 'Gender aspects of labor allocation during structural adjustment. A theoretical framework and the African experience', in S. Horton, R. Hanbur and D. Mazumdar (eds), *Labor Markets in an Era of Adjustment*, Vol. I, Washington: World Bank.

3. Walters, B. (1997) 'Engendering macroeconomics. A reconsideration of growth theory', in *Gender and Macropolicy*, Eschborn, Germany: GTZ.

CHAPTER 5

Economic Policies, Public Spending and Gender-differentiated Effects

REBECA GRYNSPAN[1]

Legend has it that half the sky
Rests on us women.

§ This chapter presents a brief reflection on economic policies and public spending, touching upon issues such as privatization, streamlining and decentralization of the state. It does not view macro-economic policy and fiscal adjustment as data merely sharing a general design. If this were true, examining their effects on women and on gender relations would only be an intellectual pursuit. It rather brings gender issues into a broader debate on development, critically reviewing the practice of state modernization processes, such as decentralization, thought of as being especially apt to promote gender equality.

ECONOMIC POLICIES AND PUBLIC SPENDING

The current debate on economic policies and the allocation of public spending, especially with respect to social investment, is divided into two main themes:

1. The kind of insertion into the world market promoted. Will it be a type of insertion that allows our countries to compete on the basis of low wages or on the basis of productivity and technology?
2. The demand for state resources versus the fiscal balance. Present conditions demand earmarking additional state resources for social investment, at the same time that the need for fiscal discipline exerts its pull in the opposite direction.

As a response to these themes, a general proposal has emerged, which may be summarized in the following points:

1. Liberalization is enough to determine the type of market insertion sought; generating employment is the main objective and thus achieving it based on low wages is a better result than stagnation, which is the alternative.

2. Service privatization, streamlining of the state, funnelling of expenditures and administrative decentralization simultaneously help tackle fiscal restrictions, satisfy the needs of low-income groups and promote the participation of civil society. Measures taken in this sense are bound to yield extra resources. These should be allocated exclusively to the delivery of basic services for society's most vulnerable groups, a task that the state must continue to perform. These services are mainly primary education, water and minimum health and social security packages. Local governments should be the ones providing these services wherever possible.

Under the criteria of this 'general' proposal, *it would seem feasible* to sustain, or even increase, the growth rate while simultaneously catering to society's poorest groups, all within a climate of macro-economic stability and equilibrium. This proposal *would also seem* to respond to women's needs. Some arguments used in this sense are:

- Controlling inflation tends to benefit women more, since women are more likely to be found in low- or fixed-wage sectors incapable of protecting themselves against inflation.
- As women tend to work in the informal sector or in small-scale enterprises, an overvalued currency confronts them with imports kept inexpensive artificially, making foreign exchange policy have significant consequences on the women active in these sectors.
- The costs of economic and state reforms during periods of transition may negatively affect women, requiring the development of social safety nets and programmes specifically geared to women (especially aid programmes).
- It is commonly acknowledged that social safety nets are not a substitute for a more integral approach to economic and social policy. Thus public spending should be redirected to primary education, primary health services and water supplies, particularly in rural areas. Likewise, emphasis should be made on the need to upgrade agricultural extension services for rural women and to improve women's access to credit by eliminating the restrictions they usually face, particularly those involving collateral.

Although surely some specific points of this 'general' proposal may be shared – and I am also aware that this description somewhat caricatures the situation – it is important to refer to the other side of the coin with the intention of provoking discussion; that is, to refer to the effects that putting into practice this type of economic and fiscal proposal may have on the economic model in general, and on women in particular.

TOWARDS THE ATTAINMENT OF GENDER EQUALITY

The package promoted in this 'general' proposal (privatization, streamlining of the state, funnelling and decentralization of services) may have perverse effects on women, in terms of their access to quality services and of the increasing and unpaid workload implicit in many reforms. In the first place, one of the proposal's obvious weaknesses is that poor women are its main focus. This prevents discussing gender equality and equal opportunities as strategic issues, substituting these aspects for a problem that is no doubt important but does not necessarily lead to 'gender equality'. The tendency to limit the emphasis on gender to the feminization of poverty is a trap that humanity has stumbled into many times and diverts the question of strategy.

PRIVATIZATION OF SERVICES AND FUNNELLING

The privatization[2] and funnelling proposal is geared to solving budgetary restrictions. As such, it does not pretend so much the inclusion of sectors (which would demand an expansion in public spending) or improving their efficiency, but the exclusion of some sectors from the provision of services (especially the middle sectors). With the exception of countries where most of the female population is poor, the net effects of this proposal hinder women's access to quality services. This may clearly be seen when health services are privatized, which still leaves the state in charge of providing a basic health package for the poor. In a budgetary proposal of this type, the first programmes to be eliminated, and not necessarily taken over by the private sector, tend to be those geared to treating specific female diseases, such as the early detection and treatment of breast and uterine cancer, requiring a public system of routine care and control. In this scheme, what Hirschman[3] so forcefully described many years ago tends to hold true: when a public service deteriorates, the first to be expelled from its benefits are those who can afford to pay for the service privately. If the system continues to deteriorate, the next-in-line excluded are those who have a say in demanding quality services (the middle sectors). At the end of the line, those who are completely destitute and voiceless remain, which accounts for the service's further deterioration until it is simply a poor service provided only for the poor.

A proposal advocating the privatization of health and education services and the dismantling of basic service delivery should be thoroughly reconsidered in the light of market flaws and the non-equitable selection such markets generate. Experiences seeming to ratify Hirschman's forecast must be weighed most cautiously. The middle sectors tend to be the most affected with this proposal, but so are the more vulnerable sectors, given the deterioration of service delivery in question. Market flaws doubly affect women, since they also tend to affect them in gender-specific ways.

Reallocating resources to primary education usually does not stem from assigning new resources to education, but from withdrawing them from other levels in order to reinforce primary education. This type of proposal is not valid in the case of Latin America, at least under the criteria of gender equality. Though no one would oppose making an added effort to reach 100 per cent coverage of primary education, the greatest disparities between women and men in Latin America are not found at this level. It is more at the level of secondary and adult education programmes, including training in order to gain access to the labour market. The effects of cutting back public university funding must also be weighed most carefully, since a very high percentage of those enrolled in universities are women (50 per cent in Colombia and Costa Rica, for example). To achieve gender equality, it is wiser to stimulate the presence of women in higher secondary education and to include more women in learning and training programmes geared towards a more demanding labour market (computer sciences being crucial), as well as to promote literacy programmes for adult women so that they may qualify for better-paying jobs. These options should not disappear under the guise of a general proposal for universal primary education coverage.

Similar reflections can be made with respect to pension scheme reforms in which individual capitalization does not resolve the access of the informal sector to social security schemes, while the reforms proposed never take into account gender equality. If individual capitalization is not complemented by taxation and some degree of solidarity, the long-term effects in terms of scope and equity will strongly hit broad middle sectors, the informal sector and women in particular.

The debate about investment in education and health is also related to the discussion on productive insertion, which attributes priority to the creation of any kind of employment and not to the quality of employment generated. Although such job-creating schemes may work in countries with a very low level of development, at least initially, they pose substantial problems for many Latin American countries. It is worth asking several questions in connection with the following: the level of real wages to be achieved in order to compete on the basis of cheap manual labour, if we think of countries such as Colombia, Argentina or Costa Rica; the insertion of the modern female labour force into the worst-paid activities; and the education and training carried out by individual countries in order to make a genuine investment in human capital, promoting a qualitative leap in the quality of investment and thus consequently affecting productivity and the national aggregate value.

In terms of employment opportunities, evidence points to the fact that women are more prone to join the labour market via the *maquila* or agricultural export industry (in what amounts to the final stages of the process). Since such investment is volatile and much competition exists to keep its wages low, women are thus condemned to jobs in which they are exploited, get minimum working and social security benefits and earn very low wages. Attempts made to raise salaries for these activities, not accompanied by technological changes increasing their added value and productivity, will tend to provoke the flight of investment fostering even more unemployment. It is doubtful whether schemes designed to promote greater gender equity can be based on the use of cheap manual labour and minimum education and health service packages. These may initially improve poor women's living conditions but will most likely prevent them from bettering their situation and that of the population at large.

STREAMLINING THE STATE APPARATUS

Streamlining the state also has significant effects on women when it comes to reducing the bureaucratic apparatus in sectors with a large female participation, or when there is a cut in services based on the underlying assumption that its absence will be filled through individual or communal voluntary work. This type of work is usually transferred to women, since it tends to be viewed as an extension of unpaid domestic labour. There is a huge difference between promoting community organization and, in general, giving women and citizens on the whole more voice and participation, and attempting to substitute the state's roles and its obligation to finance programmes. We are not casting doubts on the need for the state and its institutions to change, beginning with the acceptance that social development is not only the state's responsibility. Just as the state is not a body outside the social structure, civil society is also a main actor in the struggle against poverty and in favour of social development. Entrepreneurial, grassroots, peasant and workers' organizations, as well as women's organizations, should have specific opportunities to contribute to this perspective from their specific areas of activity.

This protagonism, however, does not condone the idea of a subsidiary state, limited to granting subsidies and transfers to the poor and otherwise delegating the delivery of social services to the private sector. The question is not whether the state should shrink from performing its tasks, but that it be complemented by, and articulated with, the rest of society. The state is bound to continue being the main financier of social programmes for a long time. To promote gender equality, we should draft public policies that raise to the level of institutional policies the actions tending to improve opportunities and overcome the specific obstacles encountered by women at the sectorial level of public administration (and not remaining at the level of satellite programmes). Examples to be cited are the actions demanded from the various ministries of agriculture geared to promoting the access of women farmers to productive resources, especially land and credit, or to extending female access to housing programmes that take into account the specific needs of groups such as women heads of households.

It is not to women's benefit that the state be a dinosaur or a weak state. On the contrary, a strategic state capable of concertation is desirable, one that does not shrink from its responsibility to apply social rights or burden women with an excess of unpaid work; a state that includes women in the drafting of public policy and 'institutionalizes' and internalizes the programmes it is meant to advance in order to satisfy the needs of the whole population. The above implies combining selective programmes geared to overcoming the extra obstacles women face due to their gender, with universal programmes geared to the rest of the population. This design makes integration *versus* marginalization possible. It promotes access to mainstream development and not the isolated execution of loose projects that never make a holistic impact on people's reality.

DECENTRALIZATION

In the search for a renewed type of public institution, Latin American states confront the task of promoting administrative decentralization and strengthening local governments. The idea is to get closer to the users in order to respond to their particular demands and avoid drafting homogeneous policies ignoring heterogeneity and the local specificity. It is argued that decentralization can generate greater social consensus through increased citizen participation, while exercising a stricter control over the local bureaucracies that seek refuge in the maze of centralism to avoid accountability. Working in smaller territorial units and catering to more manageable numbers of inhabitants makes it easier to quantify costs and benefits, and to experiment with innovative forms of management that may eventually be replicated elsewhere. Obviously, the relative sizes of the different countries impose limits on these processes and differentiated results.

Although I tend to sympathize with the objectives put forward in this type of proposal, I have enormous doubts regarding its design. The danger of a badly managed decentralization is that it may actually increase inequality, by leading to an unacceptable fluctuation in the quality standards of service delivery. This usually affects the poor sectors to a much larger extent. The same thing can happen when finances are delegated to local units. The classic example of this type of decentralization is education in the United States: how it is managed and how its funds are collected. Both aspects are subject to very few general guidelines. This is regarded as the main reason for the educational disparity prevalent throughout the country.[4] In the political sphere, decentralization may consolidate forms of oligarchic domination already present in certain regions, which erode democracy and the values of the nation-state. In Raczinski's analysis of decentralization in Argentina and especially Brazil, 'clientele-like' pressures and practices are very often much stronger at regional, provincial or local levels than at the national one. This warning may be extended to broader territories. The pressures exerted by powerful elite groups in towns and regions may cause a 'hoarding' of decentralized resources towards economic or power-related concerns, a state of affairs degrading the decentralization process significantly.

We should keep in mind, therefore, that it is not the transfer of formal power from the central government to the local government that furthers democracy, since this may only lead to locally reproducing, or even aggravating, the problems caused by centralism. If power and resources are to be transferred to local governments, the process must be linked to creating consultation and concertation mechanisms involving grassroots organizations, strengthening community-based social organizations and among these the participation of women. Communities and local governments are not synonymous. We should not forget that it is at the community level where the greatest citizens' participation and women's participation take place.

The whole range of community organizations must be taken into account, if furthering democracy is truly desired. Greater *empowerment* of women can be achieved at this sphere: it is here that women may have more *voice*. At the municipal level, women's participation is quite often displaced when local governments are granted more power and resources. If greater participation and empowerment are not achieved, decentralization may bring about the exclusion of women from the local political processes, deepening social and gender inequalities even further.

ALTERNATIVE PROPOSALS

We must draft alternative proposals that contemplate social investment in human capital and the construction of greater social capital, while addressing the demands of a more exacting world, more technologically oriented and competitive. A design concentrated on basic services will not yield a qualitative leap in production, technical progress or more productivity. Thus it will also not bring about better wages. An alternative proposal must seek complementarity between universal and selective programmes, especially with respect to education and health. It must make room for the inclusion of vulnerable sectors and address the specificity of the situations faced by women and men alike. It should further democracy by supporting grassroots organizations, and women's organizations and participation, while respecting everyone's social rights. Such a proposal should promote cooperation among families and societies, abolishing the prevailing patterns of excessive exploitation of women's domestic and voluntary work.

This economic and social proposal is feasible, but it is also not easy to carry out. Some countries are already defining strategies to make it possible. Even during its structural adjustment period, Costa Rica increased social investment and the amount of resources for education and health, promoting a growth process based on investment in high technology that may serve, once more, to unite the social and the economic as two sides of the same coin.

The ongoing debate in Latin America is not a proposal against liberalization or macro-economic stability. It concentrates rather on how social policy should be designed, especially the social protection schemes to be implemented during the next century. Merely advancing reforms is not bound to lead to the development desired, or to create a more prosperous and equitable society, one displaying solidarity and in which gender equality is a basic condition. A new type of proposal must combine the demands posed by market liberalization with adequate levels of social protection and investment, leading us to higher levels of shared well-being while building a common zenith of cooperation and progress.

NOTES

1. Rebeca Grynspan, an economist, was vice-president of Costa Rica. She now acts as a consultant for several international agencies and is professor of economics at the University of Costa Rica.

2. This document refers to the privatization of social services and not to the privatization of state enterprises.

3. Hirschman, A. O. (1986) *Interés privado y acción pública*, Fondo de cultura económica, México.

4. Owen, J. D. (1974) *School Inequality and the Welfare State*, Baltimore, MD: Johns Hopkins University Press.

CHAPTER 6

Unpaid Household Labour: A Conceptual Approach

FABIOLA CAMPILLO[1]

§ The real economy fluctuates between the production economy and the economy associated with care, reproduction and human welfare. As Diane Elson so aptly defines it, 'We have two economies: the economy in which people earn wages in order to produce things to be sold on the market or financed through taxation. This is the economy based on goods, which everyone considers "the economy". On the other hand we have the hidden economy, the invisible one, the one devoted to care' (Elson 1995). What sets these two economies apart is that housework tends to be unpaid and difficult to quantify: it is a form of labour that shares the nature of a handicraft; is carried out within the home mainly by women and girls and by its members and linked to the market as an input for the sale of another product, working force or capacity; is regulated by ideological and normative mechanisms, and is not assigned a value except as long as it is substituted by goods or services to be found on the market.

This chapter intends to show that unpaid domestic labour in conjunction with the subordinate role of women has relevant effects for the national economy. These effects are linked to:

- market production subsidies;
- gender-differentiated alternatives in the labour market and wages;
- the organization and orientation of social policies and services;
- the camouflage of some types of productive work; and
- the upholding of rigid work and employment patterns.

Decisive factors for understanding the link between the sexual division of labour and the national economy are in this context the *invisibility*, *non-accountability* and *non-remuneration* of household work, three features that are interrelated. *Invisibility* relates to patriarchal ideology having managed to include and legitimize under female roles everything connected with the care of the family and its social reproduction. *Non-accountability* refers to the assumption that whatever does not directly produce wealth cannot be recorded as an economic process. Thus accountancy systems are geared towards traditional economic units, their purpose being to record the production of goods and services tradable on national or international markets. And finally, *non-remuneration* refers to the abundance of manual labour available to perform domestic work for free and its almost infinite elasticity to adjust to the changes taking place in the macro-economic environment.

In it second section, this chapter also attempts to give some conceptual ideas on how and why non-paid household production has to be measured in order to formulate adequate policy recommendations.

EFFECTS OF UNPAID HOUSEHOLD LABOUR ON THE NATIONAL ECONOMY

Unpaid household work as a subsidy to capital accumulation   Its first effect is subsidizing market production. This is carried out in several ways:

1. Domestic labour subsidizes the entrepreneurial sector through the unpaid segment of the workforce. Relying on the abundant, sometimes excessive, amount of female manual labour, especially that of housewives, means that a transfer of value from the household economy to the market economy takes place.
2. Under conditions of economic crisis, housewives must intensify their domestic labour in order to counteract a loss in the acquisition power of salaries (Torres 1977); this still holds true in the cases of women who work outside the home.
3. Domestic labour affects wages. As De Barbieri highlights in her article 'Note for a Study of Women's Work: the Problem of Domestic Labour', this type of work has 'the effect of depressing' the wages for such work, since while a contingent of unpaid or 'invisible' women workers exists, salaries are regulated only by the supply and demand of the workforce exerted outside the home, as if a relation of interdependence did not exist between both labour spheres.

Opportunities differentiated according to placement and permanence of women and men in the labour market   Assigning women the main responsibility for the care of household members no doubt restricts their chances of gaining access to more dynamic employment sectors, working full-time, increasing their training levels and not having to interrupt their working lives. In many regions those in charge of taking decisions in the home hold that sending girls to school is useless, since there do not seem to be options for them to join the labour market. Thus they are considered unable to compensate for the investment made in them by earning additional income in the future.

It is therefore not by accident that the largest share of women's participation remains at the base of the occupational pyramid, or that the conditions under which women are hired and paid their wages tend to be less favourable than those for men.

Housewives face a complex added dilemma in times of crisis: they are forced to enter the labour market because the household income is not enough, and at the same time they have to invest more time in domestic labour since the production of services and goods formerly carried out by the state is transferred to the home. The latter may be alleviated, as happens mainly in developing societies, wherever an abundance of the labour force allows paying for domestic activities by hiring help of both sexes, although this still has a depreciating effect on the new incomes generated.

Gender biases in labour opportunities have become stronger in recent years, since economic crises and social changes have generated a significant rise in the number of households in the whole world single-handedly supported by women. Female-headed households in Latin America were close to 25 per cent in the 1990s, reaching even higher percentages in countries such as Honduras and El Salvador. According to the Latin American Economic Commission, 'extreme poverty, particularly in urban areas, above all affects households where there is no male partner and the female head of the household must take charge of the domestic chores besides earning enough money to live on'.

Building social services and policies on the invisible foundations of domestic labour The state does not consider the possibility of socializing a series of services in the domestic sphere, since unpaid domestic labour is a cushion for the satisfaction of human needs. Most public policies today are drafted under the implicit assumption that the state has an obligation to fill the gap left by those women who can no longer cope with their burden, either because increasingly they choose to work outside the home or because they are forced to do so by their personal circumstances.

Thus, some social policies include in their justification the changes generated when women stop doing all the domestic chores (neglected children, teenage drug abuse, school truancy and so on.).

Within the framework of privatization and the delegation of service delivery to organizations in civil society, the state shifts another burden on volunteer work, which it presumes has no cost and can be carried out by women and other members of the community guided by altruistic reasons of the same tenure used as a rationale for domestic labour. This is a way of making that much cheaper the tasks related to public welfare rightfully corresponding to the public sector.

The productive work concealed in domestic work   In production units that are not completely entrepreneurial, such as peasant production economies, indigenous communities and small-scale ventures in the informal sector, many activities that are strictly productive and linked to the market are not quantified or considered as work but are made to appear as an extension of domestic labour instead. This is the case in the raising of small livestock, or growing vegetable gardens, or having women and children help do harvesting and weeding, or running the corner grocery shop with the cooperation of several family members.

A study carried out by the ICCA and the IDB in 18 Latin American countries in order to re-estimate women's participation in agricultural work demonstrated that nearly 5.5 million women in rural areas had not been counted as workers either because their activities were seen as an extension of domestic labour or because those who did the survey themselves underestimated the share of domestic labour involved. Officially, these 5.5 million women appeared as inactive for statistical purposes (Kleysen and Campillo 1996).

In Pakistan, where the official index for women's economic participation in agriculture was only 7 per cent, the World Bank re-estimated this figure to be 73 per cent upon the basis of the agricultural census carried out in 1981. Official figures had failed to register the work of nearly 12 million agricultural workers (quoted in British Council 1995). If the trend to identify formerly uncounted female rural workers continues, a radical change in rural and agricultural development policies would surely be warranted.

The combination of making merchandise and producing it at home is also a high source of under-registered female labour. Studies of the informal sector have generated data and indicators to this respect. To give only one example, more than 50 per cent of the women employed in small shops in Brazil's urban sector carry out their work at home (Abreu 1995: 86). The result may be that their activity is not registered as economic, or that it is registered but underestimated and simply seen as an aid to producing other merchandise. This work, which remains hidden, is not added to the costs of production of the economic units comprising the economy's informal sector. That accounts for a distortion in the sector's dynamics and in the possible incomes generated. By holding prices below real market prices, these non-entrepreneurial units also transfer value to the rest of society.

Even where statistics include the category 'unpaid family helper', some household members may not be included in them, especially women if they declare themselves to be housewives, or if they lack the means to measure the number of hours or days that they devote to producing the merchandise in question

A rigid definition of the concepts of work and employment is maintained The economic concepts of work and employment have been formulated within the context of industrial, urban processes with a high level of organization with respect to how the work is performed. Clear-cut hiring guidelines are established between employees and employers, even though in the world at large other forms continue to exist in which working sites and processes do not necessarily follow these guidelines. Upholding a rigid work code has meant ignoring the work that is carried out under the non-industrial modes of production.

This factor is both cause and effect in upholding the sexual division of labour as something natural, viewing the specialized tasks assigned to the sexes as practically biological in nature. It is a cause due to the fact that since it is not recorded as work, it is ideologically justifiable that women – idle in essence – and children of both sexes help men carry out their own tasks, which generate the household income in the most efficient way possible. It is an effect because what remains invisible lacks the force to change the approaches and guidelines that might chart the way for the registration and evaluation of all economic activities.

Another important aspect is that statistics and economic analyses, in general, start out from the erroneous premise of dividing the population into active and inactive according to whether people produce goods and services tradable on the market or not. The mistake is to believe that women who work outside the home do not also devote themselves to domestic labour. A study carried out in Argentina by the Inter-American Development Bank showed that, if the time dedicated to domestic chores was added to the time spent at work, 'women with paid jobs have an invisible working week of 13 hours and a full working week of 91.3 hours' (IDB 1995).

Advances have been achieved in this area in spite of everything. A study by Anker and Hein (1987) included a typology of definitions of manual labour, ranging from paid work to work consisting of paid and unpaid labour alike. The ILO definition is the most inclusive with respect to the unpaid activities that women perform. This definition is as follows: 'People whose activities generate products and services, regardless of whether these are sold or not, activities that should be included in national accounts' (Anker and Hein 1987: 17).

As we can appreciate, it is not possible to reveal the true dimension of the invisible work represented by domestic labour without making substantial changes in work and employment statistics (in the concepts, the methodologies used to record the data, the selected informants, the types of tabulation and analysis). A change in national accounts systems as they are now designed is also called for (in the definition of recorded units and in the methods used to report the values generated in the production of goods and services).

LEARNING FROM SOME ECONOMIC MEASURING INSTRUMENTS

The United Nations and INSTRAW in particular, individual women authors and governments from different countries alike have all developed schemes to measure how unpaid domestic labour contributes to the economy. Tatjana Sikoska, for instance, offers in this volume (Chapter 7) a good methodological contribution to the measurement and valuation of unpaid household production. As a result of these efforts, today different methodologies exist to measure domestic labour, based on the units of working time invested in the production of goods and services to be consumed by household members – attributed wages – or in units of value similar to those used on the market.

In studies on household production, Goldschmidt-Clermont identifies four methodologies useful for the assessment of unpaid domestic labour, according to how we desire to measure it:

1. the volume of labour inputs (work and goods consumed in the production process), measured with respect to the time spent or the number of workers;

2. the volume of the product – that is, of the goods and services produced – measured in various physical units;
3. the value of the inputs, according to a series of labour estimates such as the wages earned by workers performing substitute tasks, salaries in kind seen as non-monetary benefits, opportunity cost of time and labour incurred by market enterprises for a similar volume of the product in question; and
4. the value of products (goods or services) generated, according to the price of similar products on the market.

In the first two points, the volumes of domestic labour may be compared with the values generated on the market economy. In the following two points, we find monetary values that give us an idea of the real total value of what a given society produces, and of the contribution that invisible work makes to its total wealth production (Goldschmidt-Clermont 1982, 1987). In the study carried out by INSTRAW on the valuation of household production and satellite accounts (1996), significant details on methodological approximations are found that were used in three case studies in Canada, Nepal and Finland.

In its 1995 *Human Development Report* devoted to gender equality, the United Nations Development Programme (UNDP) reveals striking data about the contribution of domestic work to the economies.

The first aspect observed when attempting to measure the volume of domestic work is that, in all the countries under study (nine developing nations, among them Colombia, Venezuela and Guatemala, and 13 industrialized nations), women work more hours than men. Although the differences among countries or among regions of the same country may be substantial, on the average in developing countries 'women devote 13% more time to market and non-market activities together' (UNDP 1995: 102). Of the total volume of work, 53 per cent corresponds to women and 47 per cent to men, a difference that broadens to 55 per cent versus 45 per cent in rural areas. In developed countries, women perform 51 per cent of the total workload.

These differences in the distribution per sex of the total work volume do not correspond with the differences found when paid and unpaid labours are separated. In developing countries, women devoted on average one-third of their working time to paid activities, and two-thirds to unpaid housework. For men, the proportion was reversed.

Contrary to what might be expected in developed countries, given their greater flexibility in the sexual division of labour, the relation remains similar: 66 per cent of the time worked by women stays excluded from national accounts systems, while for men it is 34 per cent (ibid). In other words, development alone does not eliminate the main gap between the sexes, although it may somewhat reduce its severity. Meanwhile, development paradigms have not sought to find the way to destroy the roots of women's subordination, which are economic to a great extent. Women mainly continue performing work that is neither taken into account nor valued, though the conditions under which this labour process takes place may be better in industrialized economies.

Another interesting aspect is that when the non-monetary contribution generated by domestic work is estimated globally, it reaches the impressive sum of US$16 billion. This represents 70 per cent of the official gross world product, calculated at 23 billion dollars (UNDP 1995: 110). Even more significantly, 11 of these 16 billion dollars correspond to the contributions made by women through activities that remain invisible and are absent from national accounts systems.

It is worth mentioning that even the UNDP, which is dedicated to the promotion of human development, has difficulties recognizing the subversive effect that the systematic recording of unpaid domestic labour would be bound to have on the current world order. The UNDP does ask itself how the broad contribution made by work with no monetary value attached to it might be recognized and assessed, but it does so without attempting to tackle the main bias, which is based on gender differences; that is, 'without promoting a radical change in the way families organise their work'. It also does not accept the possibility of paying the cost of non-commercial labour 'given that, if all activities penetrated the market, the structure of wages would change completely' (ibid.: 110). It certainly would change. Society and capital would have to pay the cost of the population's social reproduction, in other words, instead of leaving it in the hands of women so that they continue to carry it out for free.

Considering how impressive the data compiled are, the UNDP does wonder how to correct miscalculations, but at the same time it expresses reservations about the possible solutions, especially not wanting to introduce radical changes. This is analogous to treating a fever without curing its causes.

Some countries also make allowances for the contribution of non-commercial goods and services to the gross national product. In the article 'Gender and macroeconomics', Renzi (1997) informs us that, during a recent research programme undertaken by the International

Foundation for the Global Economy (FIDEG) in Nicaragua, the share of domestic labour was estimated to be between 22 per cent and 27 per cent of the gross national product, according to whether it was estimated through the cost of opportunity or through the replacement cost.

A survey carried out by the CIEDUR in Montevideo, Uruguay, shows that if domestic work was included when estimating the rates of economic activity (of the work carried out by housewives and pensioners), women's participation rate in the total social production rose to 81 per cent, surpassing that of men. If women pensioners with no domestic help are incorporated, the rate rises to 88 per cent. The same study indicated that women dispatch their domestic responsibilities in a relatively independent manner from their participation in the labour market: 85 per cent of women workers are also housewives. The variable that defines this relation seems to be the presence of children and the women's own personal circumstances (Torres 1977).

In Australia, women's share in GNP with respect to care in the home and in the community was estimated at 65 per cent, in a survey carried out in order to estimate the use of time (Pollard 1997). Women carry out the greatest share of unpaid work in Nepal, Canada and Finland, between 67 per cent and 69 per cent (INSTRAW 1996).

Please note that the figures above differ widely according to the countries they originate in. This also has to do with the methodologies used and the absence of a single comparative and universal system. This lack of standardization also reflects an absence of the political will needed in order to produce guidelines that might put an end to the invisible nature of unpaid domestic labour.

The figures just quoted are evidence of the two-fold discriminatory reality of female labour: 'Women's economic contribution in the market is sub-recorded because their "main" role is in the home, but their contribution at home is underestimated because their place in the market is considered as only secondary' (Goldschmidt-Clermont 1982: 37).

Besides the technical and theoretical elements mentioned here, there are also the ideological and value-ridden aspects of patriarchal culture deeply embedded in the collective conscience and unconscious and that fuel the divide between work in and outside the home. Men and women are different, and we acknowledge this difference. The problem is that we also value ourselves differently according to what we do. A typical answer when women who work part-time are asked what they do is 'Nothing, I'm a housewife'. As Helen Safa so aptly puts it, 'Men see themselves and are seen as workers having family responsibilities, while women are seen and see themselves as wives and mothers having economic responsibilities' (Safa 1995: 179). On the other hand, the family offers women a social identity that paid work has not been able to provide for them.

The tension between women and the main instruments that states use for purposes of accountancy is framed within a never-ending debate. The National Accounts Systems (UNSNA) promoted by the United Nations and the International Monetary Fund, in spite of the great sophistication and technical development that they have demonstrated during the last years, by progressively including more services and some goods formerly just considered to be outside the market, still do not contemplate guidelines or methodological tools to measure unpaid activities (keep in mind that it is close to 70 per cent more than what has been accounted thus far). According to Waring, the UNSNA and the way they have been applied in the different countries precisely leave out the social objectives and values connected with the reproduction of the human race, that is: the living conditions of women and children of both sexes, the conservation of natural resources and the costs of environmental damage (Waring 1988, quoted by Koch 1996).

As far back as the first half of the twentieth century, some countries, such as Norway, attempted to estimate the value of unpaid work in their national accounts. From 1935 to 1943 and from 1946 to 1949, Norway's SNA included the estimated value of the caring economy. However, this advance was dismantled when the need arose for the country to make its records comparable with the national accounts standards created by the United Nations system (UNSNA). At that point, Norway discontinued the inclusion of values relative to unpaid domestic labour (UNIFEM 1997).

Some progress has been made with respect to methodologies and measuring schemes, but their application still seems limited to case studies and special surveys. No large-scale body of work on the subject of unpaid labour has been integrated to the central systems measuring the production of goods and services. As suggested by the UNSNA, some countries are trying to fill the gap of not placing a value on the domestic economy by drafting 'satellite or complementary accounts'. These accounts are kept separately so that they do not modify the structure of the systems, but they are consistent with central accounts as far as the recording of non-monetary work is concerned. The 'satellite' category indicates that, at least for now, these accounts will be segregated from central accounts relative to national, regional or world production. Due to this circumstance, they may either be taken into account or ignored when macro policies are being drafted, and they may continue to remain invisible according to the criteria of those in charge of taking decisions.

It is not superfluous, therefore, to stress the political difficulty and the technical complexity involved in finding ways to support more decisively the dismantling of practices that help sustain and reproduce inequality and the lack of equilibrium in the social and economic relations between women and men.

CHANGES IN THE CARING ECONOMY?

No doubt the changes that took place during the 1990s are reflected in how labour continues to be divided, in the existing intensity and forms of domestic labour. The economy's globalization, characterized by the expansion of transnational corporations, the global expansion of financial capital and a growth in the commercial exchange of goods and services, together with the consolidation of regional trade blocs, have all been accompanied by social conditions unfavourable for the majority of the poor and for women as a whole.

Huge social costs are implied in the greatest expansionist venture aiming to integrate regions, organizations or people via sophisticated technology, the use of which is propagated at a devastating speed: less pay for workers of both sexes through the reduction and increased precariousness of employment (according to the ILO, 30 per cent of the world's economically active population are unemployed or under-employed); the erosion of social conquests and achievements; the reduction and privatization of social security and the rising income concentration. According to the World Bank, 20 per cent of the poorest population sector in Latin America earns 4 per cent of the region's total income, while 10 per cent of the richest population sector earns 60 per cent of the region's total income. This is one of the most unequal distributions on the planet (Minsburg 1997). It is worth stressing that a huge amount of women form part of this 20 per cent, a phenomenon giving origin to the so-called 'feminization of poverty'.

One of the most remarkable changes involves systems of production and the demand for manual labour. According to van Osch, the new systems of production have generated a new structure in the employment pyramid: the non-qualified workers at the base, who previously had a steady job, are being substituted by 'a heterogeneous, multi-insertable mass, under unstable working conditions and with the growing presence of women and other discriminated social groups', either by reason of origin (immigrants) or racial and ethnic origins (van Osch 1996: 26). The middle stratum formerly composed of qualified workers tends to shrink, among other things due to technological changes, with the introduction of more 'intelligent' systems that are less dependent on human decisions. At the top of the pyramid, a segment of highly qualified people is expanding, in charge of planning, coordinating and controlling processes that very often transcend national borders. The old pyramid is thus acquiring the profile of an 'hourglass' in which women abound at the base, especially due to the proliferation of free-trade zones and *maquilas* that represent 'the new lever for the insertion of peripheral economies into the globalisation process' (ibid.: 27).

Gender differences tend to be expressed in polarization between the layer of highly qualified workers with very high incomes, most of whom are men, and the growing periphery of non-qualified workers having unstable jobs, with an excess of female representation. In almost every region in the world women's work has increased, but the conditions of their insertion into the labour market are becoming less and less favourable.

Budgetary cuts affecting the delivery of social services, due to modifications in how public spending is allocated, are one of the clearest aspects of the structural adjustment policies. This economic proposal does not lend any express attention to the activities related to social reproduction and performed by women. Numerous studies have shown that extra workloads are being transferred to women: the care of sick patients who formerly qualified for hospital care, or increased child care due to the shortage of child care centres; double school shifts or the privatization of education, for example.

In the absence of substantial modifications to the sexual division of labour, all these changes mean the following for women:

1. They have to confront additional restrictions when attempting to substitute domestic labour for market goods and services.
2. They are forced to intensify the production and transformation of goods in the domestic sphere, due to the fact that working conditions and salaries outside the home are uncertain and do not offer enough stability.

3. They must take up old habits pertaining to care that had already vanished.
4. They have to expand the number of working hours/days.
5. Their physical and mental health is negatively affected.

Not everything is negative in the current crossroads, however. Some women researchers have pointed out that in industrialized nations women are responding with an improved capacity of adjustment to changes in the working sphere, given the flexibility in managing their time that they have already acquired through their double status as producers and reproducers. Thus Gardiner reports that, in England, women are better fit to cope with labour deregulation and job insecurity than men, since women are more capable of resorting to flexible strategies. Men, says the author, 'have been defeated to a greater degree than women by the culture of dependence on jobs and on women to take care of their personal needs' (Gardiner 1996: 167).

As a working hypothesis – and only reality can confirm it – men will have to acquire the flexibility and self-sufficiency that women have already been forced to develop. Will this support a better distribution of domestic chores among all the household members?

The increasing elimination of steady paid work, which is highly protective of the individual, as a labour paradigm of what people might achieve in life, in contrast to non-regulated, non-remunerated work carried out in the domestic sphere, might eventually change the division of labour between men and women, in spite of the high social costs entailed. Both sexes are increasingly being forced to work more flexible hours, without having any certainty of permanence or enough social security guarantees. This is bound to make their ways of relating to the street and to the home as working sites more balanced, as long as it is accompanied by: a) strategies designed to raise and expand awareness of gender disparities and their possible solutions; and b) specific measures to quantify and remunerate work carried out in the domestic sphere.

CONCLUSIONS

Examining the close interdependent relationship between unpaid domestic labour and the dynamics of the productive economy, and its condition as a source of inequality between the sexes, it is obvious that any paradigm of human development attempting to be equitable and sustainable must promote substantial changes in the estimation and handling of the economy devoted to social reproduction and human care.

A first reason is linked to equality and rights that can no longer be postponed in this day and age. Acknowledging and paying the work done by everyone who works is something that has been recognized in all the human rights charters and documents ratified internationally. Economic rights are viewed as central rights in the declarations launched at the Human Rights Conference in Vienna (1993) and at the Social Summit in Copenhagen (1995).

Another reason refers to the need for efficiency evident in economic policy trends. Guaranteeing an adequate interpretation of reality based on more complete data that reflect what is truly happening instead of what we are in the habit of believing is bound to support more adequate decision-taking and facilitate the making of more reliable provisions regarding the effects of any macro-economic measures adopted.

Last but not least, human sustainability is a powerful incentive. The end of the twentieth century showed us the irresponsible uses that humanity has made of all its resources: water, air, forests and so on. In all these cases there was a common factor: the resource was abundant and presumed to be non-extinguishable. This assumption was incorrect. Something similar may happen with women's unpaid labour: it may seem infinitely elastic, but there are already signs of its depletion. If poverty persists and becomes more widespread, as is happening right now, the mental and physical conditions of women in the impoverished sectors, who now tackle double workloads in and outside the home, are bound to deteriorate irrevocably.

A new development paradigm that promotes and encourages equality and equity between the genders should advocate not only the fulfilment of the basic rights conquered by women during the last decades, and adequately subscribed in the Action Platform of the Fourth Women's Conference in Beijing (1995). Radical changes with respect to unpaid domestic labour must also be undertaken:

1. In all spheres, *from invisibility to visibility*: through surveys and censuses, national accounts systems, the use of language, correctly naming and identifying housewives as workers, and so on.
2. In national accounts systems, the *universality of systematic register in every country; the transition from satellite accounts to central accounts.*
3. In society, leaping *from substitution to co-responsibility.* Going from the stage of paying other women to do domestic labour, to having

the awareness and responsibility to share the costs, management and benefits of the economy devoted to care and social reproduction between men and women alike.

4. In public spending, *from voluntary work to paid work*: identifying and developing direct and indirect mechanisms to pay women for the work they perform at home or in the community.

The following question comes up for those involved in the theory and design of development models. Is economic inequality based on gender one of the last barriers to be eliminated? Can this barrier be overcome? Everything tends to indicate that it can.

NOTE

1. Fabiola Campillo, MA in rural development, is Executive Director of FUTURA, a consultancy firm located in San José, Costa Rica.

BIBLIOGRAPHY

Abreu, A. Rangel De Paiva (1995) 'América Latina: globalicación, género y trabajo', in R. Todaro and R. Rodríguez (eds), *El trabajo de las mujeres en el tiempo global*, Santiago de Chile.

Anker, R. and C. Hein (1987) *Medición de las actividades económicas de la mujer*, Geneva: International Labour Office.

British Council (1995) *El género y la reforma económica a través de los ojos de las mujeres*, London.

De Barbieri, M. Teresita (1975) 'Notas para el estudio del trabajo de las mujeres: el problema del trabajo doméstico', *Demografía y Economía*, XII(1), Instituto de Investigaciones Sociales (UNAM).

Elson, D. (1995) 'Alternative visions', in W. Harcout et al. (eds), *Towards Alternative Economics from an European Perspective*, Brussels: WIDE.

Gardiner, J. (1996) 'El trabajo doéstico revisitado: una crítica feminista de las economías neoclásica y marxista', in Van Osch, Thera (ed.), *Nuevos enfoques económicos: contribuciones al debate sobre género*, San José, Costa Rica.

Goldschmidt-Clermont, L. (1982) 'Unpaid work in the household: a review of economic evaluation methods', *Women, Work and Development*, Geneva: International Labour Office.

— (1987) *Economic Evaluation of Unpaid Household Work. Africa, Asia, Latin America and Oceania*, Geneva: International Labour Office.

INSTRAW (1996) *Valuation of Household Production and the Satellite Accounts*, Santo Domingo, Dominican Republic.

Inter-American Development Bank (IDB) (1995) *Women in the Americas. Bridging the Gender Gap*, Washington.

Kleysen, B. and F. Campillo (1996) 'Rural women food producers in 18 countries in Latin America and the Caribbean', in *Productoras Agropecuarias en América del Sur*, Washington, DC: IADB–IICA.

Koch, U. (1996) 'Enfoques de la economía hacia las mujeres y el trabajo doméstica', in T. Van Osch (ed.), *Nuevos enfoques económicos: contribuciones al debate sobre género*, San José, Costa Rica

Minsburg, N. (1997) 'El impacto de la globalización', in N. Minsburg and W. Valle Héctor, *El impacto de la globalización: la encrucijada económica del siglo XXI*, Argentina: Colección Temas de Economía.

Pollard, A. Q. (1997) *Australian Economics Trends, Value of Unpaid Work*, Internet.

Renzi, M. R. (1997) 'Género y macroeconomía', in I. Pineda Fermán (ed.), *Mujer y género: potencial alternativo para los retos del nuevo milenio*, Nicaragua.

Safa, H. I. (1995) 'Reestructuración económica y subordinación de género', in R. Todaro and R. Rodríguez (eds), *El trabajo de las mujeres en el tiempo global*, Santiago de Chile, Chile.

Torres, C. (1977) 'El trabajo doméstico y las amas de casa: el rostro invisible de las mujeres', in *Uruguay Hoy*, Mujer y Trabajo Series, No. 2, Centro Interdisciplinario de Estudios sobre el Desarrollo (CIEDUR).

UNDP (1995) *Human Development Report 1995*, Oxford: Oxford University Press.

UNIFEM (1997) 'Valuation of unpaid work', in *Gender Issues Fact Sheet*, No. 1, Bangkok.

Van Osch, T. (ed.) (1996) *Nuevos enfoques económicos: contribuciones al debatesobre género*, San José, Costa Rica.

Warner, J. M. and D. A. Campbell (2000) 'Supply response in an agrarian economy with non-symmetric gender relations', *World Development*, 28(7): 1327–40.

CHAPTER 7

Measurement and Valuation of Unpaid Household Production: A Methodological Contribution

TATJANA SIKOSKA[1]

§ The existing statistical recording systems remain heavily geared towards the recognition and the evaluation of productive activities within the organized, formal market arena, leaving household production unaccounted for. Consequently, as the 1995 *Human Development Report* points out, '$16 trillion of global output is invisible, $11 trillion of which is produced by women.' The magnitude of distortion of economic productivity and character of our economies is striking and calls for urgent reconsideration of the validity of current practices of development planning based upon data and indicators related to market production.

The inclusion of indicators of household production into the System of National Accounts (SNA) requires accurate collection of data and its comprehensive and compatible valuation. A few questions arise from this need. Which methodology is most appropriate for capturing and valuing the unaccounted contribution of household production to the national economies? How can such indicators be reflected in the national economic indicators and what are the implications of this for policy planning and development?

This chapter attempts to provide answers to these questions through:

1. comparative analysis of the existing methods and techniques for the measurement and valuation of household production;
2. elaboration of INSTRAW's innovative methodological contribution for the measurement and valuation of household production and its application in four countries; and
3. brief reference to methodological issues for further consideration.

Existing methods, grouped broadly in two categories, namely product-based valuation and wage-based valuation, are analysed and their suitability for generating indicators on compatible and comparable categories of productive activities with the categories of the SNA is evaluated. The analysis of existing methodologies pays special attention to their capacity to capture and value household production in developing countries.

Recognizing the specific conditions and methodological needs in many developing countries, especially in the rural areas, INSTRAW has developed a methodology that defines the concept of and the framework for establishing 'satellite accounts' for unpaid work. Central to this innovative methodological effort is the challenge of 'setting up the boundary for the definition of satellite accounts on unpaid household production'. Activities such as collection of fuel-wood, secondary food processing and so on are included in the revised SNA, but are not reflected in the calculation of the GDP. The reason for this is the lack of data and techniques for counting and accounting for these activities.

INSTRAW outlined a comprehensive listing of activities to be included in the proposed satellite SNA categories. These are: (i) household maintenance activities (meal preparation, housecleaning, simple repairing services, shopping, caring for children, sick and elderly, and related travel); (ii) personal development activities (education, skills development and related travel); and (iii) volunteer community work.

This categorization was applied in the research studies carried out in Canada, Finland and Nepal, using output- or product-based calculations. Previous time-use studies were also carried out. The product-based method used by INSTRAW combined conventional time-use accounting with the household expenditures and other production data, which were collected through additional small-scale surveys. The specificities of developing countries (as observed during the application of the research in Nepal) required that surveying techniques be accommodated to such realities. Hence a combination of diary, observation and direct interview techniques was used, in order to adequately collect and measure the widest variety of household activities performed.

The application of this methodology revealed, however, that there were persisting problems. Principally, these problems concern the process of weighting of the relative importance of the hours spent in household work and the estimation of a GDP measurement for household services for which there are no market equivalents. Such difficulties impede the establishment of comparable statistical standards on a nationwide basis. These difficulties are particularly relevant for the developing countries because of unavailability of data. Hence, in a National Time-Use Survey conducted in 1995 in the Dominican Republic by INSTRAW and the National Statistical Office, additional efforts were made and a detailed list of household production activities and related outputs was developed.

The results from these studies not only confirm gender-biased perceptions of women's contribution (or the lack thereof) in national economies, but present a different perspective and understanding of the role of households in the economy as a whole and on the dynamics of their interaction. This, in turn, should constitute the basis for new practices of policy planning and development.

THE UNRECOGNIZED VALUE OF HOUSEHOLD WORK

Work, when done in the household, remains largely unrecognized, by governments, men and women themselves, especially in the developing countries. There is a large gap in the available data on what women and men do outside the formal market sphere. Moreover, there is no value attached to activities performed in the household, despite the fact that it has been recognized that they represent a substantial contribution to national economies.

The invisibility of unpaid household production in national statistics and the lack of recognition of its economic value constitute the major factors perpetuating women's inequality. When women work in the household, they are considered to be 'doing nothing'. They are housewives without a profession and are passive dependants upon the breadwinners, i.e. the men. Hence constructed social relationships based on women's subordination to men continue to be reproduced in all other aspects of human life.

For this reason, the 1985 World Conference to Review and Appraise the Achievements of the United Nations Decade for Women underlined the need to recognize the socio-economic value of domestic work, which is largely performed by women. However, in order to do so, it is of crucial importance to have data on domestic productive activities that would reflect their monetary value. Hence the Conference recommended the strengthening of the 'efforts for measurement and reflection of these contributions in national accounts and in the economic statistics' (UN 1986: 1).

Since then, efforts to measure and value unpaid household production have increased and many countries have established separate satellite accounts to reflect this production. Unfortunately, most of this information is related to developed countries. The lack of statistical information on unpaid household production in developing countries results from multiple factors, among them:

- lack of sufficient recognition of the gender implications of excluding unpaid household work from the national accounts due to a lack of sensitivity towards the issue of gender equality;
- lack of clarity on the relationship between effective and efficient development planning and knowledge of both household production and the use of time within the household by household members; this, in turn, results from a lack of straightforward analysis of the effects of the relationship between the market and the household sectors on development and development planning;
- difficulties in measuring and valuing unpaid household activities and their products due to the lack of adequate methodologies and techniques that take into account the specific conditions of the developing countries; and
- difficulties in finding an adequate conceptualization of household work and market work due to the nature of developing country economies.

However, after the Fourth World Conference on Women in 1995, interest in promoting gender perspectives in development planning has increased in many developing countries. This has contributed greatly to increasing efforts for integrating gender perspectives into the processes of reform and modernization of the state. Nevertheless, this process is in its initial stages and its effective persuasion is critically dependent upon the extent to which governments are willing to address gender inequality in the division of labour between women and men. Two aspects are crucial to this: recognition of the value of the unpaid household production to the economy and social well-being, and knowledge of the distribution of time and work among household members to household production.

If development planning is to successfully address these two aspects of current labour division, which are crucial determinants of gender inequality, it must be based upon knowledge of the interactions between the market and the household sectors. Nowadays, it is clear that the process of production extends itself in a continuous manner through the market and the household sector. For example, child care is a result of both paid and unpaid work. The extent and frequency of use of market-produced goods and services for child care influences the extent and the type of market production of child care goods and services. Moreover, the interactions between the two sectors influence the transfer of labour force from the household to the market sectors and vice versa, which, in turn, influences the types and the extent of production activities that will be performed in the market or the household sector respectively (Goldschmidt-Clermont 1982: 1). 'The increase and decrease in market output and income are offset by opposite changes in household production and unpaid income. Therefore the question we have for our data and models is, what size are these offsets?' (Ironmonger 1992: 7).

The need to acquire knowledge on household production and its interactions with the market is further strengthened by current changes induced by processes of accelerated globalization on the very nature of work itself (flexibility in geographical relocation and in length of time; increased sub-contractual nature of work; blurring of the distinction between the formal and informal labour markets and so on). The effects of this on the capacity and on the forms through which both women and men allocate their time to productive activities in the market and/ or the household are tremendous.

As a result, the need to analyse these interactions on the basis of adequate and accurate indicators on household production becomes even more important.

Measurement and valuation of household production: concepts and methodologies The process for measurement and valuation of household production and its expression in statistical indicators is conditioned by three factors: (i) the existing nature of the systems of national accounts; (ii) the interface between the market and the household sectors; and (iii) the available methodologies for the measurement and valuation of household production. The first factor defines which categories of household production are to be included within the production boundary, i.e. in the System of National Accounts or in the System of Satellite Accounts. The second factor defines the methodological steps, which are to be taken in order to properly impute value on household products. And the third factor defines the actual scope and quality of data on household production that could be generated.

THE SYSTEM OF NATIONAL ACCOUNTS AND THE SYSTEM OF SATELLITE ACCOUNTS

The current System of National Accounts (hereafter SNA) excludes the majority of productive activities undertaken in the household. Although in principle activities undertaken in the household, such as agricultural production, house repairing and remunerated services as child care, are included in the SNA, problems related to their measurement and valuation make their actual inclusion very difficult. On the contrary, services produced in the household are completely excluded. The 1993 *UN Manual on National Satellite Accounts* (hereafter NSA) justifies this exclusion in the following way:

(i) Household production of services is an activity with limited repercussions for the rest of the economy. The decision to produce a service in the household implies a simultaneous decision for its consumption.

(ii) As the majority of personal and household services produced in the household are not intended for the market, there are no typical market prices that could be used for their valuation.

(iii) The imputed values have different economic significance as compared to the monetary values. The imputed incomes generated from the value-imputed production are difficult to tax in practice ... moreover, such a process would show values which are not equivalent to the monetary values for analytical and policy-making purposes.

Because of this, the SNA recommends the use of NSA for recording unpaid domestic activities. The first argument could be contested for its validity for, as will be explained latter, household production indeed interacts in many ways with the market. Moreover, the simultaneous decision to produce and consume an output can also be applied to many market activities. Yet it remains relevant to consider the arguments related to conceptual and methodological problems as quite appropriate, as will be also shown later in this chapter. Hence the major challenge remains: that is which framework of household production activities would best reflect the scope and the value of unpaid household work?

THE INTERFACE BETWEEN THE HOUSEHOLD AND THE MARKET PRODUCTION SECTORS

Adequate imputation of monetary value to household production is crucial for many reasons. But its valuation depends upon the knowledge of the interface between the market and the household production sectors. This interface, in turn, is guided by various factors inherent in the current nature of both sectors. Goldschmidt-Clermont (1982: 7) provides a useful overview of the underlining factors that guide the extent and the character of possible interactions between the two sectors. These are:

1. Constrained work capacity allocation: increased needs for cash income which could be secured only through market-related activity, have influenced an increase in the allocation of work in the marketplace; yet time-use studies show that at least an equal amount of working time is allocated to the household sphere. This means that the work capacity allocation is guided not exclusively by economic motivations but also by complex strategies that take into account social and personal needs and preferences shaped by given environmental/cultural circumstances.

2. Limited substitution between market and non-market work: although certain substitution between the two sectors is possible, both introduce constraints that limit their substitution. For example, the nature of work performed in the marketplace (fixed working hours or flexible working hours) influences the possibility to engage in certain household activities, which are performed at a given time and with a given length. Likewise, the notion of certain household activities may require work inputs at irregular time intervals, which break up the remaining time into time-slots that do not fit in with the employment requirements. Given such time constraints, the solution has been found in a strict gender division of labour worldwide, although lately, consideration should be given to factors such as personal preference and the changing nature of work (contractual nature, blurring distinction between formal informal labour markets, flexibility and so on).

3. Different labour productivity and value of time: under conditions of limited substitution, both sectors operate in related but distinct conditions that affect their relative equilibrium and competitiveness, and bear on their respective labour productivity and value of time. Hence personal decisions on the allocation of working time influenced by consequent constrains may vary. For example, a person may opt to perform the most productive activity but s/he may also opt to perform the least productive one if s/he finds it socially or economically rewarding. Additionally, differences in the production conditions in

both sectors call for careful consideration when monetary values from the market to the household sectors are imputed.

4. Externalities and quality of life: the household sector partly operates in non-monetary circumstances, hence its products are valued not only in economic terms but in personal and social ones as well.

AVAILABLE METHODOLOGIES FOR THE MEASUREMENT AND VALUATION OF UNPAID HOUSEHOLD PRODUCTION

Input vs. output approaches to the measurement and valuation of unpaid household production The process of estimating household production requires its measurement and valuation in comparable units. Hence, it is a process of quantifying productive household activities in physical and/or monetary value units. There are various methods used for this. Goldschmidt-Clermont (1987: 10–11) has classified them in four main categories of valuation methods, on the bases of two main criteria: 1) the units used for the measurement, 2) the angle from which valuation is approached (input or output):

• volume-based measurement in inputs;
• volume-based measurement in outputs;
• value-based measurement in inputs; and
• value-based measurement in outputs.

Measurement of inputs is usually a measurement of physical units of labour inputs: the number of workers or number of working hours. Outputs are measured in a wide variety of physical units, such as the number of meals cooked, number of persons cared for and so on. Yet physical units for quantifying household production are not very convenient when aggregation, for example in national accounting, becomes necessary or when overall comparisons are needed. Hence, instead of physical units of inputs or outputs, the measurement of values of inputs or outputs becomes more appropriate. Values, expressed in monetary units, are easy to determine for market production. But the goods and services produced in the household have no implicit value since the work is unpaid and the products are not sold on the market. Hence a value borrowed from the market needs to be imputed.

The value of inputs is usually expressed in wages paid for similar work in the market. The value of outputs, on the other hand, is expressed in the price of an equivalent market product.

Data requirements for the measurement and valuation of household production In order to quantify household activities and impute monetary value on them, two types of data are needed: (i) type and quantity of productive activities carried out within the household sector in a given country; and (ii) market value for goods and services resulting from similar activities carried in the marketplace. The former is usually acquired by time-use surveys and the latter by special small-scale surveys on values of market-based products and services.

TIME-USE SURVEYS Time-use surveys record how household members allocate their time and to what activities. From there, they provide time estimations, which indicate the total time allocations of women, men and children to different standardized categories of household productive activities. Time-use data are crucial for many purposes:

1. facilitating more accurate measurement of the magnitude of work and production in the household;
2. enabling cross-checking of product-based measurements of household production that are included in the SNA, i.e. the extent and quality of measurement;
3. enabling estimations of productivity of household services, such as cooking, washing, child care, which is crucial for the determination of their value; this can tell us in what productivity setting a certain service is undertaken, which is especially important for developing countries where major discrepancies in household conditions prevail;
4. enabling separate recording of time-inputs of women, men and children to household production through which estimates of the economic contribution of each can be derived;
5. giving a complete perspective and understanding of the role of households in the total economy and the dynamics of the interaction between the household and the economy; and
6. enabling better decisions on policies over a wide range of economic sectors and public affairs issues.

Time-use surveys can be carried out using different techniques and data-collection instruments. Trained interviewers who record the information given by respondents may carry out interviews, using different instruments. The most widely used instrument in surveys on time-use allocation in the household is based on *stylized questions*, which are directly put to the respondent. Usually, these questions ask the respondent to recall the amount of time that s/he has allocated to particular household activity over a specific period of time (a day, a week, a year).

There are different approaches in using stylized questions: unconstrained and constrained. The former does not require that selected time allocations total a fixed time constant, like 24 hours, while the latter does. Hence the former is usually used for time-use studies for specific activities, such as caring for children, or cooking, while the latter is used for time-use studies of an extensive list of selected activities.

Stylized questionnaires are lists of stylized questions put in a format that enables capturing and recording of time allocations to specifically chosen activities. Usually, they contain different categories for which one seeks parallel responses set in tabular forms. This instrument is very useful when different categories of time-allocations are needed, such as working daytime allocations, weekend time-allocation, or primary and secondary activities, and so on. But it has been argued that because of their vulnerability to individual interpretations of the terminology used, there are greater chances for misrepresentation (Khan et al. 1992), or that they are not appropriate for studies on non-time-conscious respondents (especially in rural areas where time is not expressed in minutes and hours) (INSTRAW 1995).

Stylized activity matrix is very similar to the activity lists (questionnaire) but is exhaustive. It enables the recording of data in a fixed reference period (for example 24 hours) that will exhaust all time-allocations to determined categories of household activities. The respondent will have to report the time allocated within 24 hours to each of the predetermined activity categories. A variation of this is a time matrix that enables the respondents to check off the activities of each category that they have undertaken in given time-slot (an hour-slot, for example). As such, the activity matrix is considered to provide greater accuracy than the activity lists.

Time diary has become the widest and most preferred instrument for collection of time-use data since it captures all activities within a fixed period of time in succession where the beginning and ending times are clearly defined by specific time-slots (5, 10, 15 and so on minutes). As such, they allow for a continuous description of activities as undertaken by the respondent. Hence, they minimize risks of misinterpretation of categories of activities as well as time units and allow for capturing different patterns of household time allocation.

Observation, as opposed to the previously mentioned techniques, requires that a person observe the respondent for a fixed period of time and record activities as they occur. It is used for the recording of time use in restricted, particular settings, such as one household or a classroom, in order to study the behaviour of particular sub-group. Observation can be continuous or random. The former is used to record time-use in household activities in areas where the population is not very aware of the amount of time they invest. The latter could be used in order to determine behavioural patterns at a particular time of a particular group of people in a particular setting.

Observation techniques have received various criticisms, despite being recognized as very useful tools in collecting data on household activities that are undertaken in very short time segments or where several activities are performed simultaneously and respondents could not properly reflect on their time-allocation (Khan et al. 1992). Critics point out that observation makes very extensive demands on time and money as well as possibly altering the behaviour of household members because of the presence of an unfamiliar person (INSTRAW 1995).

Computer-assisted data collection includes beeper studies, where after receiving a beep respondents report on the activity undertaken at the time the signal was received; and computer-assisted interviews, where computers assist interviewers and respondents through variety of questions, while at the same time carrying out editing checks and coding the data set. Although these techniques are still in the early stages of development, they are increasingly being used in developed countries, are undergoing permanent improvements and have enormous potential for fast and effective carrying out of time-use surveys.

The advantages and disadvantages of these techniques and data-collection instruments in terms of their applicability in different contexts are addressed below.

CAN SATELLITE ACCOUNTS ON HOUSEHOLD PRODUCTION BE ESTABLISHED?

The process of establishing internationally comparable and compatible frameworks of NSA on household production requires the fulfilment of three conditions: (i) establishment of a common framework that will define activity classification in SNA and NSA; (ii) establishment of a common approach for the valuation of unpaid household production; and (iii) improvement of techniques and instruments for data collection in order to make them applicable to diverse development conditions.

INSTRAW, in the last decade, has devoted much of its research efforts to this objective. In the process, it has gained some very important insights and has suggested various improvements. These will be briefly addressed below with reference to: (i) establishment of an NSA framework for activity classifications for household production; (ii) assessment of various approaches to the valuation of unpaid household production in view of their capacity to enable the creation of NSA to the SNA; and (iii) adaptation of different techniques and instruments for data collection for this purposes and with the specific aim of adapting their application to the conditions of the developing countries.

Framework for defining activity classifications for SNA and NSA Given the need to establish an internationally acceptable Satellite Household Sector Account in order to bridge the gaps in the information base in different policy areas, INSTRAW (1996) recommended a framework for defining activity classifications for SNA and for the Satellite Accounts (see Figure 7.1).

The framework suggests that SNA activities should include all activities related to the production of goods and services for the market

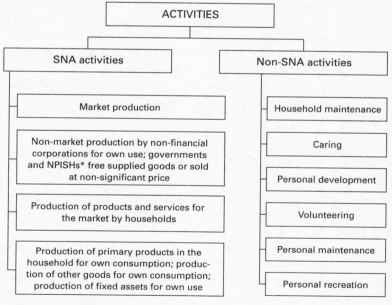

* non-profit institutions serving households

FIGURE 7.1 SNA based activity classification framework

TABLE 7.1 Advantages and disadvantages of product-based and wage-based valuation methods

Product-based valuation	Wage-based valuation
Advantages	*Advantages*
• Measures real output	• Simple and easier to handle
• Products have wider market and substitutes	• Requires fewer data once the time inputs are measured
• Compatible with the main body of SNA	• In some situations, it is the most appropriate method for valuing services
a) Real product	
b) Expenses forgone at the household level	*Disadvantages*
• Reflects household productivity situation	• Measures input and not output
• Overcomes the problems of measuring productivity of time of various individuals, simultaneous activities, and delineation of boundary between leisure and work	• Does not reflect household productivity
	• Not compatible with SNA methodology
	• There is a need for choice among multiple wage rates: polyvalent worker or specialized one; wage equivalent market function; wage for equivalent market qualification; wage forgone or opportunity cost of time
Disadvantages	• Choice required for average wages: all workers; all female workers; workers in service occupations, female, male and children
• Requires more data and effort	• Value will depend on the particular wage rate chosen
• Difficult to apply in the case of services where no comparable service exists in the market	• Problems related to productivity of time of various individuals, simultaneous activities, boundary between work and leisure, require various assumptions for solution.
• Less experience available on this methodology	

Source: INSTRAW, 1995: 42

sector (produced either in the market or in the household) as well as non-market production covered by the 1993 SNA. Non-SNA activities comprise two different sets of activities: those that can be delegated to another person and, hence, be traded in the market, and those that cannot be delegated but must be done by her/himself. Activities classified for inclusion in satellite account are household maintenance activities; caring activities; personal development activities and volunteering. Activities that can not be delegated to another person, such as personal maintenance and personal recreation, cannot be included in the non-SNA satellite accounts.

Product (output)-based valuation vs. wage (input)-based valuation   INSTRAW, in order to find out which measurement and valuation method is the most appropriate for the establishment of an internationally comparable NSA on household production, embarked on a process of extensive evaluation of existing valuation methods. Table 7.1 summarizes briefly their advantages and disadvantages.

This evaluation shows that there are two basic conceptual advantages of product-based valuation methods: they are comparable to the accounting system of SNA and they use products as the basis for valuation rather than wages. Hence problems related to simultaneous activities, individual productivity, variety of existing wages and so on can be avoided. The disadvantage of this method is in its requirements for time-use data and the data necessary for imputing of monetary values. However, there are situations in which wage-based methodologies are indeed very useful. For example, where there is no market equivalent for a household product (especially in some remote rural areas of developing countries), wages in kind or cash could be used to impute a value for a household product.

Time-use data needs and assessment of time-use data collection instruments   The applicability of current time-use instruments to the specific conditions of developing countries requires a thorough examination in terms of: (i) their requirements (inputs); and, (ii) the end products (outputs). INSTRAW (1995), on the basis of different studies evaluating data-collection instruments (Harvey and MacDonald 1976; Lingsom 1979), and its own experience, assessed the data collecting instruments. This assessment is presented in Table 7.2.

The table shows that these instruments have different advantages and disadvantages when analysed in terms of inputs or outputs. In terms of input, the criterion of cost is highly relevant for developing countries, and it shows that observation involves the highest costs as compared to other instruments. But in terms of output, instruments such as completion of diaries, activity lists or matrix and those instruments that guide/constrain the respondent to account for all activities in sequence are very highly rated as compared to others. However, certain obstacles, such as illiteracy in the rural areas of the developing countries, may require the use of observation despite its costs.

Testing the proposed methodology: creation of satellite accounts on household production in Canada, Finland and Nepal The validity of using the output-based approach in developing macro estimates of output measures using large-scale time-use data and other collateral data in order to establish NSA on household production was tested by IN-

TABLE 7.2a Subjective evaluation of data-collection instruments: input criteria

	Respondent cooperation	Respondent knowledge	Cost	Process-ability
Unconstrained stylized				
questions	medium-high	variable	medium	medium
activity list	medium-high	variable	medium	medium
activity log	medium	medium	medium	medium
Constrained				
interviewer	medium	medium	medium +	medium +
administered	high	medium	high	low–medium
activity matrix				
recall diary				
Respondent				
completed	medium	high	low–medium	low–medium
tomorrow				
diary				
Observation	low–medium	n/a	very high	medium
continuous	medium	n/a	high	medium
random spot				

Source: INSTRAW, 1995

STRAW through three case studies conducted in Canada, Finland and Nepal. The case study in Nepal attempted to develop a micro approach to output estimation, which is highly dependent upon collection at a household level of various data that are needed to calculate the quantity and the value of household production. Such micro approaches have been already used in different studies, but they focus on specific activities. INSTRAW's micro approach aimed to provide a more complete micro picture that can permit a proper overall accounting of household production. The studies carried out in Canada and Finland, on the contrary, used a macro approach. They aimed at using existing data, including data derived from representative time-diary and consumer-expenditure surveys, as the basis upon which estimates of the value of a range of activities undertaken in the household would be made.

TABLE 7.2b Subjective evaluation of data-collection instruments: output criteria

	Validity	Reliability	Usability	Flexibility
Unconstrained stylized				
questions	low	low	medium +	low
activity list	low	low	medium +	low
activity log	high	high	high	medium
Constrained interviewer	medium +	medium +	medium +	medium +
administered	medium +	medium +	high	medium
activity matrix	medium	medium	high	very high
recall diary				
Respondent completed	high	high	high	medium +
activity matrix	high	high	medium	very high
tomorrow diary				
Observation continuous	medium +	medium +	medium +	very high
random spot	very low	medium	medium	high

Source: INSTRAW, 1995

THE MICRO OUTPUT-BASED APPROACH: THE CASE STUDY IN NEPAL
The valuation process for unpaid household maintenance work in Nepal
involved the following steps:

- generating large-scale (at the national level) time-use data for all
  activities performed in the households;
- generating output data for a sub-sample of activities from the same
  group;
- deriving values for time-input on the basis of this sample, as follows:
  value of the output derived from the price of comparable or equivalent market product;
- net return to labour, exclusive of intermediate inputs used in activities
  oriented to the market but similar to domestic activities, such as
  cooking for self-consumption and for other households;
- net return to labour in other comparable non-monetary productive
  activities for which output related valuation can be performed (for
  example, if two hours are devoted to child care, this time may be
  valued at net average returns to her labour in another activity whose
  products are sold); and
- wages of polyvalent household workers (inclusive of in-kind income)
  adjusted to skill level and managerial responsibilities (INSTRAW
  1996).

In the process, data needs were identified that were necessary for the
implementation of the output-based approach. This was the result of the
lack of data crucial to the development of normative values of specific
products (prices, units of measurement, volume and value of inputs to
certain outputs and so on). Hence an additional small-scale survey that
determined normative values of outputs/products was carried out. Data
collection was carried out through structured questionnaires, focused
interviews and checklists.

One of the major problems experienced in the process of valuation
was the fact that many goods had not undertaken market transaction,
hence imputing a value on the basis of market prices to such goods
became extremely difficult. Further problems were experienced in the
rural areas, where the concept of time varies greatly as well as the
measures used to quantify cooked food. As such, the process of data
collection on time units allocated to different activities as well as the
quantification process of inputs and outputs was lengthy and often
required double-checking the collected information. Additional prob-

lems appeared due to the substantial difference in the quality of goods cooked for home consumption and those cooked for the market. Hence what was captured was the minimum value of comparable products, rather than the exact value.

Activities found in the sample households were categorized in 17 categories of different types of household maintenance work, additionally sub-classified in 132 sub-activities. The value of the outputs/ products was then calculated. Unfortunately, this was possible only for food preparation. The total volume of products generated in each household was multiplied per unit price and per unit household production costs. The difference of these sums gave the first approximation of value-added. This value minus total depreciation and fuel costs is the net value-added generated in the household. For activities other than meal preparation, such as laundry and house cleaning, wage rates of polyvalent workers were used as normative value for such activities. Although in the rural areas there was no market price for child care services, polyvalent workers' wages from the urban area were used for child care in both urban and rural areas. Child education was valued at monthly prices paid for similar services at home (INSTRAW 1996).

On the basis of such developed normative values per unit input of time in household maintenance activities, INSTRAW made an attempt to establish a global account that includes regular GDP, estimated value of non-market goods that remain outside the national accounts and a satellite account on household maintenance activities. Only a brief reference to the last point will be made in this chapter because of its innovative methodological characteristics.

The normative values derived for the major categories of household work were applied to time-use data in order to derive national averages for normative values of each unit of time input in household maintenance activities. These were classified into three major groups: (i) cooking, serving, cleaning dishes and pots; (ii) laundry and house cleaning; and (iii) child care. National averages had to be derived from regional time input data. Hence figures on regional distribution of populations were used as weights to derive first rural and urban averages for daily time input of women and men in each category of activity. These inputs were multiplied by the normative value of each hour of work in each category, and national averages were calculated again on the basis of population weights. This outcome was multiplied by the number of days in a year and number of female and male population separately in each category of activities. In order to calculate the annual value-added generated by women from meal preparation (Fcm) the following formula was used:

Fcm = (DTIUm × NVUm × PFPU + DITRm × NVRm × PFPR) × 365 × TFP

DTIUm = daily time input in hours by women in urban areas in meal preparation
NVUm = value of per hour time input in meal preparation in urban areas
PFPU = proportion of urban women (10 years and older) to the total female population
DTIRm = daily time input in hours by women in rural areas in meal preparation
NVRm = value of per hour time input in meal preparation in rural areas
PFPR = proportion of rural women (10 years and older) to the total female population
365 = days in a year
TFP = total female population 10 years and older (INSTRAW 1996).

The final outcome of such calculations shows that value-added generated by women in household maintenance activities more than doubles the regular GDP. Women contribute 27.5 per cent of regular GDP, their contribution to household maintenance activities amounts to 92.8 per cent, while their contribution to other non-market (but within SNA) products amounts to 58.3 per cent. In total, their contribution to the expanded GDP including the household maintenance satellite account amounts to 62.9 per cent.

THE MACRO OUTPUT-BASED APPROACH INSTRAW undertook a study to define the methodology for a macro approach to valuation of household production, i.e. the overall unpaid household production within a given economy. The output-based methodology for valuation of unpaid household production that was developed is based on the following formula:

The value of a non-SNA good or service was measured as:

VO = P - RME - UOD

VO = the value of 1 unit of household output
P = the market price, net of taxes and subsidies, of the good or service of like quality
RME = the cost of raw materials and energy used per unit of output
UOD = the cost of the use of dwelling per unit of output.

If value-added is defined as VA = P - RME, then the measure of household output is VO = VA − UOD, with VA being calculated net of taxes and subsidies on the product (INSTRAW 1996).

According to this formula the value of household production incorporates labour inputs, household equipment and entrepreneurship. In order to avoid double-counting of user cost of dwelling when relating GDP of the NSA with SNA GDP was substracted from the value-added, which was a very innovative step in calculating the value of household output. In contrast, user cost of household equipment, which is not included in the SNA GDP, was included in the value of household output in INSTRAW's calculation.

The procedure for estimating of value-added includes:

1. identification of broad categories of output generating activities (as mentioned above);
2. identification of items of goods and services produced within each category;
3. estimation of quantity and where possible quality of the output of each item of each category per person in a household per unit of time;
4. estimation of a market price for each good or service produced on the basis of price of market good/service of similar quality;
5. identification of the components of raw materials and energy of each produced household item subsequent calculation of value-added for each item;
6. the price of household output that was to be used in calculation VA is what SNA defines as 'basic price';
7. to measure UOD, a portion of the imputed or actual rental of a dwelling was assigned to the activity;
8. in order to arrive at the value of household production at higher levels of aggregation, the following notations were used:

- per-unit value of household output for each item in a category was calculated as: $VO = VA - UOD$, and the corresponding total value as $IVO = Q \times VO$ (where Q is quantity of output of an item and IVO is total value of output of an item).
- Total value of household-produced output in particular category of activity was calculated as $CVO = $ sum of IVO (where CVO is category-wise value of activities).
- The total value of a household's output is: $TVO = $ sum of CVO of all categories (where TVO is total value of output).
- The total value aggregated of all households in the economy was calculated as: $SACVO = $ sum of CVO (where SACVO stands for satellite account of the value of output of a category). And, SATVO $ = $ sum of TVO over all households (where SATVO stands for Satellite

Account of the total value of output of all households) (INSTRAW 1996).

This methodology was tested in two countries, Canada and Finland, using available time-use and family expenditures data, and where necessary supplementary data from secondary sources. The total estimates of the value of household work in Canada are about 42 per cent of GDP, while in Finland it is 40 per cent of GDP excluding volunteerism and education.

On the basis of the time-use data, the inputs in time of both women and men to these outputs were also determined. It was seen that in Finland there is a tendency for women to carry a heavier share of the work than in Canada, except in activities related to inside house cleaning. It is important to say that these estimates were derived on the bases of assumption of equal productivity for women and men in each activity. Measuring relative productivity levels of women and men remains as an important challenge for future research. Moreover, these studies showed that the gender division of unpaid work runs counter to that of paid work. Males account for 63 per cent of the Canadian GDP and 59 per cent of the Finnish, while females account for 61 per cent of the unpaid production in Canada and 59 per cent of the Finnish. In terms of total production (paid and unpaid) in Canada females account for 45 per cent of the total and in Finland 47 per cent (INSTRAW 1996).

LESSONS LEARNED: CONCLUSIONS AND RECOMMENDATIONS

Effective policy-making depends on accurate data and statistical indicators. Such data must reveal what type of activities are carried out and why, but more importantly what type of end products they produce and what is their contribution to the national economy as a whole. It is only then that adequate policies to improve and to change economic performance can be designed. Since women perform most of the unrecorded and unpaid household production, the issue becomes even more important when seeking ways to improve the status of women in a society.

The current SNA does not include all of the household production. It is based on marketable goods and services. Services such as cooking, ironing, child care and care of older people, which are mostly performed by women, remain excluded. Such activities, in turn, are not only crucially important for the economy as a whole, but need to be taken seriously in development planning in view of the growing dynamics of their interface with the market. Nowadays, especially in the developing countries, the line between marketable and non-marketable services is arbitrarily drawn.

But as has been discussed, the major problem of accounting for these activities is their measurement and valuation. How can internationally compatible and comparable methods to measure and value the unpaid household production be developed? INSTRAW's work in the field shows that there are indeed ways to define a common framework of household production activities for use in the creation of NSA on household production. As seen, the framework for NSA developed by INSTRAW can be used for the development of internationally comparable NSA. This framework recommends the inclusion of activities that benefit others (child care, cooking and so on), personal development activities (such as education and training) and volunteering.

But more importantly, INSTRAW's work also shows that its output-based methodology for the valuation of household production is indeed useful in measuring outputs, imputing values and calculating the total value of household production, and providing estimates on women's and men's share in it.

Being especially concerned with developing countries, where women do the majority of household work,[2] INSTRAW paid special attention to adapting measurement techniques to those conditions. The lack of resources in developing countries impedes regular time-use studies. The conditions of underdevelopment such as illiteracy, varying concepts of time and so on also impede application of techniques such as regular interviews and time diaries.

The Nepalese case study shows the following problems to be of crucial importance to the successful methodological application of the output-based approach:

- lack of or use of different units of measurements of quantities of materials used as well as quantities of time spent in a given household activity;
- problems of output quantification, since many people, especially in rural areas, could not determine the exact quantity of output produced (kg of clothes washed, kg of fuel or water fetched and so on);

- lack of market prices for some products and service and use of different in-kind payments when exchange occurs;
- difficulty in integrating the component of a quality of a product in its value;
- difficulty in applying product-based valuation for those services where the market price is non-existent and approximate value-based calculations are necessary;
- discrepancy between categorization of household production activities in time-use studies and the activities recorded in the survey may cause situations where different methods of valuation have to be applied for activities grouped in the same broad category, as in Nepal for laundry and house cleaning; the latter could only be calculated using wage-based methods; and
- inadequacy of the design of the data-collecting instruments, which may lead to failure of recording of activities that produce simultaneously few outputs and so on (INSTRAW 1996).

These problems are indeed very important and need to be addressed through further research if we are to provide accurate data on the satellite accounts on household production. It is especially important to design data-collecting instruments, which are flexible and applicable to different levels of development. Hence a combination of time-diaries, interviews and observation is highly recommended for the developing countries. This combination was used in a National Time-Use Study carried out in 1995 in the Dominican Republic in collaboration with the National Statistical Office. The experience suggests very positive results. (The final data from this study are not yet available, hence no reference is made to this case in this chapter.)

> Despite these problems, collection of time-use data remains the only valid method of capturing previously hidden activities. It can help provide the necessary alternative to the mathematical concept of time, which may be foreign to a local culture. Flexibility and a good deal of experimentation will be necessary to make the information consistent and reliable enough to permit meaningful comparative analysis. Development of general methodological guidelines, a combination of conventional statistical theory and field observation, is the necessary next step. (*INSTRAW News* 1994)

NOTES

1. Tatjana Sikoska is an adviser to the United Nations International Research and Training Institute for the Advancement of Women (INSTRAW).

2. In Africa for example, 80 per cent of food production for household consumption is produced by women as well as half of all other production, while GDP figures count only agricultural products actually brought to the market.

BIBLIOGRAPHY

Fitzgerald, J. and J. Wicks (1990) 'Measuring the value of household output: a comparison of direct and indirect approaches', *The Review of Income and Wealth*, 36(2): 129–42.

Goldschmidt-Clermont, L. (1982) 'Unpaid work in the household: a review of economic evaluation methods', *Women, Work and Development*, 1, Geneva: International Labour Office.

— (1987) *Economic Evaluation of Unpaid Household Work: Africa, Asia, Latin America and Oceania*, Geneva: International Labour Office.

Harvey, A. S. and W. S. MacDonald (1976) 'Time diaries and time data for extension of economic accounts', *Social Indicators Research*, 3(1): 21–35.

INSTRAW (1994) *INSTRAW News*, second semester, 21(9), Santo Domingo.

— (1995) *Measurement and Valuation of Unpaid Contribution: Accounting through Time and Output*, Santo Domingo.

— (1996) *Valuation of Household Production and the Satellite Accounts*, Santo Domingo.

Ironmonger, D. (1992) 'National time accounts: a focus for international comparison, modeling and methodology', Paper presented at the International Association for Time Use Research 1992 Meeting, 15–18 June, Rome.

Khan, M. E., R. Anker, E. K. G. Dastidart and B. C. Patel (1992) 'Methodological issues in collecting time use data from female labour force', *Indian Journal of Labour Economics*, 35(1): 55–72.

Lingsom, S. (1979) *Advantages and Disadvantages of Alternative Time Diary Techniques: A Working Paper*, Oslo: Statistisk Sentralbyra.

United Nations (1986) *The Nairobi Forward-looking Strategies*, Report of the World Conference to Review and Appraise the Achievements of the United Nations Decade for Women: Equality, Development, Peace, New York.

— (1993) *System of National Accounts*, Washington, DC: Eurostat, IMF, OECD, UN and WB.

— (1995) *Human Development Report 1995*, Oxford: Oxford University Press.

CHAPTER 8

Do We Have Gender Statistics?

THELMA GÁLVEZ[1]

§ The construction of gender statistics is a process involving society as a whole, as this chapter will attempt to demonstrate. It provides a brief overview of the kind of statistics normally included in National Accounts Systems. These statistics may have served to compile a great deal of information up to now, but they still fail to show how the conditions of women's lives evolve, except for touching on some isolated aspects. First we will consider the limitations of conventional statistics and then we will examine the requirements needed to produce gender statistics that might lead to a profound change in gender relations.

CONVENTIONAL STATISTICS AND GENDER

The most immediate concern when referring to gender statistics is the need to define specific gender-related situations. Quantifying how many men and women are referred to is the first question to arise when an issue affecting both sexes is involved, which can be quantified statistically. The query may also be posed in terms of averages, rates and dispersions or through the use of other tools. Just what relates to men and what relates to women?

Conventional statistics compiling information about people's various attributes may answer many such questions. Usually they are grouped under the term 'social, demographic and associated statistics' and refer to subject areas such as population, health, education, science and technology, culture, social security, justice, personal data and criminal records. Also included in the category of social statistics are matters related to economic performance such as labour, employment, salaries and incomes.[2]

Desegregation by sex is not often applied during the compilation, processing and publishing of statistics. However, modifying these statistics is always possible. Additional efforts may be needed to process or publish gender-differentiated results. Although it may mean higher costs, it is possible to change statistical guidelines so as to take gender into account. In all such cases, the two greatest difficulties are whether those in charge of producing statistics have both the political will and the financial capacity to carry out the tasks involved, and whether time series are available to know how a situation evolves over time is also relevant. Older records are not usually kept in their original form and computer processing is relatively recent. Besides, statisticians cannot actually foresee how knowledge will evolve, or how future users may examine statistics from other perspectives.

In spite of their limitations, traditional statistics contain an enormous wealth of information. Such wealth remains largely unknown but it is possible to uncover it by making additional efforts that do not always imply great costs. In fact, many demands made by parties interested in gender issues from different fields of expertise expressed as 'the need to count on sex-desegregated data' may be satisfied using conventional statistics.

Actually it should be statisticians who know best the broad possibilities offered by sex-desegregated data. Partly on this account and partly because some gender-sensitive information already does exist, it is difficult to accept that the subject of gender statistics is something new, that specialized staff are needed to prepare them and that they may require new structures and methodologies. Statisticians often believe that everything necessary has already been done and that existing publications, data bases and files already include the required information. Defining more precisely what we want enhances our opportunities to find what we are looking for.

Traditional statistics are a good point of departure, but the production of gender statistics also involves other actors. Statistics are a continuous process fed from many sources. Before going further, we will list the limitations inherent in conventional statistics, even when it is possible to desegregate them by sex:

They lack integration, coherence and an overall vision. Gender issues are seen as a specific field of expertise, practices and applications of policies needing to be matched in the field of statistics. Gender statistics form an interrelated and coherent body, usually not available as such through traditional statistics. Educational attributes, health conditions, socio-economic levels, access to and types of work and so on, produce different profiles for men and women. They show cause-and-effect relations and may reflect gender-differentiated conditions. No traditional publication has focused on the subject of gender differences or even on the subject of women.

They do not incorporate the gender issues being discussed in society. In other disciplines, statistical systems interpret information needs and adjust to them accordingly. Population studies have been crucial for collecting information through censuses and vital statistics, for example. Economic theory and policies are essential to construct price indexes, salaries and indicators of how employment evolves. Gender issues, as an academic discipline and as a social reality, should likewise inspire the creation of gender statistics.

They do not cover statistical subject matter stemming from their users. Gender studies and political practice have made advances by proposing new themes related to living in society that are not measurable with conventional statistics. The demands on the statistical system multiply when it comes to covering more areas in which the situation of men and women can be studied separately, now that more attention is being paid to finding explanations, setting up agendas and proposing actions and policies to correct disparities, injustices and discrimination. One theme emerging among many others deals with the power and influence women may have. Its first statistical expression is to measure male and female participation at various levels of representation, politics, government and so on.[3]

The concepts on which statistical registers are based do not take into account that women confront different situations. Faced with the problem of quantifying, statisticians and subject specialists ground their work in universally accepted concepts, gradually modifying them in order to incorporate the advances made in each field. With respect to statistical work, it is essential to reach agreements that allow the comparison of statistics, both internationally and with respect to time, so that changes taking place may also help draw conclusions and gauge continuity. In the case of gender studies, which is a more recent specialization, a critical study of the concepts held as valid has been carried out, since these do not convey gender awareness or give satisfactory accounts of issues pertaining to women. In other words, they have been constructed from the male perspective. One of the most well-known examples becomes evident when attempting to quantify women's economic activity. In recent years, criticisms have been made about women in production and how to assess their contribution with reference to the different ways of measuring women's economic contribution. The limits to how women's production is valued are fixed under the terms of the United Nations National Accounts System in its last review dating from 1993. Such types of measurements are adapted and reviewed at regular intervals. The recommendations resulting from such revisions should take into account the value of specific gender information and transmit this concept to those in charge of producing national statistics. The degree to which this occurs depends on the potential these representatives have to express themselves and on the power of conviction they yield in their own enclaves.

The fieldwork and procedures used to compile statistics both display gender biases. Those who carry out surveys; the civil servants who record national statistics (personal data, health, criminal records and so on) and those who lead codification, classification and computerization processes all form part of a culture that uses sexual stereotypes to study male and female activities. Although women's participation in the labour market has significantly increased, when surveyors find women at home they still tend to see them as 'housewives devoted to domestic labour' and to devote less effort to finding other explanations. When it comes to men in the economically active age range, these are just as easily visualized as working at home as unemployed, and only recently as being inactive out of personal choice, something that has not often been accepted in traditional cultures. Statisticians are becoming more aware of this bias and are taking measures to avoid making such 'non-sample errors', but screening gender biases out is not a priority with them. The language used also needs to be revised: if the question is who the head of the household is and men are still in the majority, the possibility of identifying women as heads of households is low even if this is the case, since it is seen as a transgression of the established order. Only training revealing the existence of such biases and raising awareness about them can help combat such prejudices. Similar prejudices emerge at the stage in which the information is being analysed.

Tabulation design for data publication does not take into account the need to make women visible. All intellectual disciplines are characterized by a lack of sensitivity with respect to gender differences or the need to take them into account, although this attitude is changing to various degrees. The same holds true in the field of statistics, in which a culture already exists pertaining to what should be tabulated and published by sex, since gender differences clearly do occur. Some sex-relevant data may seem useless from a traditional perspective. What is the point of finding out whether women smoke less or more than men do? What is the use of segregating infant mortality by sex? What does it matter which sex occupies what number of beds in a hospital? How does food aid differ according to sex in cases of extreme poverty? Why should we find out in what ways students profit from school according to whether they are girls or boys? How are boys and girls treated differently in the home? Segregating all data by sex is the first step towards making the changes needed in the design of tabulations. The second is the revision of causal relations between variables according to gender data. Calculating the labour rate for both sexes by marital status or number of children can be carried out when a link between work and the domestic situation is identified, yet the link has not tended to be made in tabulations for census-making. Segregating statistics per sex may rectify this shortcoming, but if the amount of information is very large and/or the series are very long, the costs involved may be prohibitively high.

THE DEMAND FOR GENDER-SENSITIVE STATISTICS

The list of limitations presented by conventional statistics might never have been formulated if progress had not been made in the demand for gender-sensitive information. This demand runs parallel to the history of the women's movement, international women's conferences and fora, gender studies and practical and academic advances. It is an issue that had already gained wide recognition by 1985, when the Nairobi strategies for empowering women stated: 'Timely and reliable statistics on women's situation play a significant role in the elimination of stereotypes and the advancement of full equality. Governments should help compile statistics and carry out periodic evaluations in order to detect stereotypes and cases of inequality, obtain specific evidence about the many harmful consequences of non-equitative laws and practices and find ways to measure progresses in eliminating discrimination.'

Although this demand arose on the fringe of National Accounts Systems, and the gaps were filled in from a collection of non-official statistics wherever possible, awareness has slowly been growing about the large amount of information already available in the statistics produced by national and international systems. There is also greater awareness of the right to expect the cooperation of official institutions, at least with respect to the recommendations pertaining to the commitment undersigned by governments at international conferences.

More recently, governments have contracted commitments by sub-

BOX 8.1 *Fourth International Women's Conference*

Extract on Strategic Objective H.3: Generation and Dissemination of Sex-desegregated Data and Information for Planning and Evaluation

209. Actions geared to national and regional services and UN agencies, in cooperation with relevant research and documentation centres:

1. To ensure that statistics related to individuals are collected, processed, analysed and presented desegregated by sex and age and that they simultaneously reflect the problems and issues relative to women and men.

2. To periodically gather, process, analyse and offer databases desegregated per sex, age, socio-economic level and other relevant indicators, including number of dependants, to be used in the design and implementation of policies and programmes.

3. To involve women's studies centres and research institutions in the development and testing of adequate indicators and research methodologies that reinforce gender analysis, and follow up whether the goals contained in the Action Platform are being implemented.

4. To appoint enough staff to strengthening gender statistics programmes and guarantee coordination, monitoring and coverage in all fields of statistics, and to prepare statistical products integrating the different subject areas.

5. To improve data collection on the full participation of men and women in the economy, also tracing their participation in the informal sector.

6. To develop more comprehensive knowledge of all work and employment modes: i) improving data collection on the non-remunerated work already included in the UN National Accounts Systems, such as agricultural work, especially with respect to subsistence agriculture and other types of production not destined for the market; ii) improving the present measurements that underestimate female unemployment and sub-employment in the labour market; and iii) acknowledging women's economic contribution and bringing to the fore the unequal distribution of paid and unpaid labour between women and men by developing methods at the relevant forums, to calculate the value of the unpaid labour not contemplated in National Accounts, such as preparing meals and

caring for dependants, and to reflect this in Satellite Accounts or in other types of official accounts, prepared separately and consistent with National Accounts.

7. To develop an international classification of activities for statistics on time use, taking into account the gender differences with respect to paid work, and to gather the corresponding data segregated by sex. At the national level and depending on existing restrictions: i) to carry out periodic studies on time use in order to measure unpaid work, also registering activities carried out simultaneously, whether they be remunerated or not; ii) to measure unpaid work not included in National Accounts and improve the methods used to reflect their value more accurately in Satellite Accounts, or in other types of official accounts produced separately and consistent with National Accounts.

8. To improve the concepts and methods used to gather data measuring poverty among men and women, including their access to resources.

9. To reinforce vital statistics systems and incorporate gender analysis in both publications and in research; to prioritize gender differences both in designing research and in data collection so as to improve morbidity statistics; to improve data collection on access to health services including access to care with respect to sexuality and reproduction, maternity care and family planning, giving special priority to the case of teenage mothers and the care of the elderly.

10. To develop better information, desegregated by sex and age, relevant to the victims of all kinds of forms of violence against women and to their aggressors, in cases of domestic violence, sexual harassment, rape, incest and sexual abuse, traffic in women and children and the violence exerted by state agents;

11. To improve concepts and data-gathering methods on the participation of men and women with disabilities, including their access to resources.

Source: B. Hedman, F. Y. Perucci and P. Sundström (1996) *Engendering Statistics. A Tool for Change*, Sweden.

scribing to the Declaration and Action Platform of the Fourth World Conference on Women (Beijing 1995). This declaration invokes governments, the international community and civil society to take action around the various critical gender issues that are currently the subject of international debate and explicitly single out actions to be undertaken by producers of official statistics.

A review of the paragraphs included in the Action Platform about gender statistics illustrates the range of potential actions connected with the different strategic objectives.[4] It refers to the need for more statistics when dealing with topics such as the feminization of poverty, violence against women and women's participation in power structures and decision-taking processes, and in order to find more effective ways of assessing the value of unpaid labour. Strategic Objective H.3 lists the agreements specifically involving producers of statistics and statistical services, giving an overview of the current demand for gender-sensitive statistics in the international context (see Box 8.1).

The Platform covers a broad action spectrum. Such actions are partly geared towards improving the production and use of gender statistics and partly towards building theory, tuning definitions, proposing classifications and collecting gender-differentiated statistics in order to study priority areas such as women's power and influence, labour and the economy, violence against women, health and disability, and so on.

The permanent debate on the different gender approaches led by the international women's movement, which runs parallel to the history of the various fora and conferences, has helped improve existing models and explore theoretical solutions. This constant progress has also influenced the perspective from which figures are constructed, shifting from the need to compile figures about women in order to further the women's cause to the demand for gender-differentiated statistics used by a much wider audience. The new approaches are more demanding with respect to quality in order to reflect each relevant subject matter and also because there is greater awareness now about the mistakes committed in the past and about the gender biases inherent in statistical production.

At almost every conference and task group dealing with issues concerning women, the need for gender-segregated statistics is felt. Most data reveal some type of shortcoming and stimulate further demands for information. More expertise has been accumulated by now on how to construct gender statistics, both at an international level and in the individual countries that have pioneered gender statistics.

STATE OF THE ART OF OFFICIAL STATISTICS

No complete inventory of the actions undertaken by official statistics services exists for Latin America and the Caribbean. The relative absence of official publications on the situation of women, or on the two sexes separately, is an indicator of this situation. No results are known, either on surveys of time allocation or on the construction of satellite accounts that run parallel to National Accounts and attempt to evaluate women's economic contribution. This shortage is evident in international statistical publications, although comparatively speaking these do have more information on developed countries.

Without having a complete list at my disposal, the examples I know of official publications including gender statistics have had external support (Mexico and Chile). In Latin America, the greatest efforts have been made outside the official sphere. Even where such statistics do exist this does not mean that the national state bodies have integrated them into their normal tasks, either financing them or guaranteeing their regularity. No institutional changes can be observed with respect to the appointment of permanent staff members to fulfil these tasks.

Another indicator of the prevalent situation are the agendas of the meetings of the Statistics Directors of the Americas supported by ECLAC, the OAS and Spain's National Institute of Statistics.[5] They meet every two years to discuss issues of common interest and draft a joint action plan. At the 1992 meeting, the main themes on their agenda were:

- Putting into effect the 1993 Review of National Accounts Systems, its demands and the examination of the basic statistics available.
- Evaluating cooperation activities related to the general subject areas: the informal sector, social and poverty indicators, short-term statistics and indicators, and statistics on foreign trade and the environment.

In 1994, the agenda contemplated making a balance of the production and adaptation of basic statistics needed to implement National Accounts Systems, the quantification of the informal economy, environmental statistics and indicators, foreign trade information geared to supporting integration processes, social and poverty-related indicators. National Statistics Directors met once more in 1996, a year after the Beijing Conference. Regional and international cooperation programmes in the field of statistics referred specifically to:

- adaptation of basic statistics for the implementation of 1993 National Accounts Systems;
- environmental statistics and indicators; and
- social and poverty-related statistics and indicators, including the informal sector theme.

Issues related to the agreements entered upon via the Beijing Platform were not discussed, nor did they form part of any action programme. Although internationally the gender issue had gained recognition and momentum, Latin American statistics offices did not seem to have heard of it. Gender statistics have not yet been incorporated as a subject area into official statistics. CESD-Madrid, which supports statistics-related training in Latin America and the Caribbean, offered a seminar on indicators concerning women in March 1995.

At the international level, more significant advances have been made. International bodies appear to be more permeable to the agreements and recommendations subscribed to by governments. From a brief summary made by the United Nations[6] it may be concluded that there has been 'considerable evolution in the statistics available about women and men, and in the way of presenting these effectively, but the main needs that have arisen as a result of the newly emerging tasks are also indicated'. These results could be observed in the NGO Forum on Women held in Beijing, during which workshops on gender statistics were organized and national and regional publications were presented, as well as the world publication we just quoted from. There was a comparative regional volume for Latin America in the series *Mujeres latinoamericanas en cifras*, which compiled national volumes from 19 countries and was carried out without resorting to official statistical services.[7]

The advances in training and methodology that have been made relatively recently are also important. The contributions made by the International Research and Training Institute for the Promotion of Women (INSTRAW) and the Statistics Division of the United Nations Secretariat should be highlighted.

PROPOSAL FOR THE CONSTRUCTION OF GENDER STATISTICS

To recapitulate, the process of constructing gender statistics is still incipient in most Latin American and Caribbean countries and has not been given priority by the official bodies in charge of producing statistics. The mandates ratified make it clear that these organizations should already have taken steps to construct gender statistics and that they should take charge of their coordination even if the data-gathering is carried out by different government bodies.

We now analyse the way to construct a process of production of gender statistics and in order to do so we base our work on the proposal developed by Statistics Sweden in its gender statistics unit and published in *Engendering Statistics. A Tool for Change* (Hedman et al.). The Swedish experience set down by these three authors (F. Perucci, one of them, is from the UN Statistics Division) has been decisive at an international level, since Statistics Sweden has cooperated in this area with training and technical assistance in several African, Asian and Latin American countries.

According to these three authors, the basic components in order to compile gender statistics are the following:

- selection of the themes to be investigated;
- identification of the statistics that need to be collected in order to reflect gender concerns;
- formulation of concepts and definitions that adequately reflect the diversity of women and men in society, in all aspects of their lives, to be used for the data gathering;
- development of data-gathering methods, taking into account the cultural and social factors and stereotypes that might determine gender biases;
- development of data analysis and presentation that can be easily understood by those who design policies or undertake planning, and by the general public.

The proposal mentioned presents the key components involved in such a process, discussed at length by the authors. The production of gender statistics is presented as a social and dynamic process in which both producers and users participate, and without whose mutual interaction it would not be possible to improve statistics, much less for them to be useful in transforming the world. We will now refer to some ideas developed on the basis of the scheme and proposals made by Hedman et al.

The project of social change   A gender statistics system is a coherent set of statistical information, desegregated per sex, which allows recognition and measurement of the disparities in opportunities encountered by men and women in various aspects of their lives. The data are produced and presented in order to reflect the conditions under which men and women struggle, their contributions to society, and their specific needs and problems.

As with any other information system, the need arises for a conceptual framework that identifies the relevant subject areas and explains the state of the art regarding the issues to be considered. Gender statistics are organized on the basis of a project to change women's circumstances with respect to men's, and in contemplation of the main, most discussed issues at the national level. As confirmed by a compilation made by FLACSO,[8] most countries have state agencies specializing in women, or women's programmes, lodged within the ministries in charge of subject areas such as education, health, agriculture, work, justice and so on. The power of each national project to effect social transformations is decided by the interaction of civil society with the official agencies entrusted with gender issues. The types of social transformations promoted will depend on the level of awareness of women in the particular country and on the approach taken by the government in question.

Theoretical explanations of women's subordinate status and discussions on ways to combat such discrimination also influence the design of gender statistics. This corresponds to the advances made in the use of the gender approach, which also penetrate and help formulate the demands for information.

Magdalena León refers to the debate taking place recently with respect to the gender-in-development approach (GID), centring on women's practical and strategic interests translated into the planning of development.[9] Quoting Molyneux, Moser and Young, León distinguishes between the practical, referring to women's material condition, and the strategic, which modifies women's status or conditions with respect to men, or to their subordinate position in society. The practical level can well have transformation potential and one of the types of transformation that can take place is women's *empowerment* (women gaining control over their lives, attaining the ability to do things and defining their own activities). This leads to the observation of the central position that power and its various manifestations have. A consequence of this for statistics is the pressing demand for gender indicators together with the shortage of theory needed to develop such measurements. Another consequence is that the need to differentiate between practical and strategic needs, between the condition of being a woman and the situation of being a woman, may find a parallel in the need to distinguish between 'practical' and 'strategic' statistics and indicators.

A proposal that reflects these distinctions from the perspective of the indicators used classifies them according to either those indicators that measure how a situation affected by gender evolves, expressing only a change in level or degree (for example, the rate of female participation in the labour market), or to those measuring a change in gender roles or in the expression of patriarchal ideology (changes in the sexual division of labour, for instance).[10]

Cooperation between users and producers The relation and cooperation between the users and producers of gender statistics allows us to identify the statistical needs in the different fields with some accuracy. Involving users with expertise on the subject in question and users with knowledge of gender issues is important. Gender studies have advanced irregularly, which means that information needs are just beginning to be assessed in some cases.

Once the needs are identified, a selection is made from the existing statistics, their sources and the quality of the data, according to the use and interpretation desired. A test of this procedure, not involving the active participation of the users, was carried out in some programmatic areas in Chile. Using some theoretical considerations as a starting point, to explain how the traceable topics were selected, a list of information needs was drafted for each area. The list contained indicators that were then confronted with an inventory of the statistical sources available. Existing knowledge and gaps in information were highlighted. This academic exercise is a guideline for the cooperation between statistics users and producers, and helps determine the availability and short-comings of statistics, evaluating them and making recommendations. In the annex, a list of indicators for the subject 'Work in Chile' is included, quoted from this source.

A more elaborate proposal is found in the work quoted by Hedman et al. Based on an issue expressing a relatively significant disparity, a classification of the different statistics and indicators needed is made, according to the clusters of underlying causes and the clusters of consequences and effects involved in the problem under study. Taking the example of occupational segregation in the labour force, since women are found to be in occupations having a lower status, it proposes the following clusters of causes:

- sexual segregation in education;
- unequal distribution of responsibilities in the family unit;
- women's reproductive role;
- prejudices and stereotypes held by employers;
- individual preferences and choices with respect to occupation, according to sex.

The following clusters of consequences are indicated:

- salary gaps according to sex;
- sex-differentiated career opportunities; and
- differences in participation at decision-making levels according to sex.

All of these points are accompanied by proposals for the statistics and indicators needed to explore their magnitude and evolution.

Cooperation to improve the conceptual and methodological framework of statistics The results found by comparing available statistics and those identified as needed but lacking supply the basis for constructing gender-sensitive statistics. Gaps and lack of quality in the available data can be identified thus. Other aspects can also be reinforced during the process.

It is important to review concepts and measuring guidelines, improve classification systems and develop methodologies for each subject area. Measuring something statistically requires concepts that are defined as precisely as possible, since such concepts will be replicated countless times by those making surveys or gathering data, and by respondents themselves. The massive nature of statistical work exposes it to the dangers of gender biases, sexual stereotypes and behaviour determined by the sexual division of roles. Those who collect data or carry out surveys can be trained and made aware of these biases, but not those who supply the basic information.

Users make their main contribution by helping to define concepts and, in doing so, by raising gender awareness among those who produce statistics. These, in turn, must review the whole process of data gathering, processing and analysis, remaining alert for the sexual stereotypes that can ruin or bias their work.

Analysis and publication of available statistics It is possible to obtain a mass of information segregated per sex, structured according to the topics first defined from the statistics available. This constitutes the raw material for gender-sensitive publications. Although the forms may widely vary according to the target group, gender statistics have a number of things in common.

To begin with, they are organized in the areas defined by traditional statistics, such as population, health, education, employment, income, and to which new aspects or aspects seen from different vantage points are added, such as power and sphere of influence, child care, families, time use, non-remunerated work, violence and criminality, population and environment, legislation, organizations and social participation. Gender-specific issues are also involved, such as types of families, household heads, sexual harassment at work, care of the elderly.

In the second place, one way or another they must all deal with the interrelation among variables. For example, are relations in the home part of demographics, time use or paid versus unpaid work? This interrelation is also expressed in the fact that such publications usually involve the cooperation of various national (the case of *Les Femmes* edited in France by INSEE, Institut National de la Statistique et des Etudes Economiques 1995) or international institutions (the case of *The World's Women 1995. Trends and Statistics*, United Nations, NY 1995).

These types of publications are among the first products of gender statistics. Although they are comparable to other statistical subject matter as far as the design of other types of products are concerned, there are specificities related to the way in which gender statistics are disseminated. Some products are geared to users with gender and statistical expertise. Others must be designed for users with no previous gender knowledge. Then the desire is simply to communicate to all how women and men fare in society or in regard to some specific area. Clear and simple designs, large-scale print runs and a wide variety of topics all form part the communicational strategy that producers of gender statistics need to adopt.

DIFFICULTIES ENCOUNTERED IN NATIONAL STATISTICS SYSTEMS

It is surprising to observe the resistance encountered when a subject such as gender, which affects everyone in their public and private, social, family and individual lives, needs to be approached, discussed and given priority to as a relevant theme.

The more professional type of knowledge and the new theories developed in gender studies seem to be confined within a circle of specialists who do not fully manage to communicate with one another.

Lack of interest among the directors and professionals in charge of national statistical systems is aggravated by the difficulties listed in the following paragraphs.

In the first place, no priority mandates emanate from the highest authorities directly in charge of statistical services. If initiatives do not stem from the authorities at the top levels, they do not arise either from within the systems themselves, because of the lack of awareness and sensitivity among the top management, since gender is not a priority theme for them. They make no effort, as leaders, to promote the subject among the rest of those who produce statistics. The argument for vertical relations between top managerial levels is based on the notion that public services are usually supplied by hierarchic, vertically structured bodies.

To the above must added the lack of knowledge and information about what might and should be done, and the lack of specific proposals to begin guiding the production of gender statistics. Resistance in the form of prejudice, *machista* biases and misconceptions is fed by the lack of specialized expertise available to respond to gender demands, the lack of sensitive gender-trained personnel and the lack of gender awareness still to be found at top managerial levels among professionals and technicians alike.

Another type of difficulty stems from the way in which statistical systems are structured. The dispersion of statistical production among several ministries or divisions makes the task of reaching their producers and raising their awareness more difficult. It breaks up statistics, because these agencies develop separate, specialized measurements corresponding to their different subjects, requiring a 'tailor-made' awareness for each agency. It multiplies the need for statistics, because it makes the demands for coordination among the different branches grows. This makes it harder to define who is responsible for gathering the data corresponding to the new subject areas proposed.

As a consequence, no finances and no internal organization are available to undertake the necessary tasks.

Some advances have been made that help to break down the prevailing inertia. One is the appearance of official users, such as women's offices or ministries, which are inserted into the public sector and have sufficient power and influence for their demands to be satisfied. In addition, the fact that some women's programmes have adopted plans in favour of women's equality facilitates the start of a process of improvement with respect to statistics.

Besides official users, women and men with gender awareness have created informal networks inside and outside the state apparatus, and these people are willing to cooperate with each other and with their users. Finally, international cooperation is creating outlets that allow taking advantage of the technical support, finances and training it has to offer.

SUGGESTIONS FOR ACTION

From the experiences undergone in other countries or by international organizations, we can extract some suggestions for producers of official statistics wishing to begin or continue the production of gender statistics.

- To publish national statistical reports on women's situation on a regular basis. In some countries, this is done in an inter-institutional and inter-disciplinary manner (France). In others, it is done under the responsibility of the Bureau of Statistics (Sweden). This is the most effective way to begin dealing with the subject. Organizing a publication of this type is a good reason to follow the steps previously described: defining subject areas, detecting gaps and inconsistencies, making an effort to unite what remains dispersed, publishing formerly unavailable gender-related data, linking various subject areas, offering the relevant information and ultimately achieving a new product.
- To unite producers around the improvement of statistical production related to gender, such as:
  - desegregation of data gathering and handling, and publication per sex;
  - rallying of consensus around concepts and classifications;
  - collection and comparison of information from different sources, in order to test validity and consistency; and
  - elimination of duplicated efforts.

Through such actions producers of statistics continue to work towards the design of a plan that will improve gender statistics. Further possibilities are:
  - incorporation of the conceptual advances in each subject area, in order to measure the situations under which men and women live better;
  - new joint records and surveys, and allocation of responsibilities in new areas of statistic collection; and

- research needed to reveal the sexist bias inherent in data gathering and processing and proposals to eliminate such biases.
- To create national associations of producers who periodically review the state of the art of gender statistics.
- To make the organizational changes required in carrying out the newly defined tasks as part of the services provided by producers.
- To give space and priority to a training plan in gender statistics for statisticians and those who register primary data: administrative personnel and surveyors.

ANNEX *An exercise in the production of statistics and indicators in keeping with the demands expressed in the labour field*

The necessary themes in relation with the demands: the themes found in diagnoses, proposals and requests relative to women's work may be grouped under the following topics, with which the indicators listed below may be associated:

1. *Measurement of unpaid work and its interrelation with paid work*

1.1 Visualization of the work performed within the home:
- Estimate of the value of domestic work as a share of the Gross National Product.
- Studies on time allocation by women and men and distribution of domestic chores: number of hours devoted to domestic work per sex and quantification of total workload for men and for women.
- Linkage between time use and: socio-economic level, presence of children, age of children etc.
- Types of household chores performed by men and women.
- Participation of male and female children in domestic chores.
- Opinions of sons and daughters about the participation of the father and mother in domestic chores.
- Use of existing social facilities for child care and care of the elderly: coverage at nurseries and kindergartens, potential population and available places.
- Children in nurseries and kindergartens, per sex and per age, according to socio-economic strata and the occupation of their parents.
- Electrical appliances in the home and their distribution.
- Staff, per sex, employed to do paid domestic work in or outside the home.

1.2 Inter-connection with paid work.
- Absence from work and causes, per sex.
- Use of maternal benefits, per activity branch, and relation with total female employment.

2. *Level of participation in the labour market and its changes*
- Rates of labour participation per sex and age.
- Estimates of rates according to differentiated factors such as education, number and age of children, urban or rural areas.
- Follow-up of rate of labour participation among spouses, in order to measure cultural changes.
- Average duration of economically active life, according to sex.
- Part-time work per socio-professional category, per occupational category, for single or married women with or without children.
- Duration of unemployment: average duration in months, proportion with duration of one year or more, per sex.
- Reasons for not working, per sex.

3. *Visibility of women's contribution to market production*
- Female participation rate in branches according to dynamism of branch.
- Absence from work and reasons: link between absenteeism and sex, age, occupational level (greater absenteeism at lower occupational level).
- Quantification of non-declared work: surveys made among unemployed.

4. *Gender discrimination in the labour market*
- Concentration in branches per sex: what branches are 80 per cent of the women concentrated in, and what branches are 80 per cent of the men concentrated in?
- Measurement of sexual segregation in the labour market; male and female participation per branch and per occupation.
- Measurement of segregation per level: female and male participation in higher echelons of occupational hierarchies.
- Proportion of women employers, per enterprise size and per branch of activity.

5. *Vulnerable work and unprotected forms of employment according to sex*

- Sub-employment rate per sex.
- Participation in the informal, or non-structured, sector per sex.
- Quantity of personnel hired (and proportion of women) and quantity of non-remunerated working relatives (and proportion of women).
- Proportion of female labour force occupied in domestic service in the home, as an indicator of the quality of work available to a given group of women and, at the same time, as an indicator of how domestic work needs are solved in the home.
- Average duration of work shift and distribution of labour force according to duration of work shift per sex.
- Proportion and regularity of temporary work, classification of temporary jobs according to production phases or types of contract: fees, training, substitutes (replacements), temporary workers, apprentices, scholarships, subcontracts for fixed terms, average duration of temporary contracts, per sex.
- Temporary work/regularity: work with no contract, piecemeal work in the home, per sex.
- Distribution of those working, according to modalities of work, per sex.
- Number of people who carry out more than one job, per sex.

6. *Working conditions*

- Proportion of wage earners, per sex, per working contract, with insurance.
- Assessment of physical and health conditions.
- Assessment of unfavourable environmental factors: noise, exposure to dust, extreme temperatures, accidents at the workplace.
- Statistics overseeing working conditions and types of omissions sanctioned.
- Sexual harassment at work.
- Opinions of workers about their working conditions: autonomy, initiative, responsibility, level of communication, pressure to perform, physical workload and new technologies.

7. *Income derived from work and economic participation*

- Average salary ratio per sex.
- Average income ratio for the self-employed per sex.

- Total income distribution per sex.
- Occupational pyramid according to income level and male/female participation
- Income per hour and per sex, in order to desegregate the effect of different work shifts.

Source: Taken from Gálvez, T. (ed.) (1997) *Propuestas para un sistema de estadísticas de género*, Instituto Nacional de Estadísticas de Chile and UNICEF, Regional Office for Argentina, Chile and Uruguay, Santiago de Chile.

NOTES

1. Thelma Gálvez is an economist and was technical sub-director of Chile's National Statistics Institute. She currently works as a consultant.

2. Classification of statistical subject areas according to the *The International Statistics Guide*, UN, New York, 1984.

3. Paragraph 190 of the Declaration and Action Platform adopted by the Fourth World Conference on Women: Equality, Development and Peace, in Beijing, 1995, states that: 'The institutions in charge of national and international statistics have not been able to resolve how to present the issues pertaining to the equal treatment of women and men in the economic and social spheres. In particular not enough use is being made of existing databases and of the methodologies used in the fundamental sphere of decision taking.'

4. Hedman, B., F. Perucci and P. Sundström (1966) *Engendering Statistics. A Tool for Change*, Sweden.

5. Final report of the Meeting of Statistics Directors of the Americas, November 1992; joint OAS/ECLAC meeting on the subject of statistics, October 1994; final report of the second joint OAS/ECLAC meeting on the subject of statistics, October 1996.

6. United Nations (1995) *Situación de la mujer en el mundo, 1995. Tendencias y estadísticas*.

7. Teresa Valdés and Enrique Gomariz (coordinators) (1995) *Mujeres latino-americas en cifras*, comparative volume, Spanish Ministry of Social Affairs-Women's Institute and Latin American Faculty of Social Sciences, FLACSO, Santiago de Chile.

8. Valdés and Gomariz.

9. León, M. (1998) 'Empoderamiento: relaciones de las mujeres con el poder', *Revista Foro* No. 33, December 1997–January 1998.

10. Galvez, T. (ed.) (1997) *Propuestas para un sistema de estadisticas de genero*, Santiago: INE–UNICEF.

PART TWO

Gender and the State

CHAPTER 9

Gender and the State: Between Disenchantment and Hope

MARIA CRISTINA ROJAS AND
ELVIA CARO[1]

§ Academics and feminist activists question the role of the state *vis-à-vis* women's achievements and limitations regarding equality, as well as their own position before the state. Echoing Sonia Álvarez's words,[2] the central questions are whether 'feminists should approach the state or not, get involved with/in the state'; whether 'a policy of change implying the broadening of women's citizenship can be promoted from within the state itself'; whether 'we should propose having specialised women/gender bodies or just incorporating a gender perspective into global policies' and whether 'we should reject, co-operate with or critically assess what these agencies do once created' (1998: 1).

Rather than answer these questions, the objective of this chapter is to draw a map of some of the conceptual approaches on the subject of gender and the state. Contrasting visions of the state and of women's role in it are implicit in these concepts. The answers also fluctuate between hope and disenchantment, as so many things pertaining to women do.

This chapter presents four of the conceptual approaches used to interpret the link between gender and the state. These approaches are not presented in a hierarchical way, nor are they mutually exclusive. Each one, from its own standpoint, seeks to explain a highly complex relationship.

THE STATE AS A REPRODUCER OF GENDER RELATIONS

One of the first debates concerning the relation between gender and the state takes place around the discussion of the state's purported neutrality in the design of public policies. The opposing view is that the state promotes certain interests given its role in a capitalist and patriarchal society. In this debate, Marxist authors have held that the state reproduces capitalist relations in production. Raising a parallel discussion, Marxist feminists developed the concept of the patriarchal state, in order to demonstrate that states reproduce gender roles and disparities by acting in the public sphere as substitutes for male domination in the private sphere. Some of the arguments that favour this *reproductivist* approach of the state are very convincing. Its supporters contend that the sexual division of labour assigns roles to women in the private sphere (child care and domestic work) and that the policies related to salaries and social conditions are based on the model of the male breadwinner. This model has served as a pretext to justify wage differences and differential treatment within the same social security system.

Linda Gordon[3] summarizes the disenchanted part of this *reproductivist* vision of the state, when she affirms that 'arguing that the state acts objectively to maintain male dominance, suggests *either* that women have never progressed and we are not much better off than we were a century ago, which invariably contradicts all the evidence, *or* defines male supremacy so as to include in it all the concessions made to women, which would amount to a tautological argument'. Without doubt, the most common criticism of the *reproductivist* vision of the state is that it ignores the fact that some state policies have managed to transform some male-dominated relations. This approach also obscures the contributions women make to such transformations.

GENDER-NEUTRALITY AND DISTENSION IN PUBLIC POLICY

An advance in the discussion on the relation between gender and the state is the application of the concept of the state's *relative autonomy*. This concept, developed by Nicos Poulantzas, looks at the state not as a monolithic unit but as an apparatus that reflects and condenses the contradictions inherent in a society divided into classes. Thus the state acts as a factor of class cohesion. It can settle disputes and formulate policies internally with a certain degree of autonomy, in accordance with the balance of social forces. To the degree that the state reflects class contradictions, its *relative autonomy* hinges on the balance between social forces.

Magdalena León's work[4] can be located within the context of this approach. She distances herself from the position that the state and its policies represent a mechanism to control women characterizing it as patriarchal, seeing the state, instead, as a complex network of power relations whose legitimacy is partly determined by its ability to include class, ethnic origin and gender interests. For the state, this means making concessions to the groups exerting pressure to advance their demands. For women's groups, it means understanding the context and the pull of social forces, expressing and achieving the representation of their interests.

León introduces the concepts of *gender-neutrality and distension*, seeking to explain 'the emergence of signs of political will to formulate women's programmes and projects among governments ... and the structural difficulties inherent, for states, in formulating macro policies that promote changes geared to women' (p. 34). The concept of *gender distension* is defined 'as a way of aiming at the process that is being consolidated in public policies, tending to reduce the tension around the subject of gender expressly and directly ... [which implies] that a tense or friction-ridden situation already existed ... framed within the alleged neutrality of policies, which led to the denial of unequal gender relations' (p. 38). Latin American states are *gender-neutral* at the level of macro-economic and macro-social policies but they practice *gender distension* in certain specific actions geared to women, particularly since 1975.

The state therefore represents a double dimension, as a vehicle of change and as a system of control over women's lives. Viewed as a vehicle of change, public policy is susceptible to change within certain limits, through factors of a structural nature that govern state actions. These factors influence the political will to implement changes associated with several traits, such as the state's limited function, given the social marginalization typical of contemporary neo-liberal states. The rigidity and hierarchization of the state apparatus, with its heavy bureaucratization and clientele-like practices, allows room for very few new policies. Finally, the sexual division pervading social relations and manifest in the state's institutional inertia does not favour changes in how tasks are allocated to men and women within the family or in society. In spite of such limitations, public policies can promote women's interests under certain circumstances.

Several factors may be identified when attempting to make a synthesis of the process of distension taking place within states. There is the commitment of states to several UN initiatives, such as the International Convention for the Elimination of All Forms of Discrimination Against

Women and the world conferences on women. Many countries are also undergoing economic and social crises that force large groups of women, whose very survival is under threat, to pressure the state. Their proposals are beginning to be taken into account in the drafting of public policies. The Latin American women's movement is an important factor in the promotion of these demands, which initially were for civil and political rights and then tackled labour rights, human rights and various specific feminist claims.[5]

Magdalena León affirms that the purported presence of gender-neutrality has led to macro-economic policies that disregard women's interests during the current changes, as well as ignoring the consequences of these policies for women. The state has taken some positive actions towards gender distension throughout the region, mostly channelled via several institutional schemes and sectorial plans and a large amount of specific projects. These projects view women as an objective of social policy, just when the social dimension is being crowded out in favour of planning and resource allocation. The regional controversy taking place at the moment about women's projects shows the difficulty and complexity of regarding such projects as the only way to raise gender awareness. It also shows the diversity of women's interests, which also fluctuate, over time, according to the social context.

The last problem we will focus on here concerns the divergence between state policies based on a gamut of projects for women and the integration of projects and programmes that may affect mainstream development, rethinking development itself in the light of women's interests. In accordance with this, 'the integration of macro policies makes sense, as long as gender differences are always taken into account ... the real social differences existing between men and women ... (as well as) the sexual division of labour on the material, cultural and symbolic planes alike; and of course accepting that global development projects refusing to consider this set of facts may contribute to reproducing women's subordination' (p. 42).

The main question in the debate about macro or micro projects 'is the potential that a particular policy or project has to alter or reproduce the sexual division of labour ... It is an alternative for the women's social movement to participate in the state, accepting that the patriarchal state is not so monolithic and all-encompassing that it cannot alter its own logic according to the requirements of the different forces and circumstances required for its reproduction' (p. 42).

Magdalena León's work is a significant advance in analysing the relations between gender, the state and public policies, due to its recognition of the fact that the state also has non-monolithic features, and that a rich variety of approaches, and even contradictions, exist when policies geared to women are drafted. Disenchantment is reflected in the structural limits encountered, which simply do not allow women's programmes and projects, or women's participation in politics, to bring about effective changes, since 'it is not the sex of the actors, but the gender system that must change'. This points to the institutional changes needed in order to both carry out gender analysis and formulate policies with the potential of transforming gender relations in society and culture.

The *relative autonomy* approach has some intrinsic difficulties, since it uses a combination of structural and circumstantial factors. It also tends to find socio-centric explanations, displaying a strong bias for what actually takes place in society. Usually it ignores the autonomous role that states can play in drafting public policies and in the design of independent actions that integrate the interests of specific groups.[6]

Finally, introducing processes of constitution of subjects through discursive strategies can establish great dependence on social mobilization to achieve transformations.[7]

THE STATE AS A CONSTITUENT PART OF GENDER RELATIONS

Instead of assuming that the state is a neutral instrument, or that it simply reproduces relations of inequality, defenders of this approach look at the forms and circumstances that make it possible for states to formulate independent policies with the capacity to transform gender relations. More than searching for homogeneous answers and making generalizations, some of this stream's female researchers seek to identify the differences between countries in the drafting of specific policies, in the assignation of subsidies to single mothers and female breadwinners, in maternity leave and abortion legislation. In this connection it is fitting to ask, for example, why some states decree measures that encourage women's incorporation into paid work, while others try to *discourage* them.

This approach centres on the state and, in particular, its capacity to draft and implement policies that can affect women positively. The state is seen as an actor having its own interests and thus also the capacity to act independently. Those who support this approach believe that public policies do not simply reflect the interests of the various actors in civil society, but that interests and circumstances within the state itself induce the differences in the type of policies pursued.

Two important proposals converge here: that the state itself is an actor, and that the state and its policies shape gender relations. At the same time gender relations also shape the nature of the state. Ann Orloff, one of the main defenders of this approach, argues that 'understanding the state and politics without gender is as impossible as understanding the family and the economy without gender'.[8]

The state not only has the capacity to act with autonomy; the policies it promotes also have an impact on gender relations. From this point of view, no such things as neutral policies exist, since the nature and definition of the state also affects how policies are drafted. As Jane Lewis[9] illustrates, not only wage policies but also policies on welfare and non-remunerated work affect how women join the labour market. In Great Britain, for example, policies hinge on men as the main breadwinners and there are fewer child care facilities. This may explain why women often have part-time jobs there. The socio-democratic Scandinavian states have moved towards policies that presume that two people earn the family income. This motivates women to join the labour force by making use of double exemption tax policies or 'maternity' leave for either fathers or mothers. Such states also provide enough and adequate child care services. Conservative-entrepreneurial states such as Germany and France, on the other hand, promote subsidiary relations with other members of the family, reinforcing female dependency on the family. In liberal states such as the United States, women's progress has been subordinated to the market.

The theoretical approximation of the state as a *constituent part of gender relations* also allows examining the effects of public policies on women's political activity and the role carried out by feminist reformers with respect to the integration of progressive policies. Theda Scopkol's analysis[10] of the welfare level shows the existence of 'paternalistic' and 'maternalistic' welfare states, whose organizations influence the way in which their citizens relate to the state. The former, generally European, have structured their programmes around male workers organized in trade unions or labour parties. In 'maternalistic' welfare states, such as the United States, social institutions tended to be dominated by women when it came to implementing welfare programmes for women.

Comparative analyses of states and their gender relations also allow us to understand why groups of women who are organized in similar fashions can produce radically different policies, as Jane Jenson describes in her comparative study on France and Great Britain.[11] According to her, a wide range of factors influenced how policies were formulated: among others, population concerns (low birth rates and high mortality rates within the context of the threat of war), the ensuing maternity discourse and the workers' association capacity.

Social forces promote policies in different directions also, as Penderson illustrates in a comparative study on the balance of power between workers, employers and the state in France and Great Britain.[12] According to this study,

> men workers wanted women to be their wives, men employers wanted women to be their workers (cheap and submissive labour), women themselves wanted to be recognised as mothers or as workers ... the rank and file of the British and French trade unions preferred their wives to keep outside the labour market ... Given the capitalistic and strong state that France is and the strength of its working class, and the slightly less powerful British state, the French state yielded its authority over women to those who wished to exploit them, and the British state yielded its authority over women to those who wished to exclude them.

Within the approach that considers the state as an agent affecting gender relations, it is also possible to include variations with respect to a differentiation among women through characteristics involving class, ethnic group, race or religion. In this context, Fiona Williams's work is worth highlighting. According to Williams, the conditions under which British women were able to join the labour force were different for white working-class women from those for Afro-Caribbean women. While the first joined the labour market under conditions that did not interfere with their domestic circumstances, the second, who arrived in England as migrants, were forced to take on full-time jobs. They worked irregular shifts or night shifts that were not even legal by labour regulations: 'the immigrants were treated as working units more than as individuals having their own welfare needs, and since it was assumed that they had arrived voluntarily, no special provision was made for low-cost housing or for childcare'.[13] Welfare policies in the United States were influenced by the fear of extending citizenship rights to new migrants and the Afro-American population.

Although the theoretical approach that the state affects gender relations is an important contribution, it is worth pointing out some of the fallacies of this approach. The first flaw lies in the approach itself, which stresses two analyses: studying social policies, the welfare state being the reference point, but leaving out economic policies and their impact on gender, and analysing the decisions taken in high government spheres or by groups of organized women. Both tend to ignore subordinate voices such as those of grassroots organizations. The second flaw is external to the approach and has to do with what Robert Cox calls the purpose of theory.[14] The question about the state's capacity to act independently seeks to solve the problems related to the conditions that increase or inhibit the effectiveness of gender policies in order to maximize their power to transform. Applying the two types of purposes, as Cox proposes, the attempt would be to leap from the question of what gender is and how gender policies work, to the question of how the present institutional order was created and which factors can transform it. More specifically, the approach of the state as a constituent part of gender relations does not explain why and how the state awards itself the right to represent the interests of subordinate groups and in what way these groups are *reinterpreted* in and outside the state.

GENDER POLICIES AS INSTITUTIONALIZED INTERPRETATIVE SYSTEMS

Interpretative approaches are the result of two types of theoretical considerations, with the result that the paradigm used to reflect on politics undergoes a revolution. The first proposal comes from the post-structuralist stream, concretely the philosophy of Michel Foucault. This author shifted the theoretical discussion about the state from its being a problem of jurisdictional sovereignty to its being a problem involving domination practices and techniques. Foucault also referred to the microphysics of power, through which the study of power is privileged from the extremities towards the centre. The various forms of power are related to the way in which the discourse is organized and to how knowledge is produced and generated. A second proposal stems from feminist theory and, in particular, from how the subject of identity, understood in essentialist terms, is questioned. In this approach, the subject is what it means to be a woman, and these concepts are linked at the same time to the subject of women's subordination, as is the case when reproduction and the feminine are identified with the private sphere. In this way, large areas of the political universe are excluded and the benefits women gain from the state are as limited as those linked to labour.

Following the Marxist tradition, Nancy Fraser provides a theoretical contribution by attempting to make a synthesis between post-structuralism and feminism, to which she adds her concern regarding the effects of the yielding of power on social inequality. The approximation that Fraser makes to the subject of 'satisfaction of needs', as object of the intervention directed towards women, reflects this triple synthesis.[15] Fraser advocates a change in approach, in which not only the satisfaction of needs is catered for, but there is also a 'policy of interpretation of these needs'. The discourse on the needs to be satisfied, and the institutions and experts that are to be in charge of doing this, is the product of a struggle in which groups of various discursive capacities compete with each other in order to make their own interpretation prevail. It is this interpretative discourse that allows some needs to be de-politicized, others hidden or simply left in the hands of the experts to be resolved.

For Fraser, policies are *institutionalized interpretative systems* that construct women and their needs according to certain arguable interpretations. The programmes have cultural effects upon the ways of solving the 'problems' and 'needs' of poor women and upon how a differentiated citizenship is (re)constructed according to gender, class, race and sexuality, as is the case with Black and Latin women in North American society.

For her part, Sonia Álvarez makes a valuable contribution to the interpretative perspective. In '¿En qué estado está el feminismo? Reflexiones teóricas y perspectivas comparativas'[16] Álvarez explores the concept of the state as an organization that creates new meanings – among these that of gender – maintaining an internally contradictory and polyphonic discourse with frequent shifts in perspective, which may range from power relations to complementarity between the sexes, and from emphasis on women's rights to negotiation in order to make the interests of the whole family compatible.

This work inspires us to a lucid disenchantment regarding the state's gender policy. In her words,

> each time, there are more and more feminists looking towards the state as the arena in which to promote changes in unequal gender relations ... those acting from a feminist perspective are revising their former practices ... towards states that now appear to be speaking their own language ... and that have taken up the promotion of gender equity [through] an impressive number of policies and programmes supposedly aimed at improving women's conditions ... and the creation of specialised

machinery designed to foster and monitor gender programmes and policies. (p. 3)

Álvarez warns against the effects of having gender become a mere fad in countries aspiring to 'modernity', showing how the feminist critique of women's subordination takes on a completely different meaning in the state's discourse. The same thing is happening with the use of the 'gender perspective' discourse, which mitigates clashes and ideological confrontation by making use of analytical categories that portray no existential or political commitment. For some public servants, 'gender' seems more a term for technical planning jargon, a neutral indicator of 'modernity' and 'development' than 'a terrain or domain heavily mined with unequal power relations between men and women' (p. 5).

By the same token, the 'New Agenda of Public Policies', promoted on a worldwide scale by liberal economics and liberal democratic theory, tries to create a sense of 'comfort' with some proposals made by the women's movement and to foster interest in the recent official concern with gender issues. A series of national and local government policies has increased the demand for women and gender specialists, especially those involving actions oriented to 'vulnerable populations'. Local and international feminists are becoming more appreciated for their technical capacity, and as key state partners in modernization programmes, than as members of civil society organizations or of feminist movements whose objective it is to promote women's full citizenship. The problem of cooperating with the state is that these organizations rarely participate in the orientation and design of plans, particularly when it comes to working with grassroots women and interpreting and articulating their needs. Participation is usually limited to providing training with a gender perspective, an activity that is fast becoming a genuine growth industry (p. 7).

The new meanings that the state attributes to discourse have their most graphic expression in the policies for 'vulnerable women', those notoriously excluded from the mainstream development model. In this context, the author exposes the forms adopted by the state to regulate the fertility, sexuality and morality of poor women, by redefining their productive and reproductive roles in the name of gender equity. From a feminist perspective, these programmes have little relation with the *empowerment*, equality or citizenship of grassroots women. This is obvious in the new welfare policy of the current United States administration, which prescribes as the state panacea for black and poor women that they 'take "personal responsibility" for the improvement of their living conditions' (Personal Responsibility Act 1996). This norm *requires* poor and unmarried mothers to join the labour market and stop depending on the state (to stop being *welfare mothers)* through *workfare* jobs: work that is not of a permanent nature and has very low standards. The work makes no tough demands on these women but it also does not upgrade their training or working skills. Poor married women and mothers not depending on public welfare have the right to work from home or outside the home, which goes to show that for the state the problem is the women's dependence on the state, not their dependence on their husbands.

Likewise, the new *welfare* legislation in the United States attempts to regulate the sexuality and 'morality' of poor women/mothers, imposing strict conditions on childbearing out of wedlock, such as forcing women to reveal the paternity of their children in order to receive benefits, and to cooperate with welfare agencies in order to make them pay child support. This forces poor women to have contact with the fathers of their children whether or not these men represent a threat of violence to them or to their children: 'The rules about the determination of paternity compel poor mothers to reveal their private affairs in exchange for money or medical assistance, being forced to answer questions about who they've had intercourse with, how many times, how, where and when' (p. 19).

The above leads Álvarez to the conclusion that 'the state is a site of discursive-cultural production, a crucial site in which gender and citizenship are constructed, gender (and/or class, race and sexual) relations are re-signified, re-coded and shaped ... [which has] consequences for the chances that different "categories" of women have of gaining access to full citizenship and human dignity' (p. 20). The importance of this reflection for feminist practices is undeniable, as the author makes clear when she proposes that it is necessary to discard any type of liberal feminist strategy, in relation to the state, in which the state is viewed as a neutral actor in the organization of power relations based on gender, class, race or sexuality. As far as post-structuralist and Marxist feminists are concerned, 'gender-friendly' states promote policies having little to do with equality and even less with feminism. This creates the risk of surrendering to the state the normalization of such matters as reproductive rights, sexual liberty, affirmative action or female employment.

Sonia Álvarez's marked pessimism regarding the possibilities of becoming involved with the state is somewhat mitigated when she takes up the arguments of political-theory feminist Shirin Rai, concluding that feminists in the 'South' cannot afford the luxury of ignoring the state, since 'the state is simply there'. Cooperation must fulfil some requirements (pp. 21–5), while:

- avoiding Manichaean and instrumentalist visions of the state, paying attention to the political junctures that open points of access for feminists to promote policies that favour women;
- being alert to the ways in which the state (re)positions female subjects through the *institutional interpretative systems*, whether a specialized apparatus or greater 'opening to gender' exists or not;
- remaining wary and aware with respect to institutional and social representations;
- pondering the political consequences of the growing tendency among feminist NGOs to cooperate with the state – the delicate balance between their technical relation with the state and the more rebellious activities of the movement must be maintained;
- carrying out effective feminist lobbying and a constant process of 're-translation', through which the limitations of 'policies with a gender perspective' are questioned or contested by institutions, society and culture; and
- redrafting strategies and discourses that will fight the tendency to standardize feminism and render it harmless.

CONCLUSIONS

The objective of this work, to identify theoretical ways to explain or interpret the complex relation between gender and the state, or gender and public policies, led to a review of four approaches: the state as a reproducer of gender relations, the relative autonomy of the state, the state as a constituent part of gender relations, and the state as an institutionalized interpretative system. Factors that sometimes only allow limited analysis emerge in all four approaches. At other times, strategic analyses can be made to envision the linkage between gender and the state and guide the actions undertaken by the *women's social movement* towards their objective of transforming gender relations. The conclusions, likewise, originate in the various approaches.

The state is a vehicle of change   The state has a double dimension, as a vehicle of change and as a form of control over women's lives. It is possible to work with or within it, seeking ways to broaden the opportunities women have to apply the rights that claim. In the same manner, the supporters of this approach affirm that the state is not monolithic; it has cracks through which the demands posed by social forces can penetrate and the women's social movement can play a significant role in exerting this pressure. The state's legitimacy is partially determined by its ability to include class, ethnic and gender interests, indicating that the state can alter its own logic according to circumstances and to the forces exerting pressure to gain their demands.

States are not really neutral with respect to gender   The approaches reviewed allow us to infer that the state is not neutral, either because it reproduces conditions of inequality; or because it is a player defending its own interests and with the capacity to act autonomously; or because its policies influence gender, race, class and ethnic relations and sexuality; or because, within its interpretative schemes, it creates new meanings and it is a site of cultural-discursive production in which gender relations are shaped, allocated new meanings and new codes.

Representations are contestable   The state's representations/interpretations are questionable and may be contested, making it possible for a discursive feminist overseeing role, within or outside the state, to present alternative visions and articulations through dialogues with the state or by way of collective struggles. These standpoints require new proposals, both from academia and militant feminism, in order to overcome notions of the state as a simple reproducer of gender relations, as a homogeneous and all-encompassing instrument/apparatus and as a terrain far removed from class, ethnic and gender interests. It also requires re-examining the actions of women's civil society, one that keeps a check on the forms in which the state reinterprets and repositions female subjects and that remains alert to the political conditions that might open points of access for feminists to make policies more favourable to women.

'The state is simply there'   It does not matter how far women position themselves from it, what the state does exerts an influence on gender, ethnic and class relations. This has two types of implications. On the one hand, it is necessary to maintain a critical distance from the state, which means that it is important to know how it runs, in what ways the state restructures its social relations and what its own capacity to implement policies that affect women is. On the other hand, it is necessary to ponder deeply on the political consequences of the growing tendency,

observable among feminist NGOs, to cooperate with the state, in such a way that a balance is always maintained between their technical relation with the state and non-comformist activities. It is also important to carry out feminist lobbying stemming from a feminist 'retranslation' of positions and actions that leads to a re-elaboration of alternative feminist strategies and discourses.

States are not homogeneous In order to bring alternative strategies before the state, knowledge of the internal dynamics that states develop during the course of their political and democratic, economic, institutional and social processes is required, as well as of the external dynamics connected with the process of insertion into a globalized world. On the basis of this knowledge, it is necessary to propose comparative analyses that lead to identifying the limitations and potentials inherent in the undertakings of the (different kinds) of states, in order to promote equality between the genders. *There are no such things as formulas: only cracks to filter through.*

NOTES

1. Maria Cristina Rojas, professor at the Norman Paterson School of International Affairs, Ottawa, Canada; Elvia Caro, sociologist, MA, international consultant. Both authors are partners of the firm FUTURA Consultorías.

2. Álvarez, S. (1998) '¿En qué estado está el feminismo? Reflexiones teóricas y perspectivas comparativas', mimeo, Paper presented at the First International Seminar on Research Experiences from a Gender Perspective, National University of Colombia, Gender, Development and Women Studies Programme, April.

3. Gordon, L. (1990) 'The new feminist scholarship on the welfare state', in L. Gordon, *Women, the State and Welfare*, Madison: University of Wisconsin Press, p. 16.

4. León, M. (1993) 'El género en la política pública de América Latina: neutralidad y distensión', *Revista de Análisis Político*, IPRI, 20, Bogota, September–December.

5. The *women's social movement* includes a wide spectrum of groups with a diversity of approaches and action forms according to their various interests, contributing from their diversity to changes in public policy. This endeavour recognizes how complex the composition of the women's movement is and the differentiated action of NGOs and women's organizations in their struggles and demands, but it still does not seek to broaden the discussion.

6. A critique of this 'socio-centric' position appeared in a volume entitled *Bringing the State Back In*, ed. P. Evans, D. Rueschmayer and T. Skopcol, Cambridge: Cambridge University Press, 1985.

7. This is the key emphasis of the critique made by Ernesto Laclau and Chantal Mouffe in their book *Hegemony and Socialist Strategy*, London, New York: Verso, 1985.

8. Orloff, Ann Shola (1997) 'Relaciones de género y política social', in María Cristina Rojas and Adriana Delgado (eds), *Política social: desafíos y utopías*, Bogota: Universidad Javeriana, p. 156.

9. Lewis, Jane (1992) 'Gender and the Development of Welfare Regimes', *Journal of European Social Policy*, 2(3).

10. Skocpol, T. (1992) *Protecting Soldiers and Mothers: The Political Origin of Social Policy in the United States*, Cambridge, MA: Harvard University Press.

11. Jenson, J. (1986) 'Gender and reproduction: or babies and the state', *Studies in Political Economy* 20, Summer.

12. Penderson, quoted by Orloff, p. 167.

13. Willams, F. (1997) 'Raza, etnia, género y clase en los estados de bienestar: un marco de análisis comparativo', in *Papel político*, Javeriana University, April, Bogota, p. 63.

14. Robert Cox distinguishes between two types of purposes in one theory: 'problem-solving' and criticizing the framework, which makes part of the 'critical' theory. The first takes the world as it finds it and asks how its different parts can function together more effectively, given a source of problems previously identified. The critical purpose does not take as given the existence of institutions or power relations but questions them, examining their origin and their reason for being in the process of change. Cox, R. (1986) 'Social forces, states and world orders: beyond international relations theory', in R. O. Keohane, *Neorealism and Its Critics*, New York: Columbia University Press, p. 208.

15. Fraser, N. (1990) 'Struggle over needs: outline of a socialist-feminist critical theory of late-capitalist political culture', in L. Gordon, *Women, the State and Welfare*, Madison: University of Wisconsin Press.

16. Sonia Álvarez's work compiles the results of research done in Chile, Peru and Colombia in 1997, about 'the state of the movement and the movement of the state'. It was carried out among 130 women, many of them feminists currently working with the state or subcontracted by it to develop gender projects. Álvarez refers to some recent feminist theories about the post-welfare state in the United States, highlighting parallels between US programmes for poor women and some of the current policies with a gender perspective promoted by various Latin American governments.

CHAPTER 10

State Modernization, Institutional Change and Gender

ANNETTE BACKHAUS[1]

GENDER ON THE PUBLIC AGENDA

As long as the demands and expectations for change implying gender equality depend largely on the state's regulatory, compensatory or supervisory role, it is worthwhile to study the gender agenda and the mechanisms that facilitate or inhibit its implementation. It is also relevant to see how public institutions work. Far from being 'meek' policy executors, bureaucracies are living sets of values and attitudes that can activate, hinder or distort policies and agendas that encourage change. Institutional change is very important during state modernization processes geared towards improving public administration. These processes favour incorporating the gender issue into the state's agenda, as long as attention is paid to their paradigms, programmes and actors.

The needs that states must cater to are socially constructed, defined and prioritized by decision-making mechanisms and negotiation of the different actors in the public sphere. Women are not a part of these key actors and tend to be excluded from the informal male networks and mechanisms. Although informal, these still yield power because they are spaces for negotiation and patronage. Who decides the gender agenda therefore and, in particular, who implements it?

A global gender agenda defined approximately two decades ago and ratified by most states is still held to be valid. However, a brief review of some indicators demonstrates that this agenda has not really implied substantial changes in society's gender disparities regardless of which state model prevails.

Hence the UNDP has seen the need to construct a human development index for women (WDI) alongside its Human Development Index (HDI), using the three indicators of life expectancy, education and income. 'Human development' does not really imply an equitable gender development. An index of women's potentialization (IWP) has also been designed, since in spite of 'women's achievements' based on the three indicators, these do not automatically mean women get better decision-taking opportunities (UNDP 1995).

THE RESISTANCE OF BUREAUCRACIES

When it comes to institutionalizing women's interests in the definition of policies, no country in the world may be considered truly *developed*. Even in Scandinavia and countries such as Canada, a deep bureaucratic resistance exists with regard to the equitable integration of women as subjects of public policy (Goetz 1995: 2).

Public institutions are the link between state agencies and the population. They enforce and apply rules and regulations that help implement policies, create inter-institutional exchange and complementarity and develop communication and negotiation mechanisms with different social groups.

Institutions are not neutral actors just devoted to designing and implementing top managerial decisions or acting 'according to established procedures'. They also reflect and reproduce the values, norms and biases of the societies in which they are immersed, and that includes notions about the masculine and the feminine. This means their discretionary powers are relatively large. The resistance and mechanisms that distort or de-legitimate the gender agenda have been underestimated. Only until quite recently did attention begin to be paid to the idiosyncrasy and culture of institutions 'and their hidden agenda based on patriarchal opposition' (Longwe 1997: 149) which blocks and deviates the demands for change.

Bureaucracies tend to be hierarchical and not very democratic institutions, usually characterized by their inertia and conservatism in the face of change. It is with respect to the gender agenda that such resistances are the strongest. In a study about the incorporation of new subjects into the International Development Asociation (IDA), it was found that themes such as ecology and evaluation, which have never been too prominent, were more accepted and easier to put into practice than 'the subject of women' (Staudt 1985: 131). In the field of ecology, a topic emerging almost parallel to the 'women's question', standardized norms for the evaluation of environmental impacts are already in place (such as the European Union's Ecoaudit). No attempts have been made, on the contrary, to set the standards for a *gender audit* applicable to institutional performance and the impact of institutional policies.

Each policy promoting change that implies retargeting resources tends to be met with resistance. The processes of learning and of deconstructing identities, values and premises are long-standing, conflict-ridden and contradictory. The subject of gender necessarily affects the actors involved at a personal level. Questioning the discriminatory mechanisms in place at the institutional level inevitably implies that both

---

BOX 10.1 *Relevant Facts*

• The rate of female participation in the economically active population has increased by only 3.9 per cent in the past 20 years, from 35.6 per cent in 1970, to 39.5 per cent in 1990, with a very little difference evident between the developing and the industrialized worlds. This advance has been 'slow and incongruent with the spectacular growth in women's educational level' (UNDP 1995: 43).

• Close to two-thirds of women's work is not recorded in the National Accounts, while the proportion is diametrically opposite in the case of men's work (UNDP 1995: 99).

• Salary disparity to the disadvantage of women still exists. On average, women earn only 75 per cent of what men earn in countries like the United States and Germany; in extreme cases such as Bangladesh only 42 per cent (UNDP 1995: 43). 'Classic variables' such as education, professional experience and seniority in the workplace only partially explain this situation, since women often earn less even in cases where these variables are equal. Other studies affirm that between 30 and 60 per cent of the inequalities cannot be explained by the factors mentioned. Salary disparity is even more marked in cases where women have a better education and a higher professional level, as well as in sectors with a high percentage of female labour force (Schubert 1997: 119 ff.).

• Female representation in national parliaments is 10 per cent in developing countries and 12 per cent in industrialized ones. Only the Scandinavian countries show a higher proportion: between 35 and 40 per cent (UNDP 1995: 50). On the American continent, the

male and female managers have to reflect internally on their conduct, and not only regarding their professional or institutional behaviour.

As Staudt puts it, redistributive gender policies are just as inclined to create conflict as any other redistributive policy, but the personalized resistance is more subtle and complex. Much confusion persists about what interpersonal relations between the sexes entail (Staudt 1990: 10). In many cases, the processes stemming from a committed kind of discourse (women's empowerment, participation in policy decisions,

---

33 per cent of female senators in the Bahamas is the highest proportion among countries with a bicameral legislative branch, while the United States only has 15 per cent (INIM 1998: 7).

• Women's participation in top-level posts in the executive branch of government is still low. In the United States, it reaches 29 per cent, in Canada, Colombia, Mexico and the Dominican Republic around 20 per cent, and in the remaining countries 16 per cent or less (INIM 1998: 8).

• At a world level, women hold only 14 per cent of the administrative and executive posts (UNDP 1995: 55). In the United States, in 1995, as the result of a policy meant to promote 'diversity' (aimed at providing women and minorities greater access to work posts), only three out of every hundred chief executive officers of the 500 largest corporations were women (*Washington Post*, 22 March 1998). In a national survey done in the United States by the *Washington Post* and Harvard University, 71 per cent of the women polled, and 59 per cent of the men, answered yes when asked if they thought women were discriminated against when striving for top executive positions (*Washington Post*, 23 March 1998).

• Living with a male partner can be a high risk factor for women, as illustrated in an analysis made of 35 studies from various countries. It shows that between one-quarter and one-half of all women have been physically abused by their current partner or a past one (Heise 1994: 5ff.). This violence, often invisible and usually unpunished, has repercussions not only at the individual level of the victim, but also at the level of societies as a whole, since it represents important economic costs for them (IDB 1997).

access to resources) only result in the creation of some services for women at different institutional levels, something culled by Longwe as 'the evaporation of gender policies in the patriarchal pot'.

The following points are indicators of this 'evaporation' process with respect to gender policies in the programmes and projects advanced by institutions and organizations (see insert). These proposals are meant not to accuse but to highlight the structure of institutions 'in the profoundly embedded generic conventions of public bureaucracies' (Goetz 1995: 51), which function with the logic of 'masculine preference' even where the will for change exists.

- At the level of the objectives of a programme or project, commitment towards women's empowerment may be found, defined both by a greater participation in decisions as well as by greater access to resources.
- In the analysis of a given situation, those involved tend to reduce it to viewing the 'gender gaps' in the access to resources, without paying much attention to women's lack of power of articulation and decision.
- In the activities themselves, assigning resources to women is not usually the norm, if these are not already provided through additional resources.
- In the evaluations, the question of whether women benefited arises, but whether there was a change in the women's access of women tends never to be asked.

The most frequent arguments are:

- The access of resources is the same for everyone ('we do not discriminate').
- Women do not want to be involved.
- We have a shortage of (additional) resources.
- The 'culture' is like that and we cannot act differently if we want to respect it.

The above was revealed when a gender assessment took place during the modernization process of Nicaragua's Police Force (see Box 10.2). Through this input it became possible to incorporate the issue of violence against women at this institutional level.

Considering this 'evaporation' of the gender agenda, the deviations and resistance encountered in public entities and the fact that this significantly affects the potential to implement changes, there should be more interest in basing state modernization and institutional changes in

BOX 10.2 *Nicaragua: Women and the Police*

In a certain province of Nicaragua, a substantial increase in the number of complaints filed by female victims of domestic violence at the police precinct was observed. This very likely had to do with the fact that this police station has a Women and Children Police Station attached to it and women trusted they would be treated properly. However, this station is finding it more and more difficult to handle the growing number of complaints adequately: the interest and commitment of the head of the Police Department (DP) contrast with the shortage of personnel, which does not allow the hiring of the additional female officers required.

During a meeting of the chief of police and the head of the Women and Children's Police Station, the question arose of the number of crimes per category, and the corresponding caseload assigned to police personnel. It was then confirmed that the head of the Women and Children's Police Station had to deal with a proportionally higher number of cases.

When the hypothetical question was raised as to what might be done if crime in a certain area of the province increased substantially, the answer given was that staff would be relocated and reinforced. In the case of the rise in violence against women, however, no thought was in fact given to reallocating staff because of this increase. Not even the female staff in that particular stations had contemplated this possibility.

At another police station, the police commissioner was asked why so few women were involved in operational activities, to which he replied that he would be perfectly willing to promote greater participation, but that his subordinate, the area chief, was not so willing. In no other case would a police commissioner have tolerated such flagrant defiance on the part of one of his subordinates to his orders. In this case, the police commissioner did not insist that his command was obeyed, or that compliance to the corresponding Police Statutes (which had already been the subject of a gender assessment) was mandatory. These Statutes demanded greater female participation in police operations.

public administration on more gender-equitative approaches. Both government agencies and international cooperation should take a more leading role in it.

STATE REFORMS: NEW PARADIGMS FOR A GENDER AGENDA?

'Time and again history has shown that good governance is not a luxury but a vital necessity' (James Wolfenson, President of the World Bank, 1997).

Many countries, particularly in Latin America, have undertaken a series of reforms of varying degrees and scopes implying a redefinition and reconstruction of the state. The financial and economic crisis during the 1980s made the deficiencies shown by the state as a promoter of development, as a provider of social services and as a guarantor of equitative and sustainable development much more visible. Although during the first phase of structural adjustment a minimalist model of state policies prevailed, today even the World Bank recognizes the need for 'good governance', which cannot flourish 'in the absence of the same'.

At the risk of oversimplifying, which is always present when trying to identify common features and trends by reducing their complexity, the new political agenda might be summarized as follows:

- good governance, not governability;
- accountability of the public sector;
- efficient and effective performance;
- deregulation;
- subsidiarity both between the state and the private sector (privatization, external contracting) and among different state levels (decentralization); and
- state regulation and mediation in order to correct market flaws.

The following main instruments may be highlighted:

- reorganization and restructuring of the public sector, including the decentralization of the administration; and
- promotion of the public sector's capacity.

Countries undergo this process in different ways and with different priorities, but it is worthwhile stressing the potential benefits of incorporating the gender approach into the public administration area.

The gender proposal, with its integral and horizontal approach and its intersectorial analytic capacity, can and should be a tool used to overcome the state's fragmentary sectorial vision. The importance of 'the cultural' in society becomes clearer and gains broader acceptance. Culture can hinder or favour public policies and even influence the economic sphere. It is crucial to construct arguments. It is vital to link the desired objectives and impacts of modernization with a gender-sensitive agenda, both at the level of new paradigms and at the level of public policies.

Governability resulting from the state's 'new' legitimacy and understood as the strengthening of democracy, the participation of the population in the definition of policies, the protection of human rights without discrimination, eradication of exclusion mechanisms, the building of trust and legal guarantees will not be achieved unless gender aspects are paid attention to. Regardless of the shortcomings already mentioned, Nicaragua's police have gained legitimacy before women and their organizations, because of their growing commitment to fighting violence against women. This struggle should be a task and an obligation for every public institution and not just police precincts. The Nicaraguan police actively carry out inter-institutional efforts with the Nicaraguan Institute for Women, different women's organizations and the legal branch.

With regard to the paradigm of *accountability*, the state assumes responsibility for policies, programmes and resource allocation before both its female and male population. The 'South African Women's Budget Initiative' may serve as an example of a strategy designed to achieve a more equitable distribution of resources. It helps to analyse how the national budget is allocated according to the different population groups, beneficiaries and non-beneficiaries alike, and based on the needs and potentials of the different groups in society. This facilitates transparency in state investment, and such transparency is the first step towards attaining a more equitable budget distribution.

Efficiency and effectiveness require considering the whole range of economic actors, service and resource seekers, as well as taxpayers, with respect to development and economic growth. A state that really grants priority to these paradigms and is free of gender biases is more likely to consider women as economic actors than a welfare state is, with its emphasis on social aspects and its dominant view of women as a 'vulnerable' group. Many evaluations of agricultural development projects in Nicaragua have concluded that women behave more positively in the face of innovations and productive changes than males do. Female farmers are more receptive to change, if they consider that viable and valid alternatives are being offered to them. Women are also more steady and consistent in the use of new productive processes. Female farmers or peasants can also represent a barrier when it comes to the success of a given technological or productive innovation, if they believe such changes will affect them negatively or simply fail to appreciate the changes as something positive. This was proved again and again through the numerous failures of agro-export projects in the 1970s and 1980s. When seeking a policy to promote non-traditional production it is useful thus to differentiate between male and female economic behaviour, and especially to regard women producers as genuine economic actors and potential agents of change and development.

De-regulation, which normally includes simplification and savings of resources measures and implies that state intervention in a society's economic behaviour may be positive for women, who tend to be involved in small and micro-scale enterprises. However, it may also limit the intended effects or produce undesirable ones. Schemes introducing payment of taxes at bank counters, for example, may affect the aim to increase the number of taxpayers, if many of them and women in particular have trouble using banks or feel intimidated by them by reason of education or culture. Another example is designing measures to increase competition. This may be pivotal in favouring a small group of economic actors who usually enjoy a better relative position anyway, but may serve to expel a much larger group with no real possibilities to achieve economic insertion. More women may be affected directly or indirectly by such a measure, since women tend to work in small and micro-enterprises in both the formal and informal sectors. These ventures may seriously hamper women's capacity to take advantage of the opportunities offered.

At a macro level, these arguments will not have much impact if the specificity of the institutions involved is not taken into account, as well as their assorted practices for policy implementation, control and monitoring.

INSTITUTIONAL CHANGE: OVERCOMING THE PREFERENCE FOR MALES

In state modernization processes, increasing the state's capacity via the 'revitalization of public institutions' (World Bank 1997) is the central issue. According to the World Bank, this revitalization entails finding effective controls and guidelines to counteract corruption and arbitrariness; increasing competition in order to ensure more efficiency; improving performance through salary rises and other incentives; and responding more effectively to the needs of the population via greater decentralization and participation.

Unfortunately, the proposal of the World Bank, as a *leading agency* in modernization programmes, does not take into account that achieving such goals to a large extent depends on carefully examining the heterogeneous character of the population, its needs, problems and 'participation' potentials alike, as well as the 'generic' character of public institutions. It is likely that modernization processes will reproduce the same barriers limiting advances in the construction of equality between men and women, in spite of the paradigms that would require differentiation at the level of the population and at the level of the actors associated with the public institutions.

Let us briefly point out some basic components of a strategy to transform public institutions that allows recognizing the gender approach as a useful tool for the very success of institutional modernization. These components are derived mainly from the Nicaraguan experience and encompass three areas: gender violence, modernization of the public sector and economic policies.

It is crucial to establish the systematic link between the mandate and the general objectives of an institution or programme, and the requirements for change with respect to gender relations. The need to make this type of link at a general institutional level is clear, that is, at the level of collective responsibilities and not only with respect to one particular segment. Thus a strategy can be matched to the entire behaviour of an institution. This reduces the danger of relegating the subject of gender to only one individual or division. Otherwise there is the risk of isolation and this may even cause the institution to have conflicting policies.

The above must be associated with the process of institutional modernization, since what is being sought is the impact of institutional modernization: that is, clearly defined mandates and objectives, efficiency and efficacy, assessing needs according to population demands, the non-discretionary behaviour of civil servants and the resulting new legitimization of public entities by their citizens.

External changes must also be associated with changes from within. The civil service is a strategic ingredient in modernizing the state. Civil servants of both sexes are the actors involved. This implies a change in self-perceptions and attitudes (at the service of the population), a transformation of the 'culture of doing' to a 'culture of results and impacts', a modification of income criteria, job security and incentives based on merit and professional qualification, and a transformation of the internal culture, values and styles of management.

The need to analyse these processes and their premises using a gender approach is based on two reasons. On the one hand, an institution can hardly implement institutional policies warranting gender equity if, at its core, it does not reflect the population's diversity, their needs and potentials. In this sense, internal diversity facilitates better understanding and having a less biased approach to reality, counterbalancing the preference for males with respect to the definition of priorities, resources and arguments. On the other hand, the very premises of these reforms might not be adequately fulfilled without first identifying and overcoming gender biases present among the staff. It is highly acknowledged that the criteria for merit and professionalism are neutral only in theory. They do not escape subjectivity and discretionary behaviour in its application. Horizontal and vertical segregation and disparities in salaries are generalized procedures at the level of public employment, even in countries that do take into account these criteria (Schmid 1991), and regardless of whether women as qualified as or better qualified than men and show more reliable and consistent behaviour.

Disregarding such biases may have significant consequences for the success of a reform and modernization process of public administration seeking to develop a human resource policy that stimulates and incentivates staff performance, aims at the efficient use of the staff and attempts to overcome the state's discretionary and arbitrary attitudes.

Changes at the core of an institution are not only achieved with a 'critical mass' of 30 per cent of women, as is more and more often demanded (UNDP 1995). This is a necessary condition but it is in no way sufficient. The case of Nicaragua's civil service illustrates that, even if it is composed mainly of women (63 per cent), and even if so many women do occupy posts that imply decision-taking (52 per cent women and 48 per cent men), the 'glass ceiling' has not been broken. Using a

BOX 10.3 *Gender Assessment in the Nicaraguan Police*

During the course of its gender assessment, the Nicaraguan police force has managed to link the subject of *gender violence with that of civilian security*. The theme is no longer treated in a marginal fashion and assigned to isolated police precincts. Instead it has been adopted by the whole police force. The concept of civilian security was examined from the perspective of the differentiated risk patterns for men and women, the police's discretionary actions (resources, procedures, attitudes) and the *contradictions visible in their own goals within their modernization process* (professionalization; objective criteria for police practices; protection of human rights; the search for renewed legitimacy). This approach has permitted incorporating the subject of violence against women into all the other tasks carried out by the police, such as crime prevention, reviews of codes, procedures and information systems, and the search for solutions such as increasing the female police staff, involving more women in operational areas, introducing the subjects of 'gender violence and civilian security' during recruitment training courses and the regular training of active officers.

While making a diagnosis based on the background, professional profile and placement of female and male staff in the Nicaraguan police force, it was noticed that women had relative advantages as far as education and seniority were concerned. These capacities and expertise are still not being taken into account or fully taken advantage of, however. Women continue to be relegated almost exclusively to the service and administration areas. Their opportunities for promotion are much more limited. These features are contradictory within the framework of enhancing the process of professionalization of the police force. This led to a revision of the system of promotions, during which the need to increase the number of female staff in the operational areas enjoying the highest recognition and significance was openly expressed. Reflection was also focused on women's comparative advantages. Because of how women are socialized they are less likely to be aggressive or corrupt and they are more understanding. They treat people more 'humanly' and are less aggressive and hierarchical. Nowadays there are more and more mixed male and female teams in the traffic police, for example.

gender perspective, focal groups have been created and interviews have been compiled within the framework of an ongoing study on public employment in Nicaragua. The frequency with which women, in particular, but also men, admit that there is a great deal of resistance to accepting women on their professional merit and on their competence warrants attention. These forms of resistance include not letting women speak at meetings with the same frequency and intensity as their male counterparts; disparaging women's contributions; accepting the proposals made by women only if they also agree to assume the responsibility for carrying them out; and not recognizing that gender discrimination lies at the root of all such manifestations and goes beyond the scope of 'isolated cases'. Even where females form part of the civil service, indirect and underlying mechanisms of discrimination, segregation and undervaluation continue to be in place. The 'power to define' remains in male hands. This puts women in the ambivalent position of 'being inside' and 'being outside' at the same time.

An institutional change promoting more equality between men and women demands a transformation not only at the level of objectives, institutional structure and human resources, but in the 'culture', understood as the ideas, judgements and prejudices that may define how actors behave. Regarding the 'gender culture' to be observed in public institutions, Newman differentiates between three kinds of culture: *traditional culture*, *competitive culture* and the *culture of transformation*. While *traditional culture* is the 'classical' culture implying male and female roles and stereotypes, a slash-and-burn competition prevails in *competitive culture*. Women are granted spaces as long as they manage to withstand the competition: 'Women are allowed entry if they can prove to be capable and if they are strong enough to withstand the rhythm' (Newman 1995: 14, 16).

Finally, it is important to highlight the *culture of transformation* in this discussion because it reflects, to a great extent, the components related to change that are being sought through modernization: that is, a culture oriented towards satisfying the needs of the population, improving the quality of service, working towards administration styles based on communication and transparency, favouring incentives and promotion of civil servants with no discrimination or exclusion. In such a culture, the characteristics typically viewed as 'feminine' (communication, having a holistic vision) are explicitly visualized as key elements of a new management style. Even in the culture of transformation, however, equality is more an illusion than a reality. Women do not appear to have 'permission' to be, even when they occupy top posts or even if they work more. They usually have higher educational levels but take fewer decisions. Equality and neutrality are the notions presented as compromises of institutional 'cultural transformation'. This sometimes detracts from identifying and questioning the mechanisms fostering the inequality still observable in institutions. Nevertheless, it is crucial to take advantage of any given space, in order to contest the resistance to change: mutual respect and recognition can only be constructed by getting to know and understand 'the other' better. Frustration and anxiety will be inevitable, but not resorting to insults or de-legitimization. We must learn to know one another in order to be able to change.

It is important to promote reflection and analysis about the premises and objectives that this type of modernization is meant to achieve. It is not 'an easy thing' to carry out a modernization project favouring a real change in structures, mechanisms and individual and institutional attitudes, while at the same time promoting a vision of equality between men and women. Some experiences in this direction have certainly shown that the effects are beneficial for all those involved, and that a modernization process thus enhanced is a goal well worth striving towards.

NOTE

1. Annette Backhaus has a doctorate in political sciences from the University of Berlin. She is currently a senior adviser of the German Technical Cooperation Agency, GTZ.

BIBLIOGRAPHY

Goetz, A. M. (1995) *The Politics of Integrating Gender to State Development Processes. Trends, Opportunities and Constraints in Bangladesh, Chile, Jamaica, Mali, Morocco and Uganda*, New York: UNDP Occasional Paper.

Groult, B. (1978) *Así sea Ella*, Barcelona.

GTZ–INIM (1996) *Diagnóstico de género del Proyecto de Reforma del Sector Público. Acercándose al tema*, Managua, Nicaragua: Proyecto de Promoción de Políticas de Género.

GTZ–Policía Nacional de Nicaragua (1997) *Diagnóstico sobre factores que favorencen y obstaculizan la participación de las mujeres en la Policía Nacional*, Managua, Nicaragua: Proyecto de Promoción de Políticas de Género.

Heise, L. (1994) *Violencia contra la mujer: La carga oculta sobre la salud*, Washington, DC.

IDB (1997) *El impacto socio-económico de la violencia doméstica contra la mujer en Chile y Nicaragua*, Washington, DC: Interamerican Development Bank.

INIM (1998) *Informe hemisférico en el marco de los compromises de la Cumbre de las Américas*, Tema 18, Managua, Nicaragua.

Longwe, S. H. (1997) 'The evaporation of gender policies in the patriarchal cooking pot', *Development in Practice*, 7(2), May.

Newman J. (1995) 'Gender and cultural change', in C. Itzin, J. Newman (eds), *Gender, Culture and Organizational Change: Putting Theory into Practice*, London and New York: Routledge.

Schmid, G. (1991) *Women in the Public Sector*, OECD/GD 213.

Schubert, R. (1997) 'Labor market and gender', in GTZ (ed.), *Gender and Macro Policy*, Eschborn.

Staudt, K. (ed.) (1985) *Women, Foreign Assistance and Advocacy Administration*, New York: Praeger.

— (1990) *Women, International Development and Politics. The Beaurocratic Mire*, Philadelphia: Macmillan.

United Nations Centre for Social Development and Humanitarian Affairs (1992) *Women in Politics and Decision-making in the Late Twentieth Century: a United Nations Study*, Dordrecht: Martinus Nijhoff.

UNDP (1995) *Human Development Report, 1995*, New York.

UNICEF (1995) *Respuesta de UNICEF a las Preocupaciones de la Mujer. Exámen de la Política*, New York.

World Bank (1997) 'El Estado en un Mundo en Transformación', *World Development Report*, Washington, DC.

— (1979) *Integrating Women into Development*, Washington, DC.

PART THREE

Institutionalizing Gender in National
and International Organizations

CHAPTER 11

Gender Equality in Public Planning Institutions

BARBARA HESS AND ANA RICO
DE ALONSO[1]

§ The efforts undertaken by countries all over the world to promote the institutionalization of gender equity and equality over the last two decades may be classified into two main categories, according to their political and conceptual basis. The first sees women as a main focus of action and promotes creating new specialized bodies such as women's ministries, institutes or divisions, or women's divisions in already existing ministries and other entities. The second seeks to integrate a cross-cutting gender perspective into a much broader institutional spectrum.

Judging by the evaluations of experiences taking place in different countries, the achievements attained in Holland, Sweden and Canada are exemplary. Their creation of technical and specialized gender units has made it possible for the actions undertaken to become part of the mainstream of development. These activities have been directed towards creating or strengthening intra-institutional networks, with the support of sectorial specialists. Priority has been given to the sectors considered more receptive to the subject of gender. In general, though, examining the different efforts to gain institutional autonomy, integrating gender-oriented actions to the day-to-day practice of national or international agencies continues to be a limited affair, as Caren Levy and Caroline Moser have pointed out: 'In every country, the agencies and organisations that have adopted and institutionalised a Women and Development approach remain on the fringe of the mainstream of development activities undertaken by governments' (Levy 1996: 2).

In order to achieve greater equality and the participation of men and women alike in the development process, in both the public and private spheres, cultural changes must take place, both at the level of the population and in public institutions. Integrating gender approaches at the level of these institutions is an important and necessary condition, but this alone does not achieve equality between men and women. Equality must be framed within a broader and more complex strategy.

COMPONENTS OF THE PROCESS OF INSTITUTIONALIZATION

A policy favouring gender equality is put into operation when the public entities in charge of defining national or sectorial policies integrate the needs, interests and demands of men and women alike into their daily activities; this vision of equality necessarily implies changes in the attitude of public servants and supporting theoretical components and diagnoses in order to promote gender equality.

Integrating a gender approach in an institution means 'institutionalizing' this approach from within. In order to have internal and external effects, at the very least the three basic elements that have proven to be the most significant must be influenced: strategy, structure and culture.

- *Strategy*: analysis and revision of the objectives, procedures and tools; analysis of the information system, records and techniques used to generate information.
- *Structure*: analysis of how work is organized, how tasks are distributed and which communication mechanisms are in use.
- *Culture*: analysis and identification of modes of interdisciplinary work that can lead to new forms of working relations, characterized by greater cooperation and participation.

Although each institution has its own features and may apply the gender approach differently, several *general principles regarding the institutionalization of gender approaches* exist:

- A gender-sensitive approach must be conceived as a complex global strategy and not as a sum of isolated actions.
- It should penetrate an institution's internal logic, in relation to its areas of interest and its organizational components, at the same time that it introduces new elements.
- Its structuring should be carried out 'from within', much in the same way that a cell functions, based on a selection of the critical areas and themes in which the greatest gender imbalances persist, on the one hand, and, on the other hand, allowing for the proposal of short- and middle-term solutions.
- It must allow the institutional levels most relevant in terms of

leadership, decision-taking, technical and operational know-how, to appropriate the theme and the process.

The institutionalization *process* itself is based on a set of interrelated actions that include: the construction of political will, the theoretical and technical strengthening of gender analysis, the drafting of methodological supports, the generation of relevant information, and the putting into effect of plans for its implementation. These efforts may require the help of specialized external advisers to accompany the processes. Figure 11.1 illustrates the components of this process.

FACTORS THAT FAVOUR OR HINDER INSTITUTIONALIZATION

Factors that favour institutionalization

- the organizational expertise and technical know-how compiled by an institution;
- the existence of political will among top decision-taking levels;
- the application of participatory procedures to the design and implementation of the institutional strategy;

Political interest and will

Offer of cooperation

Negotiation of demand transformation

Mission to promote the strategy

Selection of strategic units

Officialization and legitimation of mission

Identification of experts in sectoral and gender-sensitive themes

Study of areas of interest involved in each unit

Participatory process: identification of gender inequities

Definition of priority areas in each unit

Formulation and discussion of institutionalization strategy

Creation of internal structure for advice and accompaniment

Establishment of technical and financial responsibilities

FIGURE 11.1 Components of institutionalization

- the formation of a technical team capable of developing a strategy for relevant development sectors, jointly with specialized teams; and
- international assistance, both in financial and technical aspects.

Factors that hinder institutionalization

- *political instability*: this can be generated by the frequent turnover of key personnel in top posts, or frequent changes in government teams; this situation generates the constant need to renegotiate the agreements that have already been reached;
- *limited accumulated experience* hindering the provision of guidance with respect to macro-economic and sectorial themes and to their gender links, both among national and international teams; and
- *low or non-existing level of commitment, or technical know-how, of the entity in charge* of gender-equality policy (National Women's Offices, for example).

EXPERIENCES GATHERED BY THE PRO-EQUITY PROJECT

The experiences gathered by the Pro-Equity Project, which was carried out as a cooperation between the Colombian and the German government from 1992 to 2001, show that the institutional integration of a gender approach – as a cross-cutting theme and as a trans-sectorial one – is a fundamental component of a *broader strategy* that can serve to put into operation a gender-equality approach on a nationwide scale. This strategy includes components such as: contextualization with respect to the country's political, economic and social reforms; drafting of national and sectorial gender-sensitive policies; reinforcement of 'public demand' at national, regional and local levels; development planning with a gender perspective; strengthening civil society's 'demand'; theoretical, methodological and instrumental development; human resource training.

The project allowed identifying the need to work on different levels, while seeking a vertical linkage among these levels. Interventions at each level must be made in keeping with corresponding functions or attributions:

- *International*: work is contextualized with respect to ongoing political, economic and social reform processes, coordinating actions with international entities.
- *National policies*: strategically placed entities are given assistance in order to create conditions for the population to participate equally

and efficiently in policy formulation; institutional development and the institutionalization of gender-equal policies are promoted at the inside of each institution.

- *Sectorial institutions and policies*: sectorial entities receive advisory guidance to integrate gender approaches into sectorial policies.
- *Decentralized and local policies*: conditions are created to encourage the population's equal and efficient participation in the processes of regional and local development, while catering to differentiated interests and needs; the capacity to plan and manage territorial entities is strengthened; advice is provided to the institutions responsible for executing gender-equal local development projects.
- *Organized civil society*: strengthening of participation capacity; planning, management and negotiation with other development actors; support for theoretical and methodological development is provided; appropriate instruments are placed at the disposal of the local authorities and the population.

EXPERIENCES OF THE COLOMBIAN NATIONAL PLANNING DEPARTMENT (DNP) WITH THE INSTITUTIONALIZATION OF THE GENDER APPROACH

The DNP is a strategic institution for putting into operation an equality policy because:

- It designs the government's National Development Plan and participates in the definition of state policies and reforms.
- It has the necessary competence to create conditions for planning a gender-equal-oriented development.
- It is a body entrusted with important, explicit responsibilities for the development of an equality policy.
- It is responsible for information systems at a macro level.
- It carries out an advisory role and does follow-up and evaluation of sectorial policies.
- It defines criteria for the allocation of national budgetary resources for the programmes carried out by all the state entities.
- It coordinates and follows up international technical cooperation projects and programmes.

Framework conditions for the DNP strategy   A series of framework conditions enhanced the DNP's institutionalization of gender-sensitive processes.

- The entity holds attributions and functions of strategic importance for national planning, embodied in Four-Year Development and Public Investment Plans.
- The country has drafted an equality policy and a policy to favour the participation of women, approved by CONPES, the National Council of Economic and Social Policy (CONPES Documents No. 2726 of August 1994 and No. 2941 of August 1997). This policy forms part of the social equality policy contained in the current government's National Development Plan. CONPES established the bases for the DNP's specific work through the following recommendations, made in the August 1997 document:

    — Request for DNP to institutionalize the existence of a team dedicated to the promotion and monitoring of gender equality, under the department's direction, with the aim of finding how to relate a gender-sensitive perspective to policy formulation and follow-up, and in the drafting of regional development plans. This recommendation was accepted when the DNP Gender Advisory Team was consolidated.

    — Request for the National Planning System to participate in the process of integrating gender equality to the management of national and territorial plans and programmes. This integration has become part of the activities promoted in the DNP's implementation strategy.

- The approval of the PROEQUIDAD/GTZ Project. The project provided advisory services and technical assistance to the national government, through counterpart institutions such as the DNP and the National Office for the Equality of Women. As a counterpart, the DNP has the capacity to mobilize resources for an international technical cooperation project.

Objectives of the DNP strategy

- to incorporate concepts related to gender equality, as an expression of social equality, in the central processes, mechanisms and tools of national and territorial planning that the DNP exerts authority over;
- to strengthen the DNP's technical capacity in handling gender issues, in order to promote its insertion into the National Development Plan;
- To strengthen the DNP's institutional capacity by establishing a technical team with expertise on gender meant to support DNP's staff in the daily performance of their tasks;

- To assure the commitment of DNP's executive levels in order to build an institutional gender tradition reflected in its day-to-day practice.

Priority working areas and action lines The following *working areas* were defined to have priority:

- Productive development of the urban economy: given the importance of generating resources for women's survival and growing insertion into the labour markets, sex-desegregated information was sought. In general, this information should allow gaining knowledge about the differentiated patterns of male and female labour insertion, identifying gender imbalances in specific sectors and making women's contribution more visible. It should help design methodologies to correct the underestimation and sub-registration of paid and unpaid labour, especially that performed by women.
- Social development: this sector is considered of strategic importance in the search for social equality and in the strengthening of social policies. Bearing this in mind, three areas of crucial significance for human development were selected: poverty and quality of life, education and health.
- Decentralization and local planning: Colombia is embarked on a profound process of decentralization involving the transfer of areas of competence towards regional and local levels. The drafting of development plans and the reinforcement of local planning are key activities within this process. Supporting local governments, planning councils and other strategic actors in order to incorporate a gender perspective to local plans permits influencing these actions and the levels of participation required.
- Rural development: its focus is on women's participation in productive processes in rural economies, and on women's access to technology and means of production.

The *action lines* adopted correspond to the DNP's tasks and are of two kinds:

- Cross-cutting action lines: incorporation of a gender dimension to information systems and databases; allocation of public investment resources; normative guidance of development plans; international cooperation projects; theoretical bases with respect to macro-economic and macro-social themes.

- Sectorial action lines: identification of existing imbalances and associated factors, through the construction of indicators, the carrying out of specialized research, the reinforcement of sectorial technical units and the promotion of gender-sensitive external credit projects.

In each action line, specific activities assigned according to the DNP's own units or internal divisions, or ascribed to them, were agreed upon.

Cross-cutting action lines

1. Unit of macro-economic analysis
- desegregation of national statistics per sex;
- study on value of unpaid domestic labour and its effects on national accounts; and
- development of a methodology to quantify the under-registration of the female EAP and proposed correction factor.

2. Social mission
- evaluation of the link between changes in women's well-being and social expenditure in the period between 1985 and 1998;
- identification and analysis of gender-imbalance factors related to the quality of education, upon the basis of achievement tests applied among third- and fifth-grade students; and
- international state of the art with respect to quality of life, poverty and well-being influenced by gender.

3. Indicator division
- Desegregation of socio-demographic indicators per sex;
- Preparation of 'Gender Indicator' Bulletin.

4. Regional and Urban Planning Unit
- Integration of gender equality in the definition of public policies and the drafting of territorial development plans; drafting of training guides and other training material; and
- participation in committees dedicated to the coordination of territorial planning; and
- development of training activities.

5. Special evaluation division
- Participation, with the division's team, in the evaluation methodology proposed to carry out the follow-up of policies and investment plans;

- definition of indicators to evaluate policies in favour of women's equality; and
- support to the National Women's Equality Division in the evaluation of said policy.

6. Colombian Agency of International Cooperation (ACCI)

- review of gender concepts and indicators used by the ACCI and cooperation agencies;
- support to the team in the definition of guidelines in the area of women, to be used in the management of cooperation projects; and
- support to training activities for ACCI staff and for the staff in charge of international cooperation at the various ministries.

Sectorial action lines

1. Unit of Social Development–Employment Division

- production of statistics pertaining to employment and labour markets, desegregated per sex; and
- analysis of behaviour and trends in urban and rural markets in Colombia and informal and formal markets, identifying male and female patterns of activity and changes taking place during the last two decades.

2. Unit of Social Division–Health Division

- review of the Health Information System (SIS) with special emphasis on indicators for registering and measuring morbidity and mortality according to sex; and
- drafting of recommendations for the Ministry of Health team responsible for designing the SIS, in order to adapt their methodology to gender specificities relevant to the health area.

3. Unit of Social Development–Division of Education

- desegregation of information and analysis of sector statistics according to sex;
- research on the differential behaviour, per sex, of students taking state examinations (ICFES) in order to gain access to university, identifying associated educational and socio-familial factors; and
- intervention in the design of projects geared to international cooperation agencies, in order to ensure that they include gender-equality components.

4. Unit of Entrepreneurial Development

- review and analysis of surveys: annual manufacturing, technological and micro-entrepreneurial surveys; and
- design and coordination of project for female micro-entrepreneurs.

5. Rural Development Unit

- diagnosis of women's participation in rural economies and in social and productive organization; and
- incorporation of a gender perspective in the creation of projects meant to attract international credit, especially with respect to access to technology, credit and land tenure.

6. Rural mission

- integration of gender approaches in diagnoses and action proposals of the rural mission's different agendas
- definition of the contents of a specific rural women's agenda.

Inputs for the National Development Plan 1998–2002

- a publication containing the results of the studies already carried out; and
- appointment of a gender consultant in units regarded as strategic for the definition of the Development Plan

NOTE

1. Barbara Hess has a master's degree in anthropology and Latin American history. She is presently director of the German Technical Cooperation Agency GTZ in El Salvador. Ana Rico de Alonso is a sociologist, has a master's degree in demographics. She currently coordinates the Gender Advisory Team of Colombia's National Planning Department and lectures at the Javeriana University and the National University of Colombia.

BIBLIOGRAPHY

Bangura, Y. (1997) *Policy Dialogue and Gendered Development. Institutional and Ideological Constraints*, Geneva: United Nations Research Institute for Social Development.

Campillo, F. and E. Caro (1998) *Estrategia para la Integración de la Equidad de Género en el Departamento Nacional de Planeación*, Bogota, Colombia.

Levy, C. (1996) 'The process of institutionalising gender in policy and planning: the "web" of institutionalisation', Working Paper No. 74, Development Planning Unit/DPU, University College London, March.

— (1996) 'Institucionalización del género en las políticas y planificación de los asentamientos humanos', *Asentamientos humanos, pobreza y género. América Latina. Hacia Habitat II.* Seminario Taller Latinoamericano, Santiago de Chile, pp. 47–76.

Moser, C. (1993) *Gender Planning and Development Theory: Theory, Practice and Training*, London and New York: Routledge.

CHAPTER 12

Gender Equality in Public Policies: The UN Economic Commission for Latin America and the Caribbean

JOSÉ ANTONIO OCAMPO[1]

§ In spite of the significant advances made in the diagnosis of gender inequality during the past years, we are still in the process of constructing knowledge about the relation between gender approaches and other development issues. In fact, learning about gender inequalities often goes hand in hand with redesigning the institutions and policies needed to overcome them. I will refer to some of the experiences made by ECLAC in this field.

The notion of gender is not new, and profound cultural changes are still needed for it to be accepted. The concepts proposed are also not easy to make operational. Developing indicators to measure and modify the differentiated conditions under which men and women work is still in the initial stage. The institutionalization of these indicators is recent and lacks continuity, stability and allocation of resources. This does not mean that progress in the gender area has not been achieved. It is important to remember, however, that we are involved in a dynamic process and as such we are both apprentices and builders in it.

SOME CONSENSUS

Let us now review briefly the main premises from which we address the issue of gender. We believe at ECLAC that some consensus already exists among those who carry out gender research and those who support the new and complex links between gender and public policies. These shared opinions are held by governments and the United Nations system, organizations belonging to civil society, academic centres and independent researchers who reflect about gender and are also active in the field.

The first consensus is that *equality* is the main objective of the political and social agenda of every democratic state in the region. No one currently believes that economic growth can be viewed independently from its effects on the distribution of the benefits generated and on the quality of life of women and men.

The second consensus, closely linked to the first, is that *economic growth itself does not automatically bring about equality*. The relation between growth and equality has to be built. This is particularly true in a region such as Latin America, which has the worst income distribution in the world, and in which poverty continues to prevail even beyond the levels characterizing it two decades ago. The problems caused by 'hard poverty' are increasing; that is, the problems faced by the poor, who find it increasingly difficult to participate in the development process. The state's role in building up the relationship between growth and equality is indisputable.

The third consensus is that the lack of equality *affects women and men in a differentiated way*, not only according to their socio-economic strata but also in connection with the roles that society has culturally assigned to each sex.

Consensus also exists on the need to *link economic and social policies*; that is, to use an integrated approach in dealing with the question of equality. If the objective of economic policies is to achieve human welfare, and if social policies demand healthy macro-economics, sustainable growth and stability, this link will be made possible only if policies are designed in a context that takes into account both spheres of government activity.

The above implies that the state and the market inevitably complement each other. So do the market and the private sector, as a general rule. The state's role is redefined in this context. Consensus also exists that democratic institutionality requires *the active participation* of various actors, women and women's non-governmental organizations among them.

ECLAC'S APPROACH TO THE ISSUE OF GENDER

Understanding the differentiated impacts of public policies on men and women, in both the political and academic spheres, means that any serious reflection on economic and social policies made today must include a gender perspective; that is, attention must be focused on gender equality. ECLAC is not indifferent to these reflections and shared opinions.

The basic context in which we frame our proposals at present is the assessment of healthy macro-economics, economic liberalization and globalization, and the need for an efficient state. The objective is to establish efficient state actions in tune with a dynamic market. We hold that the state should manage macro-economic flaws, stimulate dynamic economic growth and construct social and gender equality. The search for healthy macro-economics is currently combined with the high priority allocated to social expenditure, which in the past years has increased and become more specifically targeted in Latin America. More than setting out grand paradigmatic guidelines, we observe reality and try to learn from successful experiences, disseminate them and study the possibility of broadening and replicating them. Comparative analysis is precisely one of the best comparative advantages that ECLAC relies on, being a regional commission like it is.

Incorporating a gender perspective into this framework is the task at hand. In fact, our concern for women arises from the long-standing discrimination they have had to confront. We are pioneers in the region, having taken up the gender issue at the beginning of the 1970s. Our approach has gradually changed and become more solid, as we studied the interaction of gender with other development issues. We know women's status in society reflects not only their socio-economic level but also the roles that society assigns to males and females. These roles define their status and thus their options for effective participation.

Merely understanding this is not the same as coherently integrating a gender approach into public policies. The approach promoted by ECLAC highlights the need to draft integrated policies; this is no simple process. It is not enough to put cross-cutting policies into operation, resulting in sectorial actions. Ministries and sector institutions must also be coordinated. Furthermore – and here lies the greatest complexity – the design and application of policies geared to gender equality also imply substantial cultural changes in the structure of society.

THE INSTRUMENTS

In this brief overview, it is useful to recall the different instruments existing today that support the search to improve the design of gender-sensitive public policies. This is, without doubt, one of the areas in which the greatest progress has been made in the last decades, providing an important point of departure for public policies.

Among the most recent *international instruments*, the Convention for the Elimination of All Types of Discrimination Against Women, ratified by all Latin American and Caribbean countries, is particularly worth highlighting. It is one of the few binding instruments upon the basis of which countries are adjusting their national legislation. The Action Platform, approved at the Fourth World Women's Conference in Beijing (1995) and the process of Beijing + 5, are equally crucial since they are clearly action-oriented. It takes for granted that the discussion stage has already been left behind and puts forth the need to draft specific gender policies. The Platform is not binding, as distinct from the Convention, yet both tools have annual inter-governmental evaluations and follow-up mechanisms at the level of active UN commissions: the Women and Legal Status Commission and the Committee of the Convention for the Elimination of All Types of Discrimination Against Women (better known as CEDAW).

At the level of *regional instruments*, the Regional Action Programme for Women of Latin America and the Caribbean 1995–2001, ratified in 1994 by all the members of ECLAC, served as an input for the World Action Programme. It contains eight strategic areas around which consensus has been reached for the drafting of national policies in the region. Like the Platform, it is not a binding instrument. The Regional Conference on Women in Latin America and the Caribbean – an inter-governmental organ that holds a general meeting every three years since 1977 and is currently composed of eleven countries – meets twice a year to monitor the agreements reached on the basis of the Regional Action Programme. It is thus a political and technical agency promoting permanent linkages. The Board of Directors of the Regional Conference carries out analysis, follow-up and evaluation of its performance. During its Seventh Session, the Conference approved the Consensus of Santiago. It contains key guidelines for the follow-up and monitoring of themes related to poverty alleviation and power, themes that have been highlighted by member countries.

On the other hand, a great number of *national instruments* exist in the region. In the first place, *the offices, ministries or sub-secretariats devoted to gender* merit attention. In fact, all countries in the region have incorporated some sort of gender agency into their state apparatus. Conditions have changed during the past 20 years and may vary widely. There are four main institutional models: (i) ministries or independent institutes having ministerial status and thus yielding executive power; (ii) offices or independent services at the level of the Presidential Office, which coordinate, design and draft policies without being in charge of executing them; (iii) departments, divisions and focal points within sector ministries and (iv) autonomous organizations, such as the Federation of Cuban Women. Although this body officially represents Cuba, it has the rank of a non-governmental organization. Ministries in some countries have also created focal points to coordinate gender issues, either in ministries themselves or in specialized entities.

Another type of instrument is represented by the National Plans for Equal Opportunities. When the Seventh Regional Conference took place, at least eight countries had already launched their own equality plans. These are known under different names and have been created within the last decade, especially just prior to the Beijing Conference. In general, they contain guidelines for public policies to be executed by the various ministries. They are usually coordinated by the agencies in charge of women's policies. Some of them have a share in the national budget and are entrusted with specific policies. They involve legal reforms and most of them propose the general framework for a national gender policy.

Other particularly useful instruments are women's organizations and networks, and also the expertise that many women have accumulated through their participation in human rights, social and environmental movements. Women's growing educational level also constitutes a potential, as does the strengthening of democracies, which broadens the active participation of citizens and allows them to become actors with respect to public policies.

From the above we may conclude that currently there is a strong commitment on behalf of the UN, reflecting the mandate it has received from member governments to participate actively in the construction of adequate gender policies that foster equality. This political will is explicitly expressed in the support that member governments have given, in Aruba, to the creation of an independent and autonomous ECLAC sub-programme for the incorporation of a gender perspective into all our activities, as well as in their constant support to the Regional Women's Conference, our inter-governmental forum.

At the national level, a variety of state instruments exist, such as equality plans, national offices and policies. We must be very blunt about this subject, however: in most cases, the political legitimacy granted to these national instruments has not expressed itself until now in their stability or continuity, or in the provision of enough human and technical resources. Much less has it been expressed in a steady and adequate allocation of resources.

Gender does have an institutional presence, but although gender-sensitive institutions have been designed to coordinate or execute gender policies, in most cases, due to lack of funding, such institutionality simply continues to be merely an advocacy tool; that is, an instrument meant to promote the concept of gender equality or denounce its absence. This alters the essence of such institutions as forming part of the state apparatus, and many times leads them to adopting positions closer to those assumed by non-governmental organizations. In reality, many are still marginalized from ordinary state efforts.

The above is not true in every case. In some countries, national divisions do have enough authority within the government. Some have even existed for more than ten years. It is also true, for example, that the equality plans adopted by Chile, Paraguay and Costa Rica, the countries with the most advanced plans so far, include budgetary aspects and application mechanisms. They also specify actions and the ways in which these are to be carried out.

DIAGNOSES

The central question about any policy is to whom it applies, who are its beneficiaries. In this sense, the fluctuations in women's circumstances throughout the region should always be taken into account. Wide gaps exist among women themselves with respect to equality. In some segments of the female population, the fertility rate has decreased; life expectancy, education and training have improved; and women have entered a labour market that now offers them new opportunities, especially in the service sector. At the other end of the spectrum, many poor women continue to be affected by high fertility rates and the lack of opportunities with regard to education and work. Globalization has also had negative effects on those with less mobility and flexibility, almost always associated with lower qualifications. Despite the fact that gender equality evidently goes beyond socio-economic equality, poverty in the region, and in particular the poverty affecting women, cannot be ignored.

Formal education for women has increased, especially at the basic and secondary levels. In most countries, university education for women has also flourished. In fact, the economically active female population is attaining higher educational levels than the male population. Women's educational level not only influences their job opportunities: almost half the women who did not complete primary school, for example, were teenage mothers, in comparison to only 7 per cent among those who finished secondary school. As ECLAC points out in its *Panorama social de América Latina 1997* (Social Panorama of Latin America 1997), teenage pregnancy significantly affects educational and labour opportunities for the mothers involved and for their offspring. Thus problems continue to prevail among the young female population, especially in the poor strata, even though the fertility rate has dropped in Latin America and the Caribbean thanks to the higher educational levels.

On the other hand, most women entering the labour force in urban sectors are between 25 and 49 years old and have between 10 and 12 years of schooling, which implies that they are better qualified for work. Participation among those with technical or university studies is higher than 70 per cent. Nevertheless, *Panorama 1997* confirms that, in spite of the rapid increase in female employment, women with low and medium levels of education are finding it increasingly difficult to enter the labour market successfully.

The proportion of women in the economically active population continues to rise, especially in urban areas, where, in many countries, it exceeds 45 per cent. In some countries, such as Colombia, participation levels of 50 per cent have been reached; even higher levels are found in the Caribbean. However, women continue to earn lower salaries than men do, by 10 per cent to 40 per cent. Lack of training and lack of access to new technologies are still decisive factors affecting large groups of women.

The ways to measure women's participation in labour continue to be biased, however, especially for the poorest women, since many of them work in the informal sector and their activity is not reflected in the statistics. Naturally, the high statistical underestimation of female labour in the economy's rural and informal sectors has broader implications: according to the 1995 UNDP report, 66 per cent of the work carried out by women in developing countries is nowhere to be found in National Accounts Systems.

Although changes in the last decade have produced new sources of employment, for a great majority of women the conditions under which they work are unfavourable if compared to those of men. High unemployment and underemployment rates prevail, especially among younger women. Opportunities to work mainly consist of domestic labour, self-employment and wage earning in micro-enterprises, or work in small and medium-scale enterprises in the more traditional sectors of the economy, usually as part of sub-contracting systems implemented by large corporations. In many cases, employment is in the form of piece-work to be carried out in the home, which is another form of vulnerable employment. Specific problems characterize this large concentration in low-productivity, low-income sectors. Several studies indicate, for example, that when new technologies for *maquila* industries appear, and a better-qualified labour force is required, enterprises generally prefer to upgrade male, not female, training.

Although in the last years a higher priority has been granted to social expenditure, and this expenditure has increasingly been targeted towards the poor population, many such programmes do not reach poor women unless they are specifically geared to them, such as programmes for female heads of household, for example, or more traditionally as small-scale projects of limited scope. The greatest incidence of poverty and extreme poverty is still recorded among female-headed households, since these women have fewer financial backers and have to carry out domestic labour as well as outside work. Women contribute about 30 per cent of the income in households where both partners work. This means that without the income contributed by women, urban poverty would increase from 2 per cent to 7 per cent. Other estimates in *Panorama 1997* highlight that, when one household member has work, the probability that the home will be poverty-stricken is higher than 80 per cent, while if more than one family member has work, the prob-ability that the household will not be classified as poor is higher than 60 per cent.

APPROACHES AND POLICIES

How can we cope with such a complex panorama? What approaches and methodologies can be used, at present, to confront such a variety of situations that interlink social, cultural, political and economic aspects and also involve equality and efficiency dimensions? In the last decades, the perceived reasons for women's discrimination and subordination have shifted, from being relative to the *integration of women into de-velopment* to integrating a *gender perspective*. Today, the belief that discrimination can be overcome through better education, more jobs and increased social and political participation is supplemented by an analysis focusing on the relations that men and women establish in societies, due to the cultural allocation of roles according to sex, and in which power relations play a key role.

This is complemented by *mainstreaming*, or the incorporation of a gender perspective into the wider interests constituting development. *Mainstreaming* covers the complexity of the processes involved, redefining the conceptual perspective as well as the discourse and operational schemes generated by policies. Although the theory centring on these concepts continues to evolve, and is very often used in contrasting ways, mainstreaming is a great advance for the design and application of policies. It allows complementing the diagnoses, both in order to locate them within a broader perspective and in order to create the demand for more precise data that can be suitably targeted for action.

This change of approach is currently associated with better instruments for the design and application of gender-sensitive policies, as I have already pointed out. This creates a very favourable opportunity to move from advocacy to laying greater emphasis on action. We have the potential and the capacity to apply new research and advice methodologies as inseparable processes. We can better systematize successful practices and the possibilities to share them. It is also possible to view the subject of policies in various ways. Nieves Rico, from ECLAC, proposes at least two such new ways in Chapter 13. The first highlights the differentiated impacts that policies have on people; that is, it contends that policies are not neutral. The second viewpoint, the one we are gradually converging towards, is that insufficient, inexact or biased diagnoses contribute, in effect, to designing policies that will also, in essence, discriminate against women. Integrating a gender perspective into this phase will allow drafting more equitable policies.

It is clear, therefore, that changes in the ways public policies are conceived and designed are required in order to achieve efficiency. Among other factors, we must take into account the impact of macro-economic policies on domestic work; on the informal sector, mainly composed of women; on female production in the rural sector and on the service activities in which women are increasingly involved. This also means examining how families adapt to the effects of these policies, and what these effects imply for the various family members. Furthermore, the specific effects on female-headed households should be examined. In all such cases, we are dealing with links that mostly remain invisible and thus inhibit our understanding of the complex distributive effects that macro-economic policies can have.

There is an equally broad spectrum of considerations regarding fiscal policy. In its recent report, *El pacto fiscal* (The Fiscal Pact), ECLAC suggests that, just as the macro-economic effects of fiscal policies are analysed regularly, the practice of analysing the effects of equity on tributary norms and public budgets should also be adopted. Just as the incidence of social expenditure on the different social groups is examined, its impact on gender should also be considered. Furthermore, since one of the objectives of this pact is to increase the effectiveness, efficiency and quality of public expenditure, a crucial factor in this process is to guarantee the capacity to reach particularly needy target groups, in this case the female population, especially in the low-income sector.

Meso-economics equally opens essential spaces in which to carry out gender-sensitive analysis. Let us consider, in particular, a most decisive area: the functioning of factor markets. A broad range of actions has emerged in this field. These actions may target how information systems give the market fluidity, training instruments and the discriminations that may form part of social security laws (job protection during pregnancy and breast-feeding, for example). In the capital market, there are also special programmes associated with the access to credit available to small-scale producers, among these, in particular, producers in urban and rural micro-enterprises, and female heads of households. In the land market, these actions relate to the guarantee of women's egalitarian access to property, which refers us to the more general issue of ascertaining equal property rights for women and men alike. In another field of meso-economics, which is very important just now, the effects of globalization and trade liberalization policies on the different social sectors must be constantly monitored, putting into practice policies that reduce the costs to the population or improve the distributive effects of such policies.

Linking economic policies with gender is no longer a theme for researchers alone. The United Nations General Assembly, in its Resolution 50/104 of 20 December 1997, urged governments to develop and promote methodologies incorporating a gender perspective into their policies, including economic ones. At the international level, several aspects are defined as having priority today: poverty alleviation, development and growth of human capital, fiscal policies and the areas of unpaid economic work. Although none of these yet forms part of the routine work that economists perform, experience at all levels already exists that will allow advances in this area. In fact, examples are beginning to abound and there are particularly interesting experiences at the level of the Commonwealth Secretariat, well worth studying closely.

The considerations and reflections contained in previous sections of this chapter allow the drafting of the following four action guidelines:

- To stabilize the institutions that have been evolving at national and international levels, obviously incorporating the improvements resulting from these experiences and, in particular, assigning sufficient resources so that these institutions can carry out the functions for which they were originally created.

- In terms of neo-institutional literature, beyond the formal institutions there are also informal ones: common beliefs and daily practices. The new approaches, which involve dealing with the global notion of a 'gender perspective', emphasize precisely those aspects directly related to the cultural assignation of roles according to sex, and, in consequence, to the need to transform these 'informal institutions'.

- An analysis of the differentiated impacts of public policies on the population must be incorporated, including a gender perspective as a key element of this analysis. This implies, in turn, that the follow-up of the effects of policies and economic processes, in general, should include an analysis of the differentiated impact.

- Themes to be allocated priority are already defined in the world agenda and in national and regional agendas, contemplating an ambitious range of action for public policies.

A complex, innovative and challenging panorama is coming into view. It seeks nothing more than to improve our work, produce more equality and better redistribution and improve efficiency. We have accepted this challenge and adhere to the thought that equal opportunities for men and women are the basis of a more equal distribution of the benefits of development. This is what all of us are seeking.

NOTE

1. José Antonio Ocampo has a PhD in economics. He is currently executive secretary of the Economic Commission for Latin America and the Caribbean (ECLAC, or CEPAL in its Spanish form).

CHAPTER 13

The Institutionalization of the Gender Approach within ECLAC

MARIA NIEVES RICO[1]

§ Two main approaches to gender and public policy stand out from the rest. One is to concentrate on the differentiated impacts that policies exert on men and women and identify the changes needed in order to achieve gender equality. The other is to study the implications of gender imbalances and relations for economic and social analyses, examining the options resulting from these analyses and understanding that such an approach enhances analytical accuracy when it comes to achieving the objectives of equality, efficiency and growth.

Bearing this in mind, ECLAC embarked on an internal revision of its institutional capacity with the express purpose of integrating a gender dimension into the bulk of its work. Its aim was to facilitate carrying out its central task of cooperating with Latin American and Caribbean countries by also actively promoting policies that support gender equality.

This chapter presents the characteristics of institutionalizing the gender approach in ECLAC's field of endeavour.

THE GENDER APPROACH AT ECLAC

Since the 1970s ECLAC has cooperated with its member states in the integral analysis of development processes and in the design, follow-up and evaluation of public policies geared to women. In 1993, it founded a special unit to integrate women and development. This unit received a strong impulse in 1997, when it joined the Executive Secretariat and began to form part of the organization's official structure. This has made it easier to cooperate and follow up how the gender approach is being integrated into programmes and projects, along with the rest of ECLAC's divisions and units. It has also facilitated examining the issues raised at the Regional Women's Conference, the inter-governmental forum held every three years.

The incorporation of a gender dimension at ECLAC has been substantially stimulated by (i) the advance in the conceptualization of women's role in development both as active cooperators and as beneficiaries; (ii) an increased recognition of women's productive role and their relevance in development areas that previously remained invisible, or were hard to conceptualize, in terms of gender disparities; and (iii) the conviction that gender has a cross-cutting nature. In this sense, women are not just 'a vulnerable group' for ECLAC. It is not enough to promote programmes and projects having a 'women's component', just as the gender dimension should be considered not only when women clearly form part of an intended target group, but also when it comes to making analyses at the macro level.

Although some problems encountered by women are gender-specific and may be dealt with separately, evaluating the effects of the various policies implemented has proved that a separatist perspective is insufficient in reality. It does not manage to integrate a gender perspective into the mainstream of development. Furthermore, it is wrong to presume that women are not also present in sectorial policies and programmes, or that genuine links do not exist between the gender approach and macro analyses and policies. Such an attitude has significantly hindered the progress towards equality. The diagnoses reached by ECLAC show that there is a substantial imbalance between the contribution women make to development and the benefits women receive. They also point to serious problems caused by inefficiency.

The proposals adopted by ECLAC's member countries for the 1990s[2] pose the need to apply an integrated development approach, meant to eliminate the gaps between social and economic policies and also address social equality, making social integration into democratic and productive societies possible. The current challenge is finding development strategies that benefit, in a synergetic way, both the position of women with respect to men, and poverty eradication and the achievement of economic growth, assuming that these benefits are self-reinforcing.

ECLAC's commitment is not just nominal. Incorporating a gender perspective has been a slow and often difficult process, but large qualitative and quantitative advances have been achieved throughout the learning process undertaken from the early 1970s up to the present.

In 1996, ECLAC's Women and Development Unit began cooperating regularly with the Planning Division in charge of drafting programmes and operations. The purpose was to incorporate the gender approach, in an integrated and systematic manner, to all of ECLAC's sectorial projects. The work involved mainly hinges on:

- making sure *ex-ante* evaluations are carried out, making it possible to infer how the changes promoted by the projects might influence women, and how women themselves might contribute to these projects; and
- when drafting objectives, explicitly considering strategic gender needs such as the elimination of subordination and discrimination against women (which has political connotations), and the needs involving improving the quality of life and associated to technical changes.

A decisive step was taken in 1997, in the process of going from theory to action. Jointly with the German Technical Cooperation Agency (GTZ), the Women and Development Unit created the project 'Institutionalization of a Gender Approach in ECLAC' as part of its activities. Among the activities undertaken as part of this effort, the following stand out:

- An analysis of ECLAC's regular working programme for 1998–99, and of the projects to be executed. Subject areas and possible research, cooperation and related activities were identified to which the gender approach might be integrated, making use of the institutional resources available. A permanent dialogue was instituted for putting the gender approach into practice and involving the different divisions.
- Development of a study about the perceptions and contributions of the top managerial levels engaged in the key divisions, regarding the strategy designed to institutionalize ECLAC's gender approach.[3] This activity corresponded to the conviction that a process of these characteristics requires collective action and a participatory and transparent type of involvement, in which the fact that those taking the decisions display personal commitment is a key factor for change to actually take place;
- Organization of short internal workshops for top and middle management staff, in order to discuss how the gender approach might be incorporated to the cooperation and research-related activities undertaken by the organization.[4]
- The participatory and consensual design of a strategy to institutionalize the gender approach. This strategy, in compliance with

ECLAC's mandate, defined as its main objective: 'Incorporating a gender approach to the development co-operation that ECLAC lends to Latin American and Caribbean countries, so that women and men can benefit equally from this co-operation.'[5]

Currently the strategy is being tuned, consolidated and put up for internal consultation, in order for the different observations to be integrated and for its components to be planned so that it can truly be regarded as an institutional action plan.

The results of this project show that ECLAC has become flexible enough to analyse the differentiated impact of public policies on women and men, especially at the micro- and meso-economic levels, although the greatest resistance is still to be found with respect to the macro level. It is also worth pointing out that there is genuine interest in identifying the gender variables that might positively affect the growth and efficiency of Latin American and Caribbean economies, as well as their equality. The political will also exists to consider gender aspects from a cross-cutting perspective, as well as to undertake more inter-divisional work, also involving ECLAC's sub-regional offices,[6] in the belief that introducing a gender approach is bound to improve the quality of the organization's products and technical assistance. ECLAC's Secretariat is politically committed to all these endeavours.

Since gender-sensitive information and expertise are still low, the project has also permitted identifying support, training and guidance needs, as well as the procedures and instruments needed to reach the objectives proposed and break with certain institutional habits. There is a pressing need to consolidate a clearer theoretical understanding of the gender perspective and of the different sectorial themes constituting ECLAC's working areas. A new reading of ECLAC's 'Productive Transformation with Equality Proposal' – based on the gender approach – is a desired complementary measure.

Finally, it is worth highlighting that, during the 27th Assembly held in Aruba (May 1998), the member countries approved a new sub-programme as part of ECLAC's 2000–01 working programme. It extends the thematic, working, internal and external cooperation competencies of the Women and Development Unit. Express reference is made to the Unit's coordinating role in institutionalizing the gender approach, which is also bound to strengthen ECLAC's development cooperation capacity with other countries in the region.

SUSTAINABILITY

At present, ECLAC's development cooperation with the Latin America and Caribbean region, as well as the design, implementation and evaluation of public policies in these countries, lacks the mechanisms and procedures needed to ensure a cross-cutting incorporation of the gender approach into the different sectorial areas, as well as into the general notion of development. Efforts in this direction have yet to be systematized and considered an intrinsic part of 'good practice'. This might lead to analysing more accurately the socio-economic reality in these countries and support the drafting and implementation of public policy proposals much more in keeping with the needs of the different population sectors.

Other obstacles that must be overcome can also be identified: the tendency to believe that incorporating a gender approach is an extra chore, not a basic strategy in programming and policy designing; the lack of budget to ensure an effective gender analysis; the lack of a sex-desegregated information system revealing the differentiated roles men and women perform in society and helping to evaluate women's contribution to national development; the lack of permanent consultation mechanisms useful to identify the interests and needs of the different female population sectors; and the shortage of participation channels for the taking of public decisions.

Activities that take place at two complementary levels support ECLAC's efforts to institutionalize the gender approach. One of these is at the level of the organization's internal functioning. The other corresponds to the joint tasks developed alongside ministries and other government offices in the countries of the region.

In the first place, and as part of an ongoing training process of an organization wishing to be receptive to learning and innovation, the objectives/requirements are:

- Advancing in the conceptual understanding of the gender analysis within the framework of ECLAC's proposal for the region: a productive transformation undertaken with equality.
- Specifying procedures and instruments for the programmatic incorporation of a gender approach into the projects, with a heavy involvement of ECLAC's Planning Division in the programmes and operations.
- Providing systematic and hands-on consultancy and guidance

methods to ECLAC's main divisions and facilitating dialogue of a political and technical nature among experts and their counterparts in member countries, in the area of gender and in the sectorial themes of their competence.

- Improving diagnoses and expanding sex-desegregated statistical information, a task expressly to be carried out by the Division of Statistics and Economic Forecasts.

- Establishing follow-up and evaluation criteria for mainstreaming the gender approach in the design, implementation, follow-up and evaluation of public policies, especially in those countries having Equal Opportunities Plans and other institutional instruments directly aimed at reducing the existing gender gap between men and women.

- The sustainability of the process begun by ECLAC is grounded on the political will of its top management and also on the interest manifested by all its staff, so that through the incorporation of a gender approach the quality of the organization's work can improve and respond to the needs of the region in a more coherent way. It is also supported on an open debate, internally, and externally on the gender approach adopted by the different sectors, as well as by macroeconomic analysis. In the present, ever-changing scenario, and within the framework of ongoing state reforms, this is bound to contribute significantly to reaching common objectives for Latin America and the Caribbean: equality, efficiency, economic growth and sustainability. Thus modernity and modernization will help cancel out the long-standing debt to women that the previous centuries have accumulated.

NOTES

1. Maria Nieves Rico is an anthropologist. She is currently social affairs officer of ECLAC's Women and Development Unit.

2. See mainly CEPAL (1992) Equidad y transformación productiva: un enfoque integrado (LC/G.1701/1-P), Santiago de Chile.

3. The results of this study are to be found in Rico, M. N. (1998) *Estudio-consulta para el desarrollo de una estrategia de institucionalización del enfoque de género en el trabajo sustantivo de la CEPAL*, LC/R.1813, Santiago de Chile: ECLAC.

4. ECLAC (1997) *Informe de la reunión sobre estrategia de institucionalización del enfoque de género en el trabajo sustantivo de la CEPAL*, Santiago de Chile, 17 October 1997, LC/L.1088, Santiago de Chile.

5. The first version of the Strategy is to be found in Rico 1998, pp. 16–21.

6. The Sub-regional Office for Mexico and Central America has already begun an internal study with the same characteristics as the one carried out at ECLAC's headquarters in Santiago de Chile.

PART FOUR

Case Studies from Latin America

CHAPTER 14

Gender and the Labour Market in Colombia

CECILIA LÓPEZ MONTAÑO[1]

§ We must view the link between gender and the labour market within the context of the changes taking place in both areas. In the last 50 years, developments in production and trade have transformed the national and international composition of capital and labour. A convergence of economic, social and demographic factors has also progressively modified the gender division of labour, relations and roles with regard to production and reproduction at the core of the family. The development processes of the mid-twentieth century were cause and effect of large socio-demographic changes that altered gender relations: a rise in formal education, a decrease in family size and women's increasing economic participation encouraged their autonomy. A sharper division between sexuality and reproduction and the legitimization of different types of marital unions, together with other less tangible processes, have influenced men's and women's mentalities and the way in which the spaces that each gender inhabits are defined.

Liberalization, globalization and economic growth have had a combined effect, by transforming the labour market's composition and the dynamics of its sectors and the sexual division of labour. One of the most obvious developments is that women's participation in the economy's formal sector has increased in many countries. This, in turn, has decreased the traditionally high indexes of female participation in the informal sector, generating a relative growth in women's labour productivity and helping to breach their salary gap with men.

Labour demand is selective according to sex, education and life cycles. Male labour continues to prevail in some sub-sectors, while women acquire comparative advantages in others. This chapter examines some trends in Colombia's urban labour market observable in recent years, considering men and women's differential participation rates, the implications of economic and social structures and the challenges such changes have posed to the development process and to the design of sector and macro-economic policies. Our analysis is based on data collected by the Department of Administrative National Statistics (DANE) for its Quarterly Household Survey. The data processing was done as part of the Labour Market Study, undertaken by the Employment Division of the National Planning Department.[2]

One of the most revealing facts about how women's share in the economy has increased is their growing insertion into the labour market. Though this worldwide trend flourished much earlier in the developed world, the most striking advances are now taking place in the developing world. As Figure 14.1 illustrates, women's global participation rates (GPR) are still lower in developing countries but, in general, they have risen substantially during the last decades.

Colombia has not only shared this process: it has had more dynamic growth than most Latin American countries, a fact already confirmed by examining national and international diagnoses.

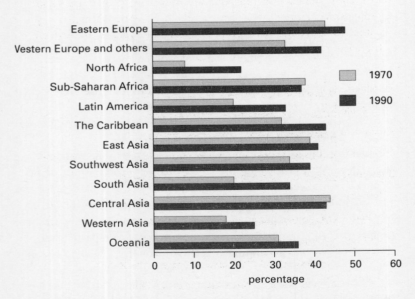

FIGURE 14.1 Women's participation in the labour force (*source*: *Year Book of Statistics*)

THE FEMALE URBAN LABOUR MARKET

In Colombia, the global urban rate of women's share in the labour market rose from 19 per cent in 1950 to 51 per cent in 1997. Although this is common to Latin America, women's share in Colombia's labour market is among the highest in the region (Figure 14.2).

Although a significant increase in women's labour participation is a generalized occurrence in Western societies, particularly in Latin America, the levels reached in Colombia have particular characteristics, related not only to the dynamics of the labour market itself but also to gains made in other sectors, such as education, demography, culture and politics, as we will now demonstrate.

• The drastic drop in the country's fertility rate, unprecedented in the entire region, has not only meant smaller families. National public campaigns, together with other social changes, have strengthened women's capacity to make their own decisions not only with respect to their sexuality and reproduction, but also to their personal life projects. Very often, this effect tends to be underestimated when it comes to analysing demographic and labour-related transitions.

• Increasing and more permanent access to education has substantially

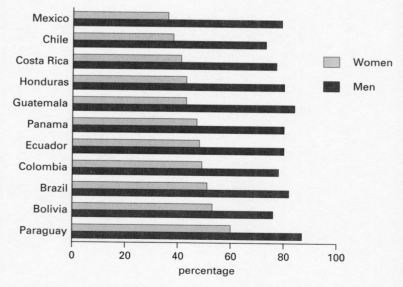

FIGURE 14.2 Participation rate per sex in urban zones, 1995 (*source*: CEPAL)

raised the levels of formal training for women, also upgrading the economic value of their time. The average years spent by women in formal education rose from 7.06 in 1976 to 9.85 in 1996, an increment of 2.79 years. It was much lower for men: from 6.98 to 8.20, during the same time span, an increment of just 1.22 years.

- The labour market's growing diversification and the expansion of sectors such as education and health, which tend to recruit a good share of female labour, partly explain the rise in women's participation rates. In the last decade, qualitative changes in the labour market have also helped to develop sectors favouring female recruitment: finances, communication, tourism and trade.
- Heading a household affects participation positively for both men and women. Consequently, the rise in the number of female-headed households has fostered women's labour participation. Although a link between women-headed households and poverty prevails, this link does not always exist, according to various diagnoses conducted. The proportion of female household heads is greater among the non-impoverished population than among the poor. Nevertheless, poverty continues to affect many male-headed households also.
- Traditionally, the presence of children under six limits female participation in the labour market. As the number of children per household decreases, it has become easier for women to work outside

FIGURE 14.3 Rate of participation per sex and marital status, September 1996 (*source*: DNP-UDS)

the home. The availability of cheap female manual labour to take over the care of home and children mitigates this effect for higher-income women. Thus, the presence of very young children inhibits women's labour participation to a higher degree in developed societies than in developing ones. In Colombia, the need for additional income has stimulated women joining the labour force, a situation further influenced by the drastic drop in fertility.

• The differential effect caused by marital status in previous decades, which accounted for women married or living in free unions having lower participation rates, tended to decrease during this decade. As Figure 14.3 shows, a remarkable increase in the labour participation of married or free-union women in the categories shown, has taken place.

There does seem to be evidence of a negative relation between income per capita and female GPR in the Latin American context, as Figure 14.4 indicates. Women therefore feel more pressure to find work in poorer societies, a phenomenon made all that much more acute by the rise in male unemployment.

In Colombia, contrary to what might be expected, male labour participation and wage earning have a positive influence on women's own

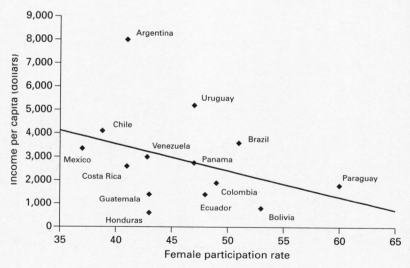

FIGURE 14.4 Rate of female participation and income per capita
(*source*: CEPAL, World Bank)

labour participation. The fact that men work or earn higher incomes does not imply that women remain inactive or withdraw from the labour market once they set up common households.

The above is evident by observing the regional GPR. Figure 14.5 indicates how female GPR is closely linked to male GPR. Both men and women have the highest GPR in Pasto and, likewise, both men and women in the Coast have the lowest GPR.

Female urban employment In the seven main metropolitan areas, two and a half million women are employed, representing 43 per cent of the total economically active population. They are mainly concentrated in the following sectors: service (37 per cent), commerce (29 per cent) and industry (21 per cent). In the productive sectors, those that have more female than male participation are services (56 per cent), commerce (48 per cent), industry (43 per cent) and banking (40 per cent).

Besides the sectors mentioned above, some macro-economic changes have also favoured women's involvement in the labour force. Reforms such as Law 50 have increased the flexibility of the labour market accompanying economic liberalization in Colombia and a good number of Latin American countries. This added flexibility has favoured the recruitment of female labour, making it more feasible for women to take part in production and reproduction activities. It is more to the advantage of entrepreneurs to hire women, since they may be just as

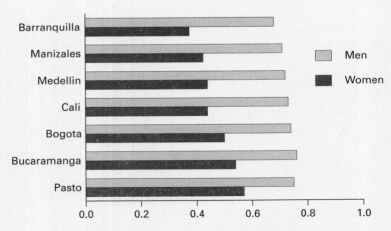

FIGURE 14.5 Rate of participation per sex in seven metropolitan areas, September 1996 (*source*: UDS-DNP)

qualified as men but accept lower wages in exchange for more flexible shifts. Such flexibility has positive and negative effects: on the one hand, it increases women's participation in the labour market; on the other hand, it increases their workload and reinforces the structures that favour paying women lower wages by hiring them as temporary workers. As Figure 14.6 illustrates, employment cycles are more striking in the case of women, since women are forced to fulfil two types of work. Because of the occupations they tend to choose, women are also more prone to lose their jobs during a crisis.

Parallel to the growing rate in female employment, there was a significant reduction in the presence of women in the informal sector during the 1990s (see Figure 14.7). While the gap in the rate of participation in the informal market between men and women was six points in 1984, in 1996 it closed completely. Contrary to previous trends and to the experiences of other countries in the region, the index of female participation in the informal market decreased much faster than the male one: the first went from 57.5 per cent in 1984 to 58.8 per cent in 1988, and from 58.8 per cent in 1988 to 52.2 per cent in 1996; for men, it fluctuated between 51.4 per cent in 1984 to 54.4 per cent in 1988 and 52 per cent in 1996.

The gap in urban salaries   The rise in women's educational level increased their relative productivity with respect to men and, consequently,

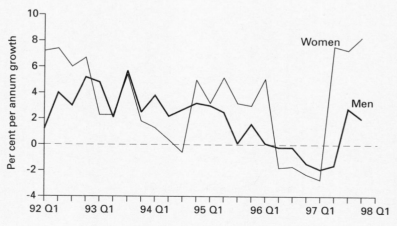

FIGURE 14.6 Growth of employment per sex in seven areas
(*source*: DNP-UDS)

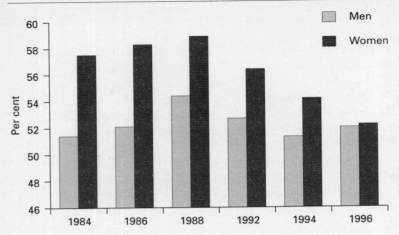

FIGURE 14.7 Rate of employment in the informal sector per sex in ten areas
(*source*: DNP-UDS)

their relative incomes. Therefore there was a large reduction in the
previous gap existing between male and female salaries. In 1982 women
earned, on average, 36 per cent less than men did. In 1996, the gap
decreased to 27 per cent. However, when discrimination by educational
level is present, substantial differences still occur.

Figure 14.8 illustrates the gaps in salaries differentiated per educational level. Thus the greatest salary gaps between men and women are

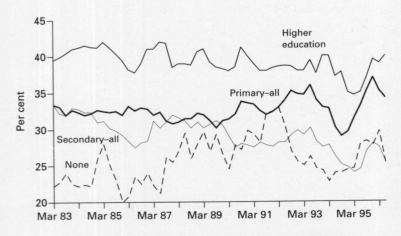

FIGURE 14.8 Salary gap per educational level (*source*: DNP-UDS)

found at the level of higher education. On an average, women earn 40 per cent less than men do at this level.

This difference may be explained by two factors: one is occupational and the other one has to do with age. Women have comparatively less access to top management postings in large companies. Such positions imply very high salaries and are still predominantly filled by men, although Colombia has practically the highest rate of female participation at the occupational summit – 27 per cent – surpassed in Latin America only by Uruguay, with 28 per cent. However, there is a link between wages and careers, and women's educational choices tend to focus on careers that are less valued and less well paid. With respect to the age variable, the reduction in the salary gap for non-single women, under 39 years old, is very sharp, while for women older than 50 the gap is almost 50 per cent. For women between 25 and 29 it is 13.28 per cent and for women between 20 and 24 it is under 10 per cent. This drastic reduction may reflect both changes in men and women's professional training and a decrease in pay for men with a simultaneous increase in women's wages (Figure 14.9).

Figure 14.10 shows the gap in salaries per city. The highest gap corresponds to Pasto and the lowest to Manizales and Barranquilla.

Female urban unemployment Traditionally, women are the most affected by unemployment, especially young women (Figure 14.11).

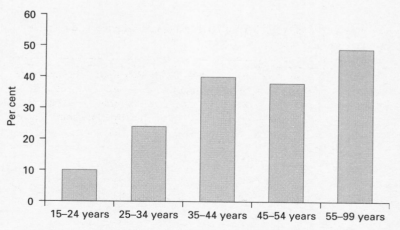

FIGURE 14.9 Salary gap between actively employed withcomplete higher education in seven areas, June 1996 (*source*: DNP-UDS)

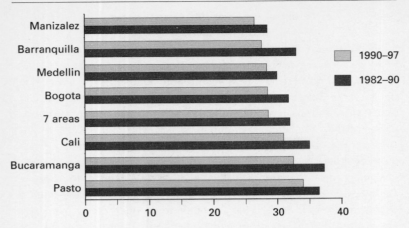

FIGURE 14.10 Average gap in salaries per city (*source*: DNP-UDS)

Nevertheless, an analysis of unemployment rates per sex and age for the seven main cities revealed that the gap between male and female rates of unemployment has been closing during the 1990s (Figure 14.12). This reduction[3] is explained by a greater rise in female labour participation and an increase in male unemployment, illustrated by the changes in labour demand according to gender.

The unemployment rate follows a similar pattern between men and women with respect to age (Figure 14.13).

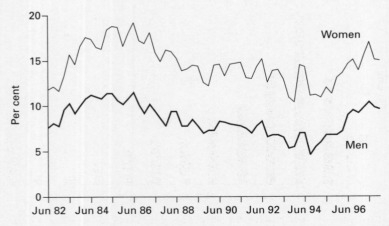

FIGURE 14.11 Unemployment rate per sex in seven areas (*source*: DNP-UDS)

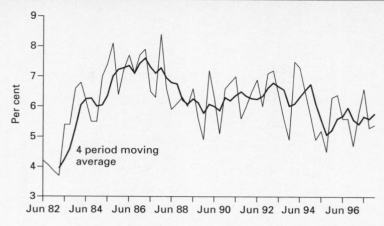

FIGURE 14.12 Gap in employment rate per sex (*source*: DNP-UDS)

The highest unemployment rates are found among women between 15 and 19 years old. Women who have not completed secondary education are the least likely to find a job, while professional women are the ones with the best chances. In general, women with the highest education and those with no education at all are the least likely to be unemployed. Women with just secondary education (complete or incomplete) do not find work easily.

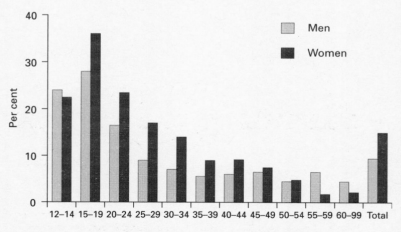

FIGURE 14.13 Unemployment rate per age group in seven areas, September 1996 (*source*: DNP-UDS)

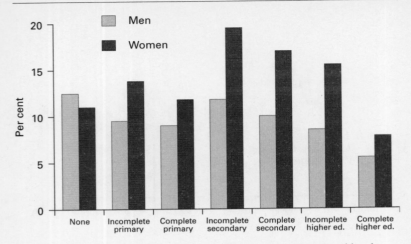

FIGURE 14.14 Unemployment rate per sex and per educational level, September 1996 (*source*: DNP-UDS)

FEMALE RURAL LABOUR MARKET

Rural women's GPR decreased in the early 1990s, therefore co-inciding with the crisis in the agricultural sector. From 1994 onwards it recovered. GPR behaviour is largely explained by the evolution of the occupational rate, which shows the same trend (Figure 14.15).

Just as in the urban area, the women more actively engaged in paid labour are those with more education and between the ages of 20 and

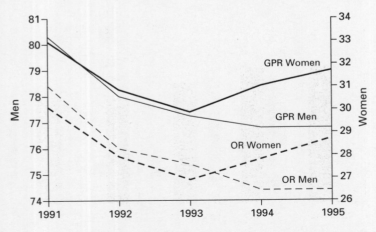

FIGURE 14.15 Rural GPR and employment rate per sex (*source*: DNP-UDS)

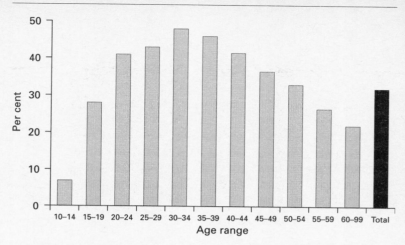

FIGURE 14.16 Rural female GPR per age, 1995 (*source*: DNP-UDS)

44 (see Figure 14.16). This implies that due to the existence of extended families, being of reproductive age does not discourage women from participating in the labour force.

Female GPR per region offers striking contrasts. The highest participation rate is found in the Pacific and eastern regions; the Atlantic region has the lowest (Figure 14.17).

Per occupational status, female employment in rural areas primarily

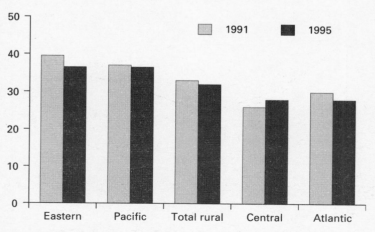

FIGURE 14.17 Rural female GPR per region (*source*: DNP-UDS)

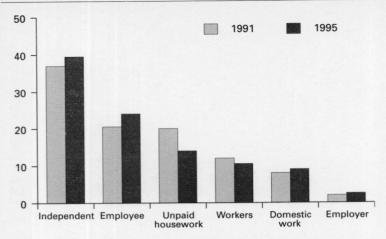

FIGURE 14.18 Distribution of economically active rural female population
per occupational sector (*source*: DNP-UDS)

consists of self-employed workers: 39.5 per cent of female rural employment. Women tend to be in charge of running small plots or holdings,
while men tend to work for wages in the agricultural sector (Figure
14.18).

Per occupational sector, as observed in Figure 14.19, female rural

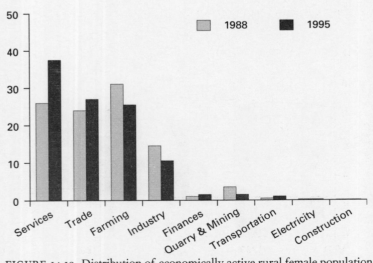

FIGURE 14.19 Distribution of economically active rural female population
per branch of activity (*source*: DNP-UDS)

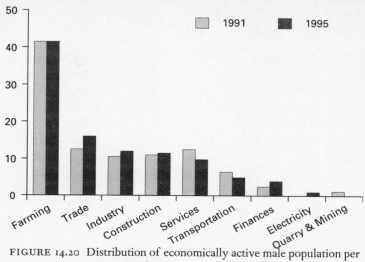

FIGURE 14.20 Distribution of economically active male population per occupational sector (*source*: DNP-UDS)

employment is concentrated in the tertiary sector (commerce and services). The same does not hold true for male employment (Figure 14.20).

Rural unemployment is higher among women than among men (Figure 14.21), just as in the urban area. Similarly, the peasant women most affected by unemployment are the very young and those who only have secondary education (complete or not) (Figures 14.22 and 14.23).

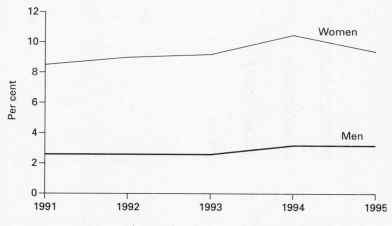

FIGURE 14.21 Rural unemployment per sex (*source*: DNP-UDS)

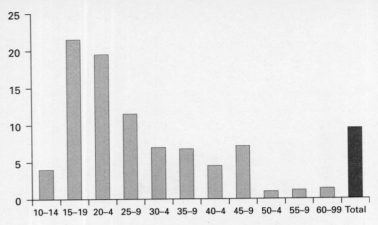

FIGURE 14.22 Female unemployment per age (*source*: DNP-UDS)

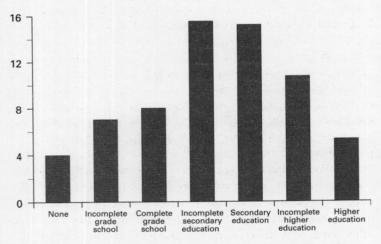

FIGURE 14.23 Female rural unemployment per educational level for 1995
(*source*: DNP-UDS)

CONCLUSIONS

Taking gender into account, the most outstanding characteristics of the Colombian labour market's behaviour during the last years are as follows:

- There has been a remarkable acceleration in women's labour participation rate, accompanied by a deceleration in the growth rate of the male labour force. By the end of 1997, the global rate of female participation had reached 51 per cent, rising from 44 per cent at the beginning of the 1990s. This is among the highest level of female employment in Latin America. Countries such as Argentina, Chile and Mexico had a 36–37 per cent rate in 1995. The masculine rate has been 74 per cent since 1987.

- Women with a higher education are strongly represented in the labour market. The greatest growth rate is to be found in the formal sector. In fact, the rate of female labour participation in the informal sector considerably declined during this period, dropping from 56 per cent to 52 per cent in the last ten years.

- These processes have been accompanied by greater productivity for women, expressed in the closing of the salary gap between men and women. There has been a rise in the wages women receive for their work, at the same time that there has been a wage drop for men. This circumstance has a levelling effect that tacitly decreases the factors related to discrimination against women by employers.

- In general, the macro-economic changes caused by globalization and the modernization of the state favour the demand for qualified labour, with a special preference for women. The expansion of health and education services as a result of increasing needs generated by modernization and health reforms produces more jobs for women since, traditionally, they have worked in these areas. The strengthening of the finance and communication sectors, for example, and more complex trade modalities, have become niches in which female labour predominates. In contrast, sectors that have historically demanded male workers are more affected by a recession in the fields of industry and construction. These changes produce both negative and positive effects. On the one hand, they promote participation in the labour market, wage earning and the building of autonomy, but on the other hand, they affect women's quality of life in terms of their income and the length of their working shifts.

- Another factor linked to the rise in female employment is the increased flexibility of working shifts product of Law 50 (reform of the Colombian labour system). This law released employers from previous commitments with regard to labour stability, hiring and wage scales. In so far as women continue to bear the brunt of domestic responsibilities and child-raising, flexible working shifts allow women to organize their time better so that their double burdens can be made more compatible, although these shifts do not necessarily reduce the amount of hours worked.

- There have also been changes in traditional trends of unemployment. Although the rate of female unemployment is much higher than the male one, the former tends to remain stable while the latter tends to increase. In 1992, the rate of female unemployment was 15.01 per cent and the male one was 8.14 per cent. In 1997, the female rate remained at 15.08 per cent, and the male rate rose to 9.56 per cent. The unemployment gap between men and women decreased from 45.7 per cent to 36.6 per cent. Those with the highest unemployment rate were youngsters of both sexes between 12 and 19 years old, followed by those between 20 and 24 years old, who had either completed or partially done their secondary education.

High female labour participation also exists in the rural sector. Rural women employment is concentrated in the tertiary sector. Most of these women are self-employed.

With respect to access to technology and less traditional occupations, peasant women have not significantly benefited from rural modernization. Women still tend to be in charge of small plots and are involved in activities very often linked to reproduction. This helps to keep invisible the economic contribution that peasant women make to the family unit and to society as a whole.

NOTES

1. Cecilia López Montaño is an economist and has an MA in population studies. She has acted as minister of planning and minister in charge of national policies for women's equity in Colombia, minister of environment and minister of agriculture. Currently she is a researcher and international consultant.

2. See Luz Henao, M. and A. Parra (1998) 'Labour markets in Colombia', *Equity, Gender and Development in Colombia*, DNP-Tercer Mundo Editors, July.

3. The gap in the rate of unemployment is defined as female unemployment minus male unemployment.

CHAPTER 15

Poverty Information, Poverty Reduction Strategies and Gender: A Colombian Case Study

ROSEMARY MCGEE[1]

§ This chapter is based on research carried out in Colombia in 1996–97 on the subject of poverty assessment, poverty reduction policies and programmes, and gender issues. The research sought to explore these issues from two angles: first, 'from the bottom upwards' – how poverty is experienced and described by poor people in rural communities of Cauca department; and second, how poverty is conceived of in Colombian policy circles – how information about poverty is constructed, and how it leads to the design and implementation of particular policy approaches to the problem. In this chapter I wish to share some insights and reflections emerging from that fieldwork, to substantiate the theoretical propositions that poverty is a gendered condition and that poverty reduction efforts must therefore take gender dimensions into account in order to succeed. This is not, of course, a condition sufficient to guarantee their success, but it is a necessary condition.

The chapter starts by spelling out basic underlying premises about poverty, gender, economics and the mechanisms of policy-formulation and policy delivery. The main theoretical elements of the gender and poverty debate are then reviewed. The essential characteristics of the contemporary approach to poverty reduction in this country – broadly similar to those applied throughout Latin America – are identified. Moving to the other end of the policy process – the poor population at whom the policies are directed – some outputs are presented from the case study research undertaken in Cauca department. The implications of these insights are discussed with reference to the characteristics of the poverty reduction approach currently under way in Colombia, and used to illustrate the importance of gender dimensions in poverty and public policy delivery. On the basis of these implications, reflections are offered as to how the contemporary approach might be modified so as to better take account of gender dimensions, thus enhancing the overall efficacy of poverty reduction measures, as well as the equity of their outcomes.

SOME UNDERLYING PREMISES

Poverty   In the neo-liberal world view that prevails today, poverty is conceived of as income deficit, leading to consumption shortfall. This conception leads directly to policy prescriptions that centre on the promotion of income-earning opportunities through labour-intensive growth models, deregulation of labour and capital markets, and basic human capital formation, with transfers for those incapacitated to work. An alternative view of poverty, one that seems to me more useful for understanding the realities of poor communities in Latin America and responding to their plight, is that propounded by Chambers (1983, 1995, 1997a, 1998), Jodha (1988), Bernstein et al. (1992), and growing numbers of poverty analysts drawing on socio-anthropological research. In this view, poverty is a complex of deprivations, varying according to location and people, and including among other facets a lack of physical necessities, social inferiority, isolation (geographical, in terms of communication, information and access to markets and social services), physical weakness, vulnerability to external shocks and personal livelihood crises, seasonality, powerlessness in contexts of exploitation and bargaining, humiliation and low self-esteem. These dimensions are mutually reinforcing, making up a deprivation trap or vicious circle of poverty (Chambers 1983: 111–12). The conventional concept reduces this complex, diverse reality to a one-dimensional phenomenon, thus simplifying the exercise of designing responses to it. The more realistic view addresses it in all its complexity and messiness, on the principle that to do otherwise would be to fail to address the real problem at all.

Gender   The roles and obligations assigned by each society to its female and male members, commonly referred to as gender identities, are different and unequal. This gender inequality – a form of power relations – manifests itself in many spheres of life but most fundamentally within two social institutions, the household and the labour market. In peasant communities in Colombia gender obligations are referred to as such, *la obligación*. For women this consists of being a good mother and a chaste and obedient *compañera*, responsible for bearing and raising children, running the household efficiently and ensuring that the resources available to the household stretch to meet its needs. For men it consists of providing a secure livelihood for their families; beyond those functional to the fulfilment of this material duty, no behavioural standards are prescribed, although extremely antisocial behaviour by men – such as wife-beating – is usually socially condemned.

Poverty as a gendered condition Gender roles and obligations mean that the two sexes experience life and interact with people and institutions differently. In the case of poor people, some of the facets of poverty mentioned above are experienced to different degrees or in different ways by each sex. Hitherto much of the gender and poverty debate has focused on the greater income poverty of women *vis-à-vis* men, especially women heads of household, often argued to be over-represented among the poor. Awareness has grown recently of the poverty of women and girls *within* households, resulting from inequitable patterns of intra-household resource distribution. Appreciation has grown, too, that whatever the relative *income* poverty of males and females, other facets of poverty – especially social inferiority, powerlessness, vulnerability, isolation, physical weakness and low self-esteem – are experienced more extensively and more acutely by women than by men. This is discussed at greater length in the following section of the chapter.

The economy as a peopled sphere Economics works through people, through their behaviour as consumers and producers, their interaction with each other and with economic institutions. Economic policy measures seek to bring about changes in economic performance by influencing behaviour at the micro and meso levels. The same can be said of all public policy: policy measures take effect when people and institutions change their behaviour in response to restrictions and incentives introduced.

The perception gap A gap exists between the perceptions of the 'experts' who make policy, and the people who are the objects of that policy (McGee 1997a, 1997b, 1998). In the case of poverty reduction policy the gap is particularly wide. Many of those who formulate poverty reduction policy have no experience of poverty. By virtue of their position, they can have only outsiders' views of the poor, which, according to Chambers, 'are distorted in many ways. Lack of contact or communication permits [outsiders] to form those views without the inconvenience of knowledge, let alone personal exposure' (Chambers 1983: 104). Given the neo-liberal stress on narrow targeting of social benefits, this perception gap has become critical. The way in which poverty is conceptualized and the form in which information on poverty is gathered and presented to policy-makers shape and limit the definition and identification of target groups, the formulation of strategies and their translation into practice. These are not the only factors, but they are very significant in determining whether and how policy-makers take up the views and positions of the poor and whether poverty reduction strategies reflect these. So the type and quality of poverty information becomes vital in the process of addressing poverty: it can be instrumental in narrowing the perception gap, and hence in making state responses appropriate and adequate.

POOR WOMEN AND MEN, GIRLS AND BOYS

Precise empirical evidence on the extent of poverty among women is in fact patchy, despite the 'feminization of poverty' thesis that became current in the 1980s. In some studies no link has been established between female household headship and poverty, or the links observed are better explained by other compositional or cultural characteristics common to female-headed households, than by the sex of the head *per se* (Baden and Milward 1995; Kabeer 1992). Since this is not the focus of the present chapter, suffice it to say that female-headed households compared to male-headed households tend to show higher dependency ratios, lower average earnings of main earners, fewer assets, less access to productive resources or high-paying employment, and longer hours of domestic labour (ibid.: 18–19). The debate about female-headed households has drawn attention to the inadequacy of the 'sex of household head' indicator, and highlighted the need for a more disaggregated analysis of the household.

All the common household-level measures of income poverty start from the assumption that intra-household differentials are insignificant (Kabeer 1991: 242). But conventional assumptions about nuclear, male-headed households, wherein altruistic male breadwinners share their income equitably between all members, have been contested and superseded. '[B]argaining and cooperative conflict models of the household, which allow for gender analysis, are now widely accepted' (Baden and Milward 1995: 13). In the light of these findings, the well-being of each household member cannot simply be extrapolated from the overall household well-being status. Using Sen's entitlements approach it has been posited that members are in fact differentially deprived, women and girls losing out to male members, due to 'asymmetries in household entitlements' – that is, gender differences in the 'implicit contracts between household members governing the distribution of food and work and of the specific responsibilities entailed in making a living and building a family' (Kabeer 1992: 10). Because of the difficulty of researching inside the household, however, few data are available on intra-household distribution and comparative well-being of individual members.

Besides intra-household inequalities, the gender division of labour, which shapes work patterns both within and beyond the household, is identified by Elson as another key to women's greater susceptibility to poverty:

> women as a gender do not enjoy the same relationship to their own labour, as do men as a gender. For women, the ability to work is not socially constituted as something they can unconditionally own and can freely dispose of. Firstly, the sexual division of labour constitutes certain types of work as the social obligation of women ... Secondly, women's relationship to their own labour is conditioned by their relationship to men ... Moreover, they may not even be able to fully control the fruits of their labours – it may be appropriated by their menfolk. The first problem of access women face is access to their own labour: and this problem of access arises in the heart of the family. (Elson 1992: 12)

Some hold that women are more likely to control the fruits of their labour when these are earned in the marketplace than when their labour is 'subsumed within the household' (Kabeer 1992: 13). However, women's position in the marketplace must not be overestimated either. Women are often propelled into the labour force under unfavourable conditions. In Sen's 'cooperative conflicts' model of the household, women's and girls' disadvantage in intra-household resource allocation is explained by their 'fallback position' being worse than their male counterparts' should the household break down (Sen 1990). Women's inferior fallback position denotes a generally inferior status beyond the household, particularly in the labour market. The notion of a 'labour tax' has been used to describe the constraints imposed on women's productive capacities in the marketplace by their socially conferred caring duties in the home (Elson 1992, citing Palmer).

In summary: gender differences exist in the extent of income poverty at both household and individual level. The cause of greater female poverty is gender discrimination, especially in the household and in the labour market. Gendered analyses of these social institutions – such as Sen's 'cooperative conflicts' model – have explained why and how income poverty is differentiated by gender and pinpointed the flawed assumptions about intra-household behaviour on which common models rest.

But a gendered analysis of poverty not only shows the conventional household model to be defective; it challenges the primacy of the economic concept of poverty in itself. The foregoing discussion reveals that individuals with equivalent labour endowments do not enjoy equal scope for transforming their capacities into improved purchasing power. Individuals' prospects for avoiding or overcoming poverty are mediated by their gender roles and relations – that is, by the lesser voice of women as a gender, and their relative lack of social standing and political bargaining power to attain satisfaction of their needs, both as individuals and as household heads. Unequal social relations are thus as much a cause of poverty as lack of income-earning opportunities. Since social relations are gendered, '[i]n the analysis of poverty a gender analysis is essential in identifying social and cultural practices which contribute to immiseration' (Goetz n.d.).

Gender analysts share the position of the alternative poverty analysts referred to earlier: that the concepts of 'deprivation' and 'livelihood' are more useful than those of income poverty and employment if development policy is to become more attuned to the needs of the world's poor (Baden and Milward 1995; Kabeer 1991, 1992, 1994). To capture gender dimensions, '[t]he conceptualization of poverty needs to be expanded to include concepts of vulnerability and powerlessness' (Goetz n.d.), as well as lack of social status and isolation. For poor women, these may constitute privations as great as shortage of income. 'Livelihood' refers to the whole range of activities in which the poor engage to satisfy their material needs, including home gardening, exploitation of common property resources, scavenging, processing, hawking, share-rearing of livestock, transporting, contract work, casual labour, domestic service, child labour, craft work and many more (Chambers 1995: 25–7). Not only does it describe better than 'employment' the realities of the poor; it also captures more of what poor women do, activities that generally lie beyond the narrow parameters of the concept 'employment'.

The issue of vulnerability to impoverishment is especially pertinent to gendered analyses. Women's independent property rights are restricted. This means that their asset bases are minimal and their capacity to survive contingent on their relationships with men. They are therefore more vulnerable than men to downturns in their livelihoods, and, by reason of their powerlessness, less able to survive livelihood or domestic crises and recover from them. Women can become poor through two sorts of process: either with the rest of the household through a decline in household well-being, or through the breakdown of the household, 'and with it, the systems of rights and obligations on which they rely' (Kabeer 1992: 5–6).

Poverty, then, is not solely about economic status but about power relations; and women's poverty is thus more complex than men's. One might deduce that efforts to reduce it will not produced sustained results unless they address this.

THE CURRENT APPROACH TO POVERTY REDUCTION IN COLOMBIA

Painting it in broad brush-strokes in the hopes that this characterization will thus be relevant to other Latin American countries as well as Colombia, the main features of the approach to poverty reduction in this country in the 1990s may be summarized as follows.

Poverty is conceived of as income shortfall with reference to a minimum family income level, measured using consumption or expenditure as proxies. In Colombia this has been expressed in the Poverty Line measure, which has increasingly supplanted the Basic Needs Unsatisfied measure.

Poverty information for planning and targeting social expenditure is gathered through large-scale household surveys, the focuses and categories of which are determined by technocrats who are separated from poor people by a very wide perception gap. In Colombia the SISBEN (System for Selection of Beneficiaries of Social Programmes) is currently being implemented for this purpose (Departamento Nacional de Planeación et al. 1994).

The information is used to construct an implicit 'ideal' poor person, a sort of *homo pauper*, ostensibly gender-neutral, for whom programmes are designed and to whom benefits and transfers are directed. Special transfers – even more narrowly targeted – are sometimes created for a prototype *femina pauper*, but these are the exceptions. The *homo pauper* is, implicitly, under-qualified, unemployed, the sole breadwinner of a nuclear family who pools his income equitably. It may be noted that this image of the household, the 'benevolent dictator' model according to Sen (1990), is no longer considered credible even in the most egalitarian of Western societies, and is less credible in the context of poorer, developing societies.

Every attempt is made to target resources for poverty reduction narrowly, at the poorest individuals. The model of resource allocation adopted is the neo-liberal model, which puts the onus on individuals to claim the goods and services they choose to consume. According to this model, demand leads to supply through the individual's exercise of his purchasing power in the marketplace. Applied in the context of social policy, the neo-liberal resource allocation model rests on the political correlate of economic purchasing power, the mechanism of 'voice'. This is the political bargaining power to hold the state to account and extract the due benefits from the system. It might be noted that just as the poor have less economic purchasing power in the market, they also have less 'voice' in the political arena, and are less able to express and satisfy their needs and preferences than the non-poor.

The poor can lay claim to resources for poverty reduction through two channels. Demand is either collective, through 'community participation', in the case of public goods – such as roads, electricity networks, local schools – or individual in the case of everything else, such as subsidies for health care, reductions in public service tariffs, transfers for population groups considered vulnerable. In Colombia the channel for collective demand is the National Cofinancing System; and for individual demand the SISBEN and the current administration's Social Solidarity Network (*Red de Solidaridad Social*).

A VIEW FROM THE FIELD

Having outlined the main features of the current approach to poverty in Colombia, let us move to the field. The fieldwork on poverty conducted in Cauca department used a combination of ethnographic research techniques and a relatively new approach known variously as Rapid Rural Appraisal (RRA), Participatory Rural Appraisal (PRA), Participatory Learning and Action (PLA), and has much in common with Participatory Action Research (PAR) as widely practised in Latin America.[2] The spread of this approach for the purpose of policy-oriented poverty analysis, and notably its adoption by the World Bank and other multilateral and bilateral development cooperation agencies, has given rise to the term 'participatory poverty assessment', which perhaps describes most closely my use of it in this fieldwork. For fourteen months I lived and researched in three small rural communities, conducting in-depth ethnographic enquiry in one location and Participatory Poverty Assessments in the others. The objective was to gain understanding of poor, isolated communities' own view of their situations, their analysis of the nature, extent and causes of their poverty and what could be done about it; and contrast these with the official perception which informs state measures for the rural poor. I wish to present three approaches to the fieldwork in synthesized form, and discuss them with reference to the foregoing discussion.

On work The question about occupation was deliberately posed as: 'What is your/your partner's occupation?' or, 'Do(es) you/your partner work?' Numerous studies have revealed that to gain any real insight into what women do all day and how they contribute to the family economy, this question should be posed very differently – especially in the case of rural women in subsistence economies. A gender-sensitive way to pose this question would be to address the woman directly (rather than a man who answers for her), preferably out of her partner's hearing, asking something like: 'Can you tell me what you do all day, from when you get up in the morning to when you go to bed at night?' Striking differences arise between the perceptions obtained through the former and the latter type of question as to the activity and time allocation of the women of the household and their contribution to the household's productive capacity as well as its reproductive function (Elson 1995; Welbourn 1991). A gender-blind question was posed in this case because people's own perceptions of what did and did not constitute work – their own or their partner's – were a matter of interest. The subsequent ethnographic research and residence in the community provided ample opportunity to supplement or revise any impressions gained through this initial survey. The few women who had given agriculture as their occupation were very poor female heads of household who spent virtually all their time farming to produce their family's sustenance that way; but it became clear that in every farming household women and girls performed a range of production-related tasks, some in the fields but more around the house, often processing rather than cultivating tasks, without which the farming unit would not have been viable. In short, the overwhelming impression given by the table is that the great majority of women in this community are less occupied than the men, doing 'housework' rather than 'work'. In fact, women were indispensable in food production for consumption and sale, and since they and their daughters alone were entirely responsible for domestic work, they worked considerably more hours than men and rested less.

On time Time allocation tables were produced by an all-women group and an all-men group during a participatory workshop in one community where participatory poverty assessment was conducted. Participants first listed all the activities they performed in their everyday lives, and then each was given 20 counters – beans, a local product – to distribute among the activities, the number placed beside each one representing how much time participants devoted to each on average. The first salient point was that women listed no leisure activities at all, until prompted – 'sleeping' and 'visiting kin/friends' were added only when the researchers suggested these. Men, on the other hand, listed sleeping first, and also listed a range of other leisure or non-productive activities – sport, resting, eating, showering.

On priorities In one participatory exercise locals classified all the households in their community in three groups, according to whether they were the poorest, the medium-poor or the least poor, and then explained which criteria they used to classify them. A comparison of men's and women's criteria reveals that the first consideration of women in categorizing households as poor was the ownership and state of the house, followed by the household's control over productive assets. Men categorized primarily on the basis of productive assets, and mentioned housing tenure and quality only as a secondary consideration or when prompted. This difference reflects the division of labours, responsibilities and space according to gendered norms. Men in these communities tend to spend minimal time inside the house, and are not responsible for those aspects of maintaining the family that go on in the house. In another participatory exercise this fact was illustrated by women's passionate desire for electricity, and men's lack of interest: they do not get up first, in the cold and dark at 4 a.m., to light wood-stoves with damp firewood, or spend whole days gathering wood far from the home. Such differences indicate that in any collective effort to establish priorities for action against poverty, tensions will exist between women's and men's priorities and interests. These tensions may be revealed or not: participatory approaches are more likely to disclose them than conventional approaches. Actions advocated by one sex may not benefit the other, and may even disfavour the other.

IMPLICATIONS OF THESE FINDINGS FOR THE EFFICACY OF POVERTY INFORMATION AND REDUCTION STRATEGIES

To discuss the implications of these insights for the current approach to poverty in Colombia, let us return to the main characteristics of that approach as outlined above.

Poverty as shortfall in family or household income The premising of poverty information-gathering and poverty reduction strategies on this limited concept carries the dual risk of failure to gather information on, and failure to design policy responses to, all the other, non-income, aspects of poverty. The consequence of treating poverty as household income deficiency – that is, stopping at the household door – is failure to perceive those intra-household dynamics which make men's and women's experience of and exposure to poverty – income shortfall and other aspects – quite different.

An information-gathering method which does not take into account the perception gap, nor significantly narrow it This carries the risk that poor people's realities will not be perceived or captured at all. For example, the only question on income in the SISBEN questionnaire is phrased in such a way that a peasant subsistence farmer cannot give an accurate answer: it presupposes a regular monetary monthly payment such as urban salaried workers receive. Since the concepts of income poverty and employment appear to be even less appropriate to poor women's realities than they are to poor men's, this leaves women's realities even more misperceived. Because women are relatively powerless compared to men and experience social constraints that prevent them from being seen and heard by researchers and survey enumerators, an information-gathering approach that does not consciously counter 'natural' biases by incorporating special efforts to see and hear women will gather only a partial picture.

The implicitly male concept of poor people informing state responses, the homo pauper This is inaccurate since at least 50 per cent of all people, and a higher percentage of the world's poor, are women. Women's gender-specific experience of poverty means that state responses and programmes designed to meet men's needs do not necessarily meet theirs. Households are not all male-headed, and even in those that are, the well-being status of household members cannot be extrapolated from the well-being status of the male head or from responses given by him, as recorded, for example, in the SISBEN survey. Nor will resources directed to him as the head necessarily benefit female members of the household.

The neo-liberal resource allocation model behind current approaches to poverty reduction, which puts the onus on the individual to claim benefits This is perhaps misguided, in that those with the least purchasing power – the economically poor – are also those with the least political bargaining power or 'voice' – the 'politically poor'. Among these 'politically poor', women have least voice of all. They cannot form networks or alliances because of social and geographical isolation; they cannot be heard in public fora because they are subordinate to the men present; they cannot defy their male partners' wishes or challenge or overtake males' superior social standing in the community.

Collective and individual mechanisms for claiming benefits from the state These are time-consuming and their effectiveness depends heavily on prevailing social and political relations. Contrary to the common stereotype of the lazy peasant awaiting state handouts instead of working for a living, peasant men work in extremely hard conditions, leaving them little disposable energy, even if they do work fewer hours than women. Women experience acute time poverty. They generally perform several tasks at once and enlist their daughters' help – frequently at the cost of their daughters' education. The kind of poverty reduction strategy that women most certainly do not require is 'that which incorporates them simply as unpaid labour for the delivery of social services, in substitutions for public expenditure' (Elson 1992: 18). Collective community action is much less likely to satisfy women's needs than men's because women are relatively muted and invisible, and because community action groups are more often led by men so tend to express men's interests and priorities. Systems for subsidizing individual demand, such as SISBEN, are less apt to satisfy women's than men's needs because poor women are even less likely than men to receive adequate information about the system and be able to fulfil its requirements, which often include travelling to municipal centres, answering questionnaires and presenting identity cards and other documentation. In the competition for resources in systems such as the Social Solidarity Network, women are easily elbowed out of the queue. As a final consideration, SISBEN and the National Cofinancing System notwithstanding, the most effective *de facto* mechanism for extracting benefits from the state in Colombia remains clientelism. This is essentially a male domain, since it is public and political rather than private and personal. Women are generally excluded from it by social convention and gendered behavioural norms.

OVERCOMING SOME LIMITATIONS OF THE CURRENT APPROACH TO POVERTY

There are clearly tremendous challenges involved in reducing poverty significantly in Colombia, which go far beyond the scope of this gendered analysis of poverty and state responses to it. However, at the level of poverty information-gathering and the design of policy responses, some suggestions arise from the foregoing discussion.

First, a process of methodological and disciplinary opening-up is required, to shift the focus of debate and of policy responses from the narrow definition of poverty as income shortfall to deprivation in the wider sense. The moment is propitious: dissatisfaction with conventional poverty measurements and with past efforts to reduce poverty has grown of late, and in other areas of the world participatory poverty assessment has been developed with the support of reputable development and research agencies and is undergoing continuous and rapid improvement (see McGee 1997b). Latin American countries, coming later to this approach, can benefit from the experience already gained with it elsewhere. Key to the reconceptualization of poverty is the dethroning of economics, traditionally regarded by many as the only serious, respectable discipline among the social sciences. Latin America has a rich tradition and considerable expertise in sociology and social anthropology that could be drawn on to diversify poverty assessment methods and enrich understandings of poverty, and would most certainly shed more light on gender differences in extent and experiences of poverty than the economistic assessment approaches used hitherto.

A better understanding of the household and of gender relations is urgently required, one that reflects reality rather than analytical expedience and wishful thinking. This is best obtained through focused micro-level empirical research, incorporating gender differences as a central interest. In addition, all other research and learning exercises conducted for public policy purposes should also incorporate attention to gender issues, if public policy is to benefit women and men equally. The underlying assumption must be that unless conscious efforts are made to counter it, male bias tends to prevail in public policy and in development efforts, skewing their results in favour of men and against women.

Second, more participatory data-gathering techniques would not only increase the validity of available poverty information, but could lead to greater public involvement in social policy-making and hence more effective policy. SISBEN, like equivalent beneficiary identification systems in countries other than Colombia, is an expensive, slow process that has not been promptly or uniformly adopted, or applied to any consistent minimum standard of quality. Five years after its initiation, critical appraisal and attempts to design complementary approaches are in order, so that the elements of poor people's realities missed by SISBEN might be captured by other means. Examples are in-depth ethnographic case studies of a sample of rural and urban poor communities; small-scale surveys applied in limited areas and focusing on locally predominant aspects of poverty such as rural livelihoods, vulnerability to violence, or environmental degradation; and focus-group discussions with groups of women supposed to benefit from state programmes. The strengthening of capacity to conduct such research should be directed at non-state agents, given that the state and its representatives are deeply mistrusted by the poor, and not without reason. Without wishing to idealize non-governmental and civil society organizations, which in their internal structures and operations often reflect the inequalities of the society around them, the bottom-up processes of poverty assessment and planning that these organizations can foster tend to be more amenable to the introduction of a gender perspective than top-down, state-led approaches. Efforts should be made to involve poor people to the maximum in this alternative poverty assessment, partly to enhance the validity of its findings and partly to ensure transparency and impartiality among the non-governmental agencies coordinating the assessments. To achieve a significant narrowing of the perception gap, not only the poor but also the top-level policy-makers should be involved in participatory poverty assessment processes, going to poor communities, staying in them for some time, watching and listening to those who have for so long been the invisible and mute objects of their policies. Nothing offers such potential as this for transforming policy-makers' 'outsider' perspectives and bringing state responses closer to people's needs.

If poverty measurement is freed from the confines of rigidly top-down, technocratic approaches such as SISBEN or poverty-line measures as calculated by the National Administrative Statistics Department (DANE), poverty can become an issue of public analysis and interest, ranging far wider than the traditional approaches, producing challenges to state resource allocation patterns and securing greater public support for increased expenditure on poverty reduction efforts. The emphasis would no longer rest exclusively on the product, a measurement; the participatory process would be an end in itself, deepening the meaning of democracy and civil society engagement with the state.

Third, a willingness to question and diverge from orthodox approaches to poverty reduction is required, if the new learning gained through innovations in poverty information is to bear fruit. A gender perspective challenges the notion that employment opportunities will lift people out of poverty, since it reveals that poor women may have no control over the remuneration their companions or they themselves receive. Gendered analysis also poses questions as to the suitability of a demand-subsidizing approach to poverty reduction. The principle of subsidies to demand rests heavily on the notions of preference-revelation and voice; the poorest – and especially women among them – lack clearly defined preferences and the voice with which to express them. If the needs of muted, invisible, subordinated poor women are to be met, these disenfranchised citizens must be actively sought out, and time, empathy and care devoted to developing rapport with them and understanding their conditions. It will surely be found that to meet their needs, given the constraints within which they live, more holistic and transformative actions are required than that of subsidy to individual demand for a pre-established menu of transfers and services.

Time needs to be perceived as an asset that is scarce and precious among the poor, especially the female poor. In designing any development intervention or poverty reduction programme, its time implications for poor women should be analysed, to ensure that the proposed measure does not simply incorporate them as unpaid labour, stretching still further their ability to cope. It should never be forgotten that reducing poverty includes reducing gender equality, since gender subordination is so central to the plight of poor women. Interventions that increase demands on women's time only compound existing inequalities.

The myth of 'community' – as a perfectly harmonious collectivity of common interests – must be rejected in favour of an appreciation that communities harbour inequalities of class, gender, race, ethnicity, age and other factors, and that community 'representatives' are not, in fact, representative. The damage done so far by the premising of the National Cofinancing System on this myth of 'community' could be reversed by efforts to nurture women leaders, and to sensitize municipal planners to gender differences among their populations. Policy-makers' eyes need to remain open to the persistence of clientelism as a major mechanism of social expenditure allocation in Colombia. Overlooking this unpalatable fact serves to perpetuate an unjust regime of male privilege, as well as all its other harmful effects.

One great step forward for poverty reduction in Colombia in recent years has been the creation of Reunirse, the network of academic social policy specialists with a government mandate to continually monitor the state social safety net programme. Reunirse's mode of working through monitors located in poor communities, and its unique scope for feeding citizens' evaluation of state performance back into the heart of the state, offer greater potential than any existing agency for detecting the gender implications of state policies and programmes and securing adjustments in these to meet gender equity criteria. A precedent has been set for citizen involvement in evaluating state management of public resources. It is important for the quality and credibility of social sector provision in Colombia as a whole that Reunirse should outlive the current change of administration and enhance its capacity and mandate for gender analysis under future administrations.

To conclude: the task is great, but so are the moral imperative and the available expertise for making state responses to poverty more gender-equitable than they have been hitherto. The incorporation of a gender perspective in poverty assessment and reduction would con- tribute not only to the increased effectiveness of poverty reduction strategies, but to greater gender equity in Colombia, surely a worthwhile aim in itself.

NOTES

1. Rosemary McGee was a fellow at the University of Manchester and currently works for the Institute of Development Studies at the University of Sussex, UK.

2. See, for example, Chambers 1992, 1994a, 1994b, 1994c, 1995, 1997a; IIED 1988–; Schönhuth and Kiewelitz 1994.

BIBLIOGRAPHY

Baden, S. and K. Milward (1995) 'Gender and poverty', Report commissioned by the Gender Office, SIDA, BRIDGE Briefings on Development and Gender, No. 90, March.

Bernstein, H., B. Crow and H. Johnson (eds) (1992) *Rural Livelihoods: Crises and Responses*, Oxford: Open University/Oxford University Press.

Chambers, R. (1983) *Rural Development: Putting the Last First*, Harlow: Longman Scientific and Technical.

— (1992) 'Rural appraisal: rapid, relaxed and participatory', IDS Discussion Paper No. 311, Brighton: Institute of Development Studies, University of Sussex.

— (1994a) 'The origins and practice of participatory rural appraisal', *World Development*, 22(7): 953–69.

— (1994b) 'Participatory rural appraisal: analysis of experience', *World Development*, 22(9): 1253–68.

— (1994c) 'Participatory rural appraisal: challenges, potential and paradigm', *World Development*, 22(10): 1437–54.

— (1995) 'Poverty and livelihoods: whose reality counts?', IDS Discussion Paper No. 347, Brighton: Institute of Development Studies, University of Sussex.

— (1997a) *Whose Reality Counts? Putting the First Last*, London: Intermediate Technology Publications.

— (1997b) 'Beyond "whose reality counts?": new methods we now need', Paper presented at World Conference on Participatory Research, Cartagena de Indias, Colombia, June.

— (1998) 'Pobreza y Sustento: ¿Cuál es la realidad que importa?', Bogotá: CINEP.

Departamento Nacional de Planeación – Unidad de Desarrollo Social and Misión Social (1994) 'SISBEN: Sistema de Selección de Beneficiarios para Programas Sociales', Bogotá, November.

Elson, D. (1992) 'Public action, poverty and development: a gender-aware analysis', Paper presented at seminar on 'Women in Extreme Poverty: Integration of Women's Concerns in National Development Planning', Division for Advancement of Women, United Nations Office, Vienna, November.

— (ed.) (1995) 2nd edn, *Male Bias in the Development Process*, Manchester: Manchester University Press.

Goetz, A. M. (n.d.) 'Gender, adjustment and poverty: issues for consideration by the SPA working groups', unpublished mimeo, Brighton: Institute of Development Studies, University of Sussex.

IIED (International Institute for Environment and Development) (1988) 'PLA notes: notes on participatory learning and action', London: IIED.

Jodha, N. S. (1988) 'Poverty debate in India: a minority view', *Economic and Political Weekly*, XXIII, special number, November: 2421–8.

Kabeer, N. (1991) 'Gender dimensions of rural poverty: analysis from Bangladesh', *Journal of Peasant Studies*, 18(2): 241–62.

— (1992) 'Women in poverty: a review of concepts and findings', Paper for seminar on 'Women in Extreme Poverty: Integration of Women's Concerns in National Development Planning', Division for Advancement of Women, United Nations Office, Vienna, November.

— (1994) *Reversed Realities: Gender Hierarchies in Development Thought*, London: Verso.

McGee, R. (1997a) 'La brecha de percepciones', *Ensayo y Error*, 1(2): 83–101.

— (1997b) 'Abriendo el proceso de las políticas públicas para la reducción de la pobreza: una perspectiva internacional', Ponencia para conferencia sobre Pobreza, Equidad y Desarrollo Social, Bogotá, noviembre.

— (1998) 'La pobreza vista desde diversas perspectivas: un estudio de caso colombiano', *Papel Político*, November, Bogotá: Pontificia Universidad Javeriana.

Schönhuth, M. and U. Kiewelitz (1994) *Diagnóstico Rural Rápido/Diagnóstico Rural Participativo: Metodologías participativas de diagnóstico y planificación para la cooperación al desarrollo*, Eschborn: GTZ – German Technical Cooperation.

Sen, A. (1990) 'Gender and cooperative conflicts', in I. Tinker (ed.), *Persistent Inequalities: Women and World Development*, Oxford: Oxford University Press.

Welbourn, A. (1991) 'RRA and the analysis of difference', RRA Notes 14, London: IIED.

CHAPTER 16

Understanding Economies as Gendered Structures: Examples from Central America

JASMINE GIDEON[1]

§ The chapters in this book have clearly demonstrated the importance of gender issues within economics. This chapter draws many of the concepts presented in the book into a framework that can be used to look at specific case studies 'through women's eyes' and draw attention to the importance of analysing both the productive and the reproductive economies in the context of economic reform processes. The analysis here uses the case of Central America in the late 1990s to illustrate the ways in which gender inequalities create distortions in the patterns of resource allocation and act as barriers to economic and social transformation, placing constraints on the achievement of development goals.

Obviously gender inequality is not the only inequality in the region that must be addressed if equitable economic growth and development is to occur, but here the focus is particularly on development constraints that stem from the unequal position of poor rural women, a group that heretofore has been neglected.

The study illustrates a framework for looking at economies as gendered structures using data from Central America. The second section discusses the economic reform programmes in the region at the end of the 1990s and the third and fourth sections present a gendered analysis of these processes. In the final section some conclusions are drawn.

CENTRAL AMERICAN ECONOMIES AS GENDERED STRUCTURES

An analysis of economies as gendered structures examines the gender balance in economic decision-making. This is particularly important because it highlights the relevance of women's empowerment in the process of economic growth and development. Raising the question *'who decides?'* highlights the important distinction between participation in the production process and control over production. When the gender balance in economic decision-making is examined it becomes clear that women lack a voice at the macro, meso and micro levels. This allows male-biased norms to persist.

This section shows some of the imbalances in Central American economies, illustrating how these imbalances relate to the gendered structure of the economies, especially the competition between the productive and reproductive sector for women's labour.

Macro-economic imbalances At the time of the study per capita GNP in the countries of Central America ranged from US$340 in Nicaragua to US$2,400 in Costa Rica (UNDP 1996). However, these figures do not give us any information on income distribution within the economies. The data in Table 16.1 show that while all the economies, with the exception of Nicaragua, expanded their output between 1978 and 1996, population growth was relatively high (see Table 16.5), so that per capita growth was only moderate. Inflation rates also showed marked differences across the region. In 1995, for example in Honduras, inflation was 29.5 per cent, while in Guatemala it was 8.8 per cent. Table 16.1 shows that all of the countries had current account deficits, much of which was attributable to high debt service repayments, especially in the case of Nicaragua, where 84 per cent of export earnings went to debt repayment in 1996. It is worth noting that there has been little improvement in Nicaragua's debt burden, and the effect of Hurricane Mitch did little to alleviate the problems; Honduras was also particularly negatively affected and its debt burden is now greater than that of Guatemala (Esquivel et al. 2001). Guatemala and Nicaragua had the largest current account deficits in the region, due to large deficits in payments for services, interest, profits, dividends, that have continued to increase (Economist Intelligence Unit 1996c, 1996e). El Salvador maintained a relatively manageable current account deficit as a result of workers' remittances, which remain the most important source of foreign exchange with flows which in 1995 were $1.15 billion (nearly one and a half times the value of goods exported) (Economist Intelligence Unit 1996b: 72).

The Central American economies are part of the Caribbean Basin Initiative (CBI), a plan set up in the mid-1980s with support from the

TABLE 16.1 Key macro-economic imbalances in the mid-1990s

	Costa Rica	El Salvador	Guatemala	Honduras	Nicaragua
Rate of growth of GDP	4.0	4.4	3.9	3.6	-0.3
GNP per capita (US$)	2,400	1,360	1,200	600	340
Rate of growth of GDP per capita	1.4	2.3	0.9	0.5	-2.8
Current account deficit as % GDP	-1.9	-1.8	-2.6	-3.5	-22.1
Trade balance (US$m)	-534	-1,147	-941	-54	-371
Total debt service (US$m)	596	300	331	360	652
Total external debt as % of GNP	49	26	21	119	306
Debt service ratio (%)	17	14	11	23	84
Budget deficit as % of GNP	9	2	-1	n.a.	18

n.a. = not available

Source: IADB (1997); UNDP (1996).

United States,[2] designed to encourage Caribbean and Central American economies to be more open and liberal, and expected to expand trade and promote economic growth and development with higher inflows of US investment in the region. However, the general consensus is that the CBI has not lived up to expectations in Central America (Hutchinson and Schumacher 1994: 131). Large trade deficits are found in all the Central American economies and in each of the countries, growth of imports has outweighed growth of exports since the mid-1980s. A variety of factors account for this: the import of inputs for agroindustry and manufacturing in the export processing industries, dramatic increases in consumer imports following trade liberalization and rising imports of basic grains due to decline in corn and bean production (Hamilton and Thompson, 1994: 1382). In addition, some products have faced problems with protectionism in target export markets.

The productive economy in Central America An examination of the structure of the productive economy from a gender perspective sheds some light on these imbalances. There are difficulties in conducting a gender analysis of the productive economy in Central America because, in common with many countries, labour force surveys and national income accounts do not fully cover women's productive activities (Benería and Feldman 1992; Benería 1995; special issue of *Feminist Economics* 1996). See Chapter 4 in this book for a more in-depth analysis of how to improve national data bases.

TABLE 16.2 Agriculture: share of GNP, exports, employment and gender intensity of production

	Share of GNP (%)	Share of exports (%)	Share of employment (%)	Male share of agricultural employment (%)	Female share of agricultural employment
Costa Rica	18	63	22	91	9
El Salvador	27	52	36	83	17
Guatemala	25	70	26	93	7
Honduras	26	68	36	94	6
Nicaragua	30	93	23	88	12

Source: Elson, Fauné et al. (1997); IADB (1997)

Most of the land in Central America is concentrated in the hands of a small number of landowners,[3] but the majority of farms are small and medium-scale production units. Table 16.2 uses official statistics to show the agricultural share of GNP in the mid-1990s and the importance of agriculture to exports across the region. In addition, the table highlights the share of agricultural employment in each country and examines the gender intensity of production; this is the percentage of female labour and male labour as a share of the total input of labour into production.

Agricultural production is a key area in which gender imbalances are evident. Official statistics suggest that agriculture is a male-intensive activity and that the female intensity of the agricultural sector ranges from 6 per cent to 17 per cent across the region (Table 16.2). Yet this is not consistent with evidence found in case studies (see for example IICA/BID studies from Central America 1993; Fletcher and Renzi 1994), which suggest that women work between four and five hours daily on family farms and that during harvest time their contribution rises. Statistical surveys are clearly failing to make visible women's contribution to agriculture, especially unpaid family work.

Food production is typically carried out by small-scale producers, although in Costa Rica only 66 per cent of them cultivate basic grains, whereas in the other countries this figure exceeds 80 per cent. Case study material from across the region reveals that women make a vital contribution to the production of food crops (Martinez and Rosales, 1995; Chiriboga et al. 1995; FAO/INRA 1995). For instance, Fauné (1997) has shown in Costa Rica that while on average men dedicate 7.5 hours daily to food production, women dedicate 8.5 hours.[4]

Coffee is a key export crop in each of the Central American economies. Despite the invisibility of female employment in official estimates, case study evidence suggests that women play a central role in small-holder coffee production, constituting up to 70 per cent of the workforce during harvesting.

Dependence on manufactured exports such as textiles and agro-exports is more important in Costa Rica and El Salvador than in the other Central American countries (Table 16.3). However, in Costa Rica at the time of the study, clothing and textiles still only accounted for 5 per cent of total exports, while in El Salvador they accounted for 15 per cent of total exports (World Bank 1993: 269). Large-scale investment has been made, especially by Asian and United States transnationals, in *maquilas* (export processing factories) and created thousands of jobs, although this has been offset in some countries, such as Nicaragua, by the destruction of jobs in the domestically oriented clothing industry due to import liberalization (Wiegersma 1994). While manufacturing remains a male-intensive sector in each of the countries, the majority of the labour force in the *maquilas* is female (Table 16.3). Although jobs are being created for women in the manufacturing sector, the quality of working conditions is poor and wage rates are low compared to those in male-intensive industries. Labour markets are characterized by gender bias and discrimination, as will be discussed below. Fauné (1995a: 109) highlights the issue of informal sector manufacturing, where women work in their own homes, often cutting out garments which are then sewn in the *maquilas*. Many of the women in this informal sector are those who are unable to arrange child care to enable them to work in the *maquilas*. Informal sector manufacturing is not reported or captured in the official data presented in Table 16.3.

One may question the sustainability of this model of industrial development, and its capacity to generate better jobs for women. Indeed, Seguino (2000a, 2000b) has argued that the rapid growth in the Asian economies was based on gender inequalities. Direct foreign investment in export processing industries has been encouraged as a result of initiatives implemented via the CBI. Inputs are imported from the United States and Asia under favourable tax regimes, products are then assembled in the Export Processing Zones and re-exported to the USA under CBI privileges. In addition, changes in tariff protection structures in the 1990s have encouraged export of output to the USA rather than

TABLE 16.3 Manufacturing: share of GNP, exports, employment and gender intensity of production

	Share of GNP (%)	Share of exports (%)	Share of employ-ment (%)	Male share of manu-facturing employment (%)	Female share of manu-facturing employment
Costa Rica	22	37	18	65	35
El Salvador	17	44	23	53	48
Guatemala	20	21	21	86	14
Honduras	27	5	17	53	47
Nicaragua	20	7	16	63	37

Source: Elson, Fauné et al. (1997); IADB (1997)

within the Central American Common Market (MCCA),[5] so trade between CBI countries is discouraged (Economist Intelligence Unit 1996a–e). Following the introduction of the North American Free Trade Agreement (NAFTA) in 1994, CBI countries are concerned over competition from Mexico. As Hutchinson and Schumacher (1994) argue, the future development of Central American economies depends, in part, on their ability to develop competitive exports in non-resource-based products.[6] Mexico's preferential access to the US market under NAFTA threatens to frustrate their progress in this direction (ibid.: 145).

It is also necessary to consider the long-term effect of dependence on foreign capital and technology.[7] As Hamilton and Thompson (1994) suggest, there is a danger that foreign corporations may add to problems of concentration and virtual monopolization in some sectors, and that the import of technology and other inputs could have a long-term negative impact on the trade balance (ibid.: 1384).

The service sector remains the largest sectoral contributor to GNP across the region. With the exception of Guatemala, it is also the sector that employs the largest proportion of the labour force, and in each country the majority of the female labour force is located in this sector. Marked differences in the gender intensity of production in the service sector across the region may be a result of different statistical definitions of the service sector. Moreover, it is likely that in Costa Rica, service sector activities are more complex and formal than those in the other countries due to its higher level of industrialization.

The service sector consists of both formal and informal[8] sub-sectors.

TABLE 16.4 Service sector: share of GNP, exports, employment and gender intensity of production

	Share of GNP (%)	Share of exports (%)	Share of employment (%)	Male share of service sector (%)	Female share of service sector
Costa Rica	60	0	60	64	36
El Salvador	55	0	41	38	62
Guatemala	55	0	53	56	44
Honduras	47	0	41	49	51
Nicaragua	50	0	61	38	62

Source: Elson, Fauné et al. (1997); IADB (1997)

Official data show that both are male-intensive, but women form a larger percentage of the informal rather than the formal service sector. Employment data show that on average, across the region 63.1 per cent of the formal sector service workers are male and 36.9 per cent are female. In comparison, 51 per cent of the informal sector service workers are male and 49 per cent are female (Elson, Evers et al. 1997). The official statistics of women's participation may be low because women are contributing unpaid labour to production in household-based enterprises and are therefore not counted. Numerous case studies attest to women's participation in micro-level income-generating activities (for example IICA/BID studies from Central America 1993). In addition, evidence from Costa Rica suggests that some female labour in the service sector may be subcontracted, again accounting for low official estimates (Fauné 1997).

In a study of Honduras (1997), López de Maizier has shown that even within the informal sector, gender distortions and barriers disadvantage women and this situation is repeated across the region. Women have less working capital and are less likely to be able to accumulate savings; they are not in occupations that facilitate skill acquisition and they are generally in poorer health. Thus gender distortions and constraints limit the growth potential of the female segment of the informal sector: it remains oriented to day-to-day household survival needs.

The reproductive economy in Central America The reproductive economy produces and maintains people. Table 16.5 provides some key indicators of the reproductive economy in Central America in the mid-1990s. Except for Costa Rica, the reproductive economy in Central America is characterized by a huge imbalance between the increase in population and the ability to maintain the population at a decent basic living standard. Women, and especially poor women, do not command the resources necessary to maintain their children in good health.

Available time budget studies from the region reveal that poor women work longer hours than men when unpaid work in the reproductive economy is taken into account as well as paid work in the productive economy (see for example IMAS 1995 on Costa Rica; AVANCSO 1995 on Guatemala; Ortíz 1994 on El Salvador; Renzi and Agurto 1996 on Nicaragua). The UNDP, in a study of SNA and non-SNA work time (see endnote three for a discussion of SNA and non-SNA work) found that in rural Guatemala, non-SNA activities were overwhelmingly female-intensive, accounting for 63 per cent of women's time yet only

TABLE 16.5 Key indicators of the reproductive economy in the mid-1990s

	Costa Rica	El Salvador	Guatemala	Honduras	Nicaragua
% population below the poverty line*	38	n.a.	75	53	50
Gini coefficient	0.46	0.50	0.59	0.59	n.a.
Fertility rate	3.1	4.0	5.3	4.8	4.9
Rate of population growth (%)	2.6	2.1	2.9	3.1	2.6
Infant mortality rate per 1,000 births	13	44	46	42	50
% of children under 5 suffering from malnutrition	2	22	n.a.	39	22

* This is the poverty line as defined by the World Bank which is the level of total per capita monthly expenditure required at which an individual can obtain the daily minimum caloric requirement (2,226 calories per adult).

Source: Elson, Fauné et al. (1997); World Bank (1996); IADB (1997).

16 per cent of men's time. In contrast, SNA activities were male-intensive, accounting for 84 per cent of men's time and only 37 per cent of women's time. The study found that on average women's daily work time was 11.3 hours and men's was 9.6 hours, and concluded that women's average work time burden was 17 per cent greater than men's (UNDP 1995: 91).

Furthermore, data on household structure from Central America show that women in female-headed households work longer hours than women in male-headed households in order to fulfil both their productive and reproductive responsibilities (Elson, Fauné et al. 1997: 279). Although there is apparently no evidence that female-headed households are poorer in terms of income than other households, it may simply be that women in female-headed households work harder and suffer more from time poverty.

The conditions of productivity of reproductive work are a critical factor in the ability to achieve sustainable and well-balanced growth. This economy is clearly vital to human well-being, but also vital to national output and exports, since it produces the human resources for employment in farms, factories and offices. Gendered norms about what is men's work and what is women's work constitute institutional biases to a better-balanced distribution of work. This would reduce the gender constraint to development resulting from the over-utilization of women's labour and the under-utilization of men's labour and some of the associated problems which are discussed in the fourth section of this chapter.

Economic decision-making in the productive and reproductive economies
As well as examining the gender division of labour it is also important to examine the gender division in economic decision-making. Even where women contribute most of the work, they do not necessarily have much say in the conditions of the production and utilization of output. Although all five countries in the region are ranked among the top 50 countries in the UNDP Gender Empowerment Measurement[9] (UNDP 1995), large gender gaps still exist.

Economic policy-making at the macro level is dominated by the ministries of finance and the central banks, where women remain relatively scarce. Government institutions responsible for women's issues have only limited decision-making abilities, and none participates in the design and implementation of economic policy reform. Women do participate to some extent in the higher echelons of political, judicial and administrative power across the region (although this is very limited in Guatemala); however, they tend to be concentrated in areas associated with women's traditional reproductive role, such as health and education, rather than in macro-economic policy arenas.

In Central America, the majority of cooperatives, trade unions, NGOs and trade and commercial organizations remain male-controlled, even where female membership is high. Active movements of women do exist in Costa Rica, El Salvador and Nicaragua. However, they tend to focus more on social issues, such as domestic violence and human rights, than on economic policy issues. Studies from the region illustrate the ways in which men dominate household decision-making, most notably over the control of resources (see for example Rojas and Román 1993 on Costa Rica; Chiriboga et al. 1995; Fauné 1995a).

ECONOMIC REFORM PROGRAMMES

Economic reform packages have been introduced across Central America with varying impact. The first country to undergo adjustment was Costa Rica, where the first stabilization programme was initiated in 1983 (Buttari 1992: 180). Guatemala's programme was initiated in 1986, El Salvador's in 1989, Honduras' and Nicaragua's[10] in 1990. The package in each country included adjustment and stabilization measures: this included exchange rate devaluation, a liberalization of markets, cuts in public expenditure and investment, tightening of credit controls and a reduction of the role of the state. One of the main objectives of the reform package of the 1990s was to further integrate the Central American economies into the world market. A key component was the creation of a number of incentives to promote the production of exports. While these programmes were partly aimed at traditional exports, the main emphasis was the promotion of non-traditional exports (Evans 1995: 17). This was especially the case in Costa Rica, where much technical assistance was given to promote non-traditional exports in agricultural commodities. In the manufacturing sector the focus was on expanding existing industrial products and encouraging foreign investment to the export processing industries and free trade zones (Hamilton and Thompson 1994: 1382).

Another key objective of the reforms was the redefining of the role of the state. As outlined by Evans (1995), the general aims of these policies was stated as the achievement of a smaller and more efficient state, directing social services at particular targets. Public expenditure cuts have continued as part of the stabilization programme, and structural adjustment measures emphasized job cuts for those in the public sector. Programmes, some compulsory and others voluntary, were initiated to encourage a transfer of workers from the public to the private sector. Within the area of social services, restructuring of public expenditure was intended to target expenditure to the poor.

However, the objectives of the reforms have not all been met and there have been both efficiency failures and equity failures. In particular, Nicaragua still has not shown any signs of economic recovery and growth and along with Honduras is currently under consideration for inclusion into the Highly Indebted Poor Country (HIPC) Initiative (Bradshaw and Linnekar forthcoming; Esquivel et al. 2001). As the figures in Table 16.1 show, all the economies ran a trade deficit, but the situation was particularly bad in El Salvador and Nicaragua. Hamilton and Thompson (1994) conclude that export promotion in Costa Rica has been inefficient, merely resulting in high government expenditure on incentive measures, extensive ecological damage and problems of protectionism. Additionally, only large-scale, particularly foreign interests have benefited, rather than the majority of medium and small-scale producers (1994: 1388), revealing that important equity failures resulted from the reforms. Furthermore, following wage cuts and increased unemployment, many households across the region faced increased poverty and have been forced to look for new means of survival; in many cases this has meant looking for alternative income-generating activities (Buttari 1992; Corral and Reardon 2001). This situation has been worsened by cuts in public expenditure on social services (Evans 1995). This too represents an important efficiency failure, since in many cases costs are merely transferred from the paid to the unpaid economy. As demonstrated in this chapter, this has negative implications for both family well-being and social and economic development.

Although Social Funds were initiated in Central America, and were intended to alleviate the worst costs of adjustment, they failed to do so. One reason for this is that, with the exception of Costa Rica, in no case has an attempt been made to specifically direct projects towards closing gender gaps. Neither gender experts nor the official WID institutions were involved in the design and assessment of projects supported by the Social Funds in the rest of the region. Benería and Mendoza (1995: 65) argue that 'the invisibility of women's poverty and women's needs remains a constant throughout the conceptualisation and operationalisation of the ESIFs. Programmes are addressed mainly to men because women's poverty is not conceptualised separately from men's – the assumption is made the reduction of men's poverty will automatically help women.' Yet evidence from the region shows that this is not the case. Fauné (1997: 100) comments that: 'while females try to stretch their family budgets, males maintain their consumption of alcohol … While females act under the logic of surviving at any cost, males tend to be under a logic of self-destruction, as shown by the high incidence of crack-cocaine consumption, whose damage is irreversible.' It is also worth noting that similar criticisms have been levelled at the Civil Co-ordinator for Emergency and Reconstruction (CCER), which was established in Nicaragua following Hurricane Mitch as part of the reconstruction process. The ability of the initiative to transform gender relations has been questioned (Bradshaw 2001).

GENDER CONSTRAINTS ON WELL-BALANCED DEVELOPMENT

An examination of the Central American economies as gendered structures reveals a number of gender constraints to well-balanced development. This section looks at gender-based price distortions and gender-based institutional biases in the Central American context and examines a number of subsequent outcomes. These include the over-utilization of women's time relative to the under-utilization of men's time, gender differences in access to infrastructure and finally gender differences in income distribution.

Gender-based price distortions   Gender-based distortions of prices oper-ate in the labour, goods and credit markets. Part of the adjustment programme in Central America has been to increase the production of non-traditional agricultural exports (NTAEs), including shellfish, horti-cultural products and fruit. Here it is possible to highlight some of the ways in which gender-based price distortions affect male and female producers' supply response. As summarized earlier, Palmer (1994) has shown how gender-based price distortions limit women's participation in and access to labour, goods and credit markets.

As argued earlier, gender bias in the labour market means that wages paid to women underestimate women's productivity and thus under-estimate the returns to women and society from employing women in paid work and from investing in the further development of women's productivity. A number of studies highlight this issue in Central America: an examination of the urban informal sector (Funkhouser 1996:

1746) reveals that the male–female wage gap is widest in the informal sector, where most women are concentrated. In Honduras the informal sector gender differential is about 40 per cent, although in the other countries it is around 25 per cent; whereas the formal sector gender differential across the region is generally around 10 per cent. Unfortunately there are few studies estimating the extent to which wage gaps are due to discrimination. However, one study in Nicaragua (Behrman and Wolfe 1991) demonstrates that gender bias accounted for 70 per cent of the difference in male and female earnings in the period 1977–78. Another study by Tzannatos (1992), covering Costa Rica, Guatemala and Honduras, shows that if gender discrimination in patterns of occupation and pay were eliminated, not only would women's income increase considerably, but also national output could be increased by up to 5 per cent because of more efficient allocation of labour.

At the micro level, women are likely to have little control over income from the sale of products. When production takes place in smallholder production units, women are often unable to market the product themselves and therefore will have no control over any income that accrues. Although poor men also lack access to goods markets, studies indicate that women are disproportionately excluded (see for example Renzi and Agurto 1993 on Nicaragua). Moreover, when women do have access to markets they are even more likely than men to find themselves in commodity chains controlled by large enterprises, often owned by foreign investors. Any benefits gained from increased income from sale of goods may not be commensurate with the amount of extra work that is created for women as a result of increased productive activities.

Gender discrimination in the credit market means that the rates of interest charged to women overestimate the cost of lending to women, and underestimate the returns from lending to women's enterprises. This is an important gender-based constraint in Central America and available data from all of the countries highlighted the gender barriers women face in access to formal credit market. For example, a study for Nicaragua (Renzi and Agurto,1993) showed that out of a total of 36,113 formal sector loans to rural enterprises, only 13 per cent went to women, while 87 per cent went to men. Although women in urban enterprises received more bank loans than men, the size of the loan was on average smaller. Rules of participation in financial markets and the structure of loan management tend to favour propertied male producers and to exclude most women (Goetz 1995). Women lack access to land ownership and consequently lack collateral necessary to receive credit. Although a number of special credit schemes have been introduced across the region that explicitly target women, the gender imbalance in credit allocation remains extremely wide. At most women receive 22 per cent of formal sector credit loan in Nicaragua. In addition, loans to women are likely to be smaller, and may be between 40 and 70 per cent of the size of loans given to men. Although it may be that women want smaller loans, institutional bias often means that formal lending services are not set up to administer small loans. Women therefore accrue higher transaction costs as a percentage of their total loan due to the fixed costs associated with lending. Another problem is that in order to receive loans from formal sector institutions collateral is necessary. Following economic reforms and the tightening of credit controls it is even harder for small-scale producers to gain access to credit and studies from the region have shown that women are more affected than men by these changes. Another study in Nicaragua by Renzi and Agurto (1994) concludes that this has been the case and that small-scale female agricultural producers are more adversely affected by the economic reforms than their male counterparts. Factors considered include less access to credit, less access to storage facilities and the higher cost of inputs.[11]

Institutional biases Institutional biases occur when institutions malfunction by operating in ways that maximize the benefits to groups controlling these institutions, rather than maximizing the benefits to society as a whole (Acker 1992; Folbre 1995; Goetz 1995, 1997). The first section illustrated the ways in which women are denied access to economic decision-making at all levels in Central America. Similarly, male-biased norms are found in many other areas, including access to jobs and access to land. While male bias in the allocation of jobs may maximize the gains to male employers and employees, it does not contribute to the most effective organization of society as a whole because women's talents are wasted. Similarly, male bias in access to land means that the productivity of women farmers is restricted.

Central American labour markets are characterized by a gender imbalance in occupational structure. For example, a fairly rigid gendered division of labour is notable in all NTAE production: while the production phase is generally male-intensive, the processing and packing is a female-intensive activity. Women are located in low-paid, low-status posts, while men dominate the higher-ranking positions, as has been demonstrated in detail in a study of NTAE production in Costa Rica (Fauné 1997).

Male-biased norms are also evident in access to land across the region. Although gender-disaggregated data on land ownership are not available, gender inequalities in land tenure have been identified in a number of studies (World Bank 1995c; FAO/INRA 1995; Deere and Leon 1999). Although land reform programmes did in principle give access to land to rural women, in practice this has not always been the case. In El Salvador men have benefited more than women over land tenure in the series of reforms that have been implemented. During one phase women represented only 11 per cent of those who gained land yet represented 36 per cent of those who lost land due to expropriation (World Bank 1995c: 31). In Nicaragua, under a land redistribution programme implemented by the Chamorro government, women received only 9.8 per cent of the land distributed between 1992 and 1994. Only 1,361 out of 12,086 beneficiaries in this period were women (Asociación de Mujeres Profesionales 1996: 26).

Outcomes It is clear that in Central America market bias gives the 'wrong' price signals (Goetz 1995) and women's participation in the production and marketing of goods and services has been seriously undervalued compared to men's. Furthermore, gender bias in institutions restricts women's productivity to a greater extent than men's productivity and economic decision-making over control of resources is dominated by men. These biases and distortions result in three gender constraints on development, which are discussed below. Yet the economic reform programmes have failed to address these issues (for a more in-depth discussion of this point see for example Cagatay et al. 1995). Indeed, the evidence here suggests that the reforms may have gone some way to intensifying some of the problems.

The over-utilization of women's time In the analysis of the reproductive economy the analysis found that women work considerably longer hours than men. Yet the economic reforms have done little to alleviate this and have in many ways added to women's time burden. Data from Central America suggest that both women's productive and reproductive activities increased following the introduction of economic reform packages. For example, a UNICEF study in Guatemala (1994: 162) highlighted the fact that women involved in the production of non-traditional agricultural exports (NTAEs), now work four hours more per day than previously. Women's reproductive burden has increased as a result of closure of child care facilities in Nicaragua.

Other studies show that the burdens of the care economy are now an important factor in drop-out rates in education. A World Bank study in Guatemala indicated that there were vast gender differences in attendance, drop-out rates, enrolments and achievement at primary and secondary-level schooling, most notably in rural areas (1995b: 10–15). World Bank surveys in Nicaragua (1995a) and El Salvador (1995c: 68) show that primary-school-aged girls are dropping out of school specifically in order to help with reproductive work. It is a major cause for concern if girls are having to undertake too much work in the reproductive economy, and is clearly an area that urgently requires further investigation.

Gender inequalities in access to infrastructure   Data from Central America can also be used to illustrate how gender-based institutional biases in expenditure on infrastructure constrain development. At a regional level, government expenditure on physical and social infrastructure declined in real terms. Reduction in government spending on social and physical infrastructure means that real costs are likely to be transferred to the unpaid reproductive economy, where women's labour is already over-utilized. In Guatemala, where health spending is still only 1.5 per cent of GNP (UNDP 2001) and social imbalances are most severe, this is of particular concern. Throughout the region, the emphasis in health care spending has been on curative rather than preventative care. This implies particular burdens for poor women, who have the major responsibility for family health care.

Following structural adjustment programmes, medical supplies are increasingly imported yet cuts in health budgets have meant that such products are beyond the reach of many health centres and hospitals; this is especially the case in Honduras and Nicaragua (Evans, 1995: 29). At the same time, in Honduras, privatization of public laboratories has also resulted in less availability of subsidized drugs. In addition, the introduction of user charges in Honduras and Nicaragua, and the possibility of similar steps in Costa Rica (ibid.: 31), further restricts access to health services. The current pattern of gender relations means that women are likely to be left to make up the shortfall in health care. Further research on this is vitally important. It has implications both for health outcomes, and also for women's productivity and ability to generate income.

At the time of the study access to safe water varied considerably, ranging from 93 per cent of the population in Costa Rica to 47 per cent

TABLE 16.6 Allocation of public spending to health and education in Central America in the mid-1990s

	Costa Rica	El Salvador	Guatemala	Honduras	Nicaragua
Health expenditure as % of GNP	6	1	1	n.a.	4
Health expenditure as % of budget	16	n.a.	9	11	13
Education expenditure as % of GNP	5	2	1	n.a.	4
Education expenditure as % of budget	15	n.a.	15	16	14

Source: Elson, Fauné et al. (1997a)

in El Salvador (UNDP 1995: 158). Little improvement has taken place, and UNDP data show that only 83 per cent of the population in El Salvador has access to improved water sources and only 74 per cent of the population have access to adequate sanitation facilities (2001: 159). World Bank statistics from El Salvador reveal the consequent gender imbalances: on average in a year, women dedicate 632 hours per year collecting domestic water, compared to 554 hours for men, and 456 hours for children. Data from the same study also show that girls are more likely than boys to collect water (World Bank 1995c: 44).

Income Distribution   Gender-based barriers in market and household institutions result in too little income accruing to women relative to income accruing to men. Two studies in Honduras (Safilios Rothschild 1988; Bradshaw 1996) suggest that typically incomes are not fully pooled within the household and that men are more likely to keep back some of their earnings for purely personal expenditure on items such as drink and tobacco. Bradshaw found that in rural areas men withheld on average 37 per cent of their earnings, while in urban areas this fell to 32 per cent. Even where women were engaged in income-generating activities, a large proportion of their income compensated only for the male income withheld from the household (ibid.: 6). Although women in female-headed households have greater control over resources than in male-headed households, the study found that their asset base was considerably smaller (ibid.: 12). This has important implications for future human development since a number of studies both from Central America and other regions show that women have a higher propensity than men to spend their income in ways that directly benefit other family members, especially children. According to the World Bank, 'evidence from Guatemala has shown it takes fifteen times more spending to achieve a given improvement in child nutrition when income is earned by the father than by the mother' (World Bank 1993: 41). In Nicaragua, a survey found better nutritional status in female-headed households, compared to male-headed households (Renzi and Agurto 1994).

TRADE-OFF BETWEEN INCREASING EXPORTS AND PROMOTION OF FOOD SECURITY

This analysis of Central America has shown how the failure to address the question of gender bias and distortions has led to their intensification following the economic reform programmes. An indication of this failure is the inability of certain Central American countries to combine export growth with the promotion of food security. This is particularly evident in Honduras and Nicaragua, where agriculture is of special importance and manufacturing growth has lagged behind that of the rest of the region, as shown in Table 16.1.

World Bank statistics for the period 1971–91 demonstrate that, within the region, food production per capita declined most severely in Honduras and Nicaragua. Food production per capita in Honduras declined by 1.3 per cent and in Nicaragua by 2.3 per cent per annum. In Honduras 39 per cent of all children under five suffer from malnutrition, while in Nicaragua the figure is 22 per cent. A study in Nicaragua also found that one in ten births that occurred within the official health service were premature and this has been linked to the nutritional status of women before or during pregnancy (Pizarro 1994: 6). Furthermore, the World Bank found that 20 per cent of total Nicaraguans are food poor – i.e. they cannot meet the daily minimum calorific requirement even if they were to devote all their consumption to food (1995a: 3). Little improvement has occurred in the last five years and 31 per cent of the population are still undernourished (UNDP 2001). Although basic food crops such as rice and beans have been imported, poor households cannot afford to pay for them. This trade-off can be partly explained in terms of gender-based inequalities and the over-utilization of women's time. Micro-level studies (FAO/INRA 1995) show that, for example in Nicaragua, women are responsible for between 38 and 60 per cent of food production and contribute up to 70 per cent of the work in coffee production. Women's labour is central to both the production of food crops and export crops but is not infinitely elastic, given that poor rural women are already working long hours, as revealed in the UNDP study cited earlier. If resources are shifted to increasing export activities the question of food security arises. The policies in the economic reform packages present a no-win situation. If production of exports increases then sufficient food crops cannot be produced; however, if producers prioritize food security this is a major barrier to shifting resources to export activities and the desired export results are not met. The evidence clearly shows that there has been a trade-off between increased export crops and improving food security.

CONCLUSION

Central America includes some of the poorest economies in the world, and many are still riven by deep social inequalities. This chapter has argued that gender inequality is among the significant constraints that hinder the achievement of well-balanced development. It has identified gender distortions, due to missing or biased markets, which give the 'wrong' price signals. A much larger amount of women's work and output than of men's work and output is given no market value, or is undervalued by markets. Gender biases from missing or biased institutions result in the 'wrong' property rights, rules and incentive structures, and economic power (in the sense of strategic decision-making about the use of all key resources) is to a large extent monopolized by men.

These gender distortions and biases result in three gender constraints on development: the over-utilization of women's time relative to the under-utilization of men's time; the under-investment in infrastructure that lessens women's time constraints and finally the distribution of too little income to women relative to that going to men.

The economic reform programmes have failed to prioritize reduction of gender distortions and biases. Indeed, there is enough evidence to cause concern that the reforms may actually have intensified some of these distortions and biases in a number of different ways: through the intensification of unpaid labour for women, men and girls; through intensification of gender inequalities in access to product markets; through intensification of gender inequalities in access to social and physical infrastructure and, finally, through intensification of gender inequalities in economic power within households.

A symptom of this failure is the inability to combine export growth with improvements in food security and nutrition. The pay-off to reducing gender distortions and barriers would be: first, a better balance between agricultural export growth and food security – more exports and better food security; and, second, a more effective allocation of household income to promote human development – more expenditure on nutrition, health, education of children.

Even within the limits of the reform proposals around which policy initiatives currently cluster there is an opportunity to obtain valuable benefits for the people of Central America, men and boys as well as women and girls, if the reforms can be refocused to include removal of gender distortions and biases. There are a number of opportunities for development cooperation to support this change of focus, with an appropriate mix of projects (both women-specific and gender-integrated) and programme aid (both balance of payments and budget support), at macro, meso and micro levels. This will include support for broadening policy dialogue; improving the design of policy; deepening the information base for policy; and empowering women in economic decision-making, as a way of reducing both gender biases and of improving the prospects for policy implementation. Ideally it would be better if alternative policies could be developed, more directly addressing the goal of well-balanced development and requiring changes in the international as well as the national economy and economic policy-makers becoming more open to these issues.

Analysing the economy from a gender perspective is far from a panacea that will solve all Central America's problems, but it does suggest ways in which economic reform can be modified and alternatives developed in ways that promote more equitable economic growth and human development.

NOTES

1. Jasmine Gideon is a fellow at Nuffield Institute in the University of Leeds. This chapter was written following a piece of collaborative research between the Gender and Economics Unit at the University of Manchester where the author was working, four Central American researchers and the Royal Netherlands Embassy, Costa Rica and first appeared in *Feminist Economics*, 1999, 5(1).

2. Nicaragua was not originally a part of the CBI, but became a member in 1990–91.

3. Although in El Salvador and Nicaragua much dispute surrounds questions of land ownership.

4. It is not clear from the study exactly what activities are covered in food production. However, it is possible that more of women's contribution is in the form of post-harvest work than is men's contribution.

5. However, the CBI has not resulted in improvements in the trade balance.

6. Hutchinson and Schumacher define resource-based industries as those which are comprised of primary product industries and those characterized by a low level of processing; this would include industries such as food processing, petroleum products, wood, cork and paper manufactures. The authors note that although one of the aims of the CBI was to promote export diversification, 20 out of the 30 leading CB exports to the United States are resource-based rather than non-resource-based products (1994: 137–8).

7. Following the Asian Crisis, Singh and Zammit (2000) point to the gendered dimensions and limitations of over-dependence on international capital flows.

8. The informal sector can be defined in a number of different ways. Menjivar and Perez (1993) look at the informal sector in six Central American countries. They

have developed a typology of three levels: a) the DYNAMIC sector, which uses some form of explicit accounting and investment; b) the SEMI-SUBSISTENCE sector, using either formal accounting or some investment; and c) the SUBSIST-ENCE sector, which lacks both of these characteristics. They found that males predominate in the dynamic sectors in all six cases, especially in Nicaragua. They also found that the salaried advantage held by men is greater in the informal sector than in the formal sector.

9. The Gender Empowerment Measurement examines whether women and men are able to actively participate in economic and political life and take part in decision-making. It focuses on three variables that reflect women's participation in political decision-making, their access to professional opportunities and their earning power. However, there are many arenas of decision-making that this measurement leaves out, since the GEM captures only what is measurable.

10. The Sandinistas implemented austerity programmes in 1985 and 1988, but these are not directly germane to the argument here.

11. Sally Baden (1996) has argued that gender differences in savings, expenditure and investment behaviour are also likely to have an impact on the outcome of reforms, yet such data are not disaggregated by gender. Better understanding of the gender-based constraints in relation to financial sector reform requires not only more systematic gender-disaggregated data, but also the integration of these data into a macro-economic analysis of how gender distortions and barriers influence underlying macro-economic trends in savings and investment.

BIBLIOGRAPHY

Acker, J. (1992) 'Gendered institutions: from sex roles to gendered institutions', *Contemporary Sociology* 21(5): 565–9.

Afshar, H. and C. Dennis (eds) (1992) *Women and Adjustment Policies in the Third World*, London: Macmillan.

Agarwal, B. (1997) '"Bargaining" and gender relations: within and beyond the household', *Feminist Economics* 3(1): 1–51.

Asociación de Mujeres Profesionales (1996) 'El ejercicio de los derechos de las mujeres en nicaragua: un análisis de género', Consultancy Report for SIDA: Managua.

Asociación para el Avance de Ciencias Sociales en Guatemala (AVANSCO) (1995) 'Trabajo y organización de mujeres', *Texto para Debate*, No. 10, Guatemala: AVANSCO.

Baden, S. (1996) 'Gender issues in financial liberalization', draft topic paper prepared for Task Force on Programme Aid and Other Forms of Assistance Related Economic Reform, mimeo, June.

Behrman, J. R. and B. L. Wolfe (1991) 'Earnings and determinants of labour force participation in a developing country: are there gender differentials?' in N. Birdsall and R. Sabot (eds), *Unfair Advantage: Labour Market Discrimination in Developing Countries*, Washington, DC: World Bank Regional and Sectoral Studies, pp. 95–120.

Benería, L. (1995) 'Towards a greater integration of gender in economics', *World Development*, 23(11): 1839–51.

Benería, L. and S. Feldman (1992) (eds) *Unequal Burden: Economic Crises, Persistent Poverty and Women's Work*, Boulder, CO: Westview Press.

Benería, L. and B. Mendoza (1995) 'Structural adjustment and social emergency funds: the cases of Honduras, Nicaragua and Mexico', *European Journal of Development Research*, 7(1): 53–76.

Bradshaw, S. (1996) 'Inequality within households: the case of Honduras', Paper presented at the 1996 Society of Latin American Studies Conference, University of Leeds.

— (2001) 'Reconstructing roles and relations: women's participation in reconstruction in post-Mitch Nicaragua', *Gender and Development*, 9(3): 79–87.

Bradshaw, S. and B. Linnekar (forthcoming) 'Challenging poverty, vulnerability and social exclusion in Nicaragua: some considerations for poverty reduction strategies', *Nicaraguan Academic Journal*.

Buttari, J. J. (1992) 'Economic policy reform in four Central American countries: patterns and lessons learned', *Journal of Interamerican Studies and World Affairs*, 34 (Spring): 179–214.

Cagatay, N., D. Elson and C. Grown (eds) (1995) *Gender, Adjustment and Macroeconomics: Special Issue of World Development*, 23(11).

Chiriboga, M., R. Grynspan and L. Pérez (1995) *Mujeres de Maíz. Programma de análisis de la política del sector agropecuario frente a la mujer productora de alimentos en Centroamérica y Panamá*, Costa Rica: IICA/BID.

Corral, L. and T. Reardon (2001) 'Rural nonfarm incomes in Nicaragua', *World Development*, 29(3): 427–42.

Deere, C. D. and M. Leon (1999) 'Institutional reform of agriculture under neoliberalism: the impact of the women's and indigenous movements', Paper presented to Land in Latin America: New Contexts, New Claims, Royal Tropical Institute (KIT), Amsterdam, May.

Economist Intelligence Unit (1996a) *Costa Rica: Country Profile*, London: The Economist.

— (1996b) *El Salvador: Country Profile*, London: The Economist.

— (1996c) *Guatemala: Country Profile*, London: The Economist.

— (1996d) *Honduras: Country Profile*, London: The Economist.

— (1996e) *Nicaragua: Country Profile*, London: The Economist.

Elson, D. (1987) 'The Impact of Structural Adjustment on Women: Concepts and Issues', Manchester, Manchester Discussion Papers in Development Studies.

— (1995) 'Gender-awareness in modelling structural adjustment', *World Development*, 23(11): 1851–68.

— (ed) (1991) *Male Bias in the Development Process*, Manchester, Manchester University Press.

Elson, D. and B. Evers (1997) 'Sectoral support: a gender-aware analysis', mimeo, GENECON Unit, University of Manchester.

Elson, D., B. Evers and J. Gideon (1997) 'Gender aware country economic reports:

concepts and sources', Working Paper no. 1, GENECON Unit, University of Manchester.

Elson, D., M. Fauné, J. Gideon, M. Gutiérrez, A. López de Mazier and E. Sacayón (1997) *Crecer con la Mujer: Oportunidades para el Desarrollo Económico Centroamericana*, San José: Embajada Real de los Paises Bajos.

Esquivel, G., F. Larraín and J. Sachs (2001) 'Central America's foreign debt burden and the HIPC Initiative', *Bulletin of Latin American Research*, 20(1): 1–28.

Evans, T. (1995) *La Transformación Neoliberal del Sector Público, Ajuste Estructural y Sector Público en Centroamérica y el Caribe*, Managua: Latino Editores.

FAO/INRA (United Nations Food and Agriculture Organization/Instituto Nicaraguense de Reforma Agraria) (1995) 'Fortalecimiento de la Gestión de la Mujer en las Unidades de Producción Campesinas', Managua, Series of Consultancy Reports.

Fauné, M. A. (1995a) *Mujeres y Familias Centroamericanas: Principales Problemas y Tendencias, Vol. 4*, San José: PNUD.

— (1995b) 'Guía Para Incorporar Género en los Proyectos agropecuarios en America Latina y el Caribe', Costa Rica, Consultancy Report for Banco Interamericano de Desarrollo.

— (1997) 'Costa Rica: gender aware country strategy report', in D. Elson et al. *Crecer con la Mujer: Oportunidades para el Desarrollo Económico Centroamericana*, San José: Embajada Real de los Paises Bajos.

Feminist Economics (1996) Special Issue in honour of Margaret Reid, 2(3).

Fletcher, S. and M. R. Renzi (1994) *Democratización, Desarrollo e Integración Centroamericana: Perspectivas de las Mujeres, Vol. 1*, Costa Rica: UNDP.

Folbre, N. (1995) 'Engendering economics: new perspective on women, work and demographic change', Paper presented at Annual Conference on Development Economics, World Bank, Washington, DC.

Funkhouser, E. (1996) 'The urban informal sector in central america: household survey evidence', *World Development*, 24(11): 1737–51.

Gobierno de Nicaragua/Instituto Nicaraguense de la Mujer (INIM) (1995) 'IV Conferencia Mundial Sobre la Mujer: Posición del Gobierno de Nicaragua Sobre la Propuesta de Plataforma de Acción Mundial', Managua: Gobierno de Nicaragua.

Goetz, A. M. (1995) 'Macro-meso-micro linkages: understanding gendered institutional structures and practices', a contribution to the SAGA Workshop on Gender and Economic Reform in Africa, Ottawa, 1–3 October.

— (1997) *Getting Institutions Right for Women in Development*, London and New York: Zed Books.

Hamilton, N. and C. Thompson (1994) 'Export promotion in a regional context: Central America and Southern Africa', *World Development*, 22(9): 1370–92.

Hill, A. M. and E. M. King (1995) 'Women's education and economic well-being', *Feminist Economics*, 1(2): 21–46.

Hutchinson, G. A. and U. Schumacher (1994) 'NAFTA's threat to Central American exports: a revealed comparative advantage approach', *Journal of Interamerican Studies and World Affairs*, 36 (Spring): 127–48.

IMAS (1995) 'Sondeo sobre perfil sociodemográfico y estrategias de supervivencia de mujeres pobres jefas de hogares', preliminary draft, Costa Rica: IMAS.

Instituto Interamericano de Cooperación para la Agricultura (IICA) and Banco Interamericano de Desarollo (BID) (1993) *Mujeres Productoras de Alimentos en Centroamérica y Políticas Secotriales*, Costa Rica: IICA.

Inter-American Development Bank (1997) Statistical Database, downloaded from the internet, IADB Webpage, September 1997.

López de Maizier, A. (1997) 'Honduras: gender aware country strategy report', in D. Elson et al., *Crecer con la Mujer: Oportunidades para el Desarrollo Económico Centroamericana*, San José: Embajada Real de los Paises Bajos.

Martinez, M. and S. Rosales (1995) 'El accesso de la mujer a la Tierra en Honduras', Tegucigalpa: Centro de Derechos de la Mujer.

Menjivar Larin, R. and J. P. Perez Sainz (eds) (1993) *Ni Heroes Ni Villanas: Genero e Informalidad Urbana en Centroamerica*, San José, Costa Rica: FLACSO.

Ortiz, E. (1994) *Mujeres del Sector Informal Urbano en El Salvador*, El Salvador: Instituto de Estudios de la Mujer.

Palmer, I. (1991) *Gender and Population in the Adjustment of African Economics: Planning for Change*, Geneva: ILO.

— (1994) 'Public finance from a gender perspective', *World Development*, 23(11): 1981–86.

Pizzaro, A. M. (1994) 'Nicaragua: Población y Calidad de Vida', Managua: S. I. Mujer.

Renzi, M. R. and Agurto, S. (1993) *Qué Hace la Mujer Nicaraguense Ante la Crisis Económica?* Managua: FIDEG.

— (1994) *Impacto de los Proyectos FISE en las Condiciones de Vida de los Nicaraguenses*, Managua: FIDEG.

— (1996) *La Mujer y Los Hogares Rurales Nicaraguenses: Indicadores Economicos y Sociales*. Managua: FIDEG.

Rojas, M. and Román, I. (1993) 'Agricultura de exportación y pequeños productores en Costa Rica', *Cuaderno 61*, San José: FLACSO.

Safilios Rothschild, C. (1988) 'The impact of agrarian reform on women's and men's income in rural Honduras', in D. Dwyer and J. Bruce (eds), *A Home Divided: Women and Income in the Third World*, Stanford, CA: Stanford University Press.

Saito, K. and D. Spurling (1992) 'Developing agricultural extension for women farmers', Washington, DC: World Bank Discussion Paper 156.

Seguino, S. (2000a) 'Gender inequality and economic growth: a cross-country analysis', *World Development*, 28(7): 1211–30.

— (2000b) 'Accounting for gender in Asian economic growth', *Feminist Economics*, 6(3): 27–58.

Singh, A. and A. Zammit (2000) 'International capital flows: identifying the gender dimension', *World Development*, 28(7): 1249–68.

Thomas, D. (1993) 'The distribution of income and expenditure within the household', *Journal of Human Resources*, 25: 635–64.

Tibaijuka, A. (1994) 'The cost of differential gender roles in African agriculture: a case study of smallholder banana–coffee farms in the Kagera region, Tanzania', *Journal of Agricultural Economics*, 45(1): 69–81.

Tzannatos, Z. (1992) 'Potential gains from the elimination of gender differentials in the labour market', *Women's Employment and Pay in Latin America Part 1: Overview and Methodology*, Washington, DC: Regional Studies Programme, Report No. 10, World Bank.

UNDP (1995) *United Nations Human Development Report*, New York and Oxford: Oxford University Press.

— (1996) *United Nations Human Development Report*, New York and Oxford: Oxford University Press.

— (2001) *United Nations Human Development Report*, New York and Oxford: Oxford University Press.

UNICEF/SEGEPLAN (1994) *Realidad Socioeconomica de Guatemala, con Enfasis en la Situación del Niño y la Mujer*, Guatemala City: Editoria Piedra Santa.

Walters, B. (1995) 'Engendering macroeconomics: a reconsideration of growth theory', *World Development*, 23(11): 1869–80.

Wiegersma, N. (1994) 'State policy and the restructuring of women's industries in Nicaragua', in N. Aslanbeigui, S. Pressman and G. Summerfield (eds), *Women in the Age of Economic Transition: Gender Impacts of Reforms in Post-Socialist Developing Countries*, London and New York, Routledge, pp. 192–205.

World Bank (1993) *World Development Report*, New York and Oxford: Oxford University Press.

— (1995a) *Republic of Nicaragua, Poverty Assessment, Volume I and II*, Washington, DC: World Bank.

— (1995b) *Guatemala Basic Education Strategy: Equity and Efficiency in Education*. Washington, DC: World Bank.

— (1995c) *Moving to a Gender Approach: El Salvador: Issues and Recommendations*. Washington, DC: World Bank.

— (1996) *World Development Report*, New York and Oxford: Oxford University Press.

Index